Mitsubishi Zero

Aviation titles by the same author:

Aichi D3A1/2 Val
Air Combat Manoeuvres
Avro Lancaster
Close Air Support
Curtiss SB2C Helldiver
Dive Bomber!
Dive Bombers in Action
Douglas AD Skyraider
Douglas SBD Dauntless
Fairchild-Republic A-10 Thunderbolt-II
Fist from the Sky
Impact! the Dive Bomber Pilots Speak
Into the Assault
Junkers Ju87 Stuka
Kamikaze!
Lockheed Martin C-130 Hercules
Luftwaffe Colours – Stuka Volume 1
Luftwaffe Colours – Stuka Volume 2
North American T-6
Petlyakov Pe-2 Peshka
Royal Air Force Squadron Badges
Ship Strike!
Skua! The Royal Navy's Dive Bomber
Straight Down!
Stuka at War
Stukas over the Mediterranean
Stukas over the Steppe
Stuka Spearhead
Stuka Squadron
T6 – A Pictorial History
The Sea Eagles
The Stuka at War
Torpedo Bombers
Vengeance!

Mitsubishi Zero

Japan's Legendary Fighter

Peter C. Smith

Pen & Sword
AVIATION

First published in Great Britain in 2014 by
Pen & Sword Aviation
an imprint of
Pen & Sword Books Ltd
47 Church Street
Barnsley
South Yorkshire
S70 2AS

ISBN 978 1 78159 319 6

A CIP catalogue record for this book is available from the British
Library

Typeset in Ehrhardt by
Mac Style Ltd, Bridlington, East Yorkshire
Printed and bound in the UK by CPI Group (UK) Ltd,
Croydon, CRO 4YY

Pen & Sword Books Ltd incorporates the imprints of Pen & Sword
Archaeology, Atlas, Aviation, Battleground, Discovery, Family
History, History, Maritime, Military, Naval, Politics, Railways, Select,
Transport, True Crime, and Fiction, Frontline Books, Leo Cooper,
Praetorian Press, Seaforth Publishing and Wharncliffe.

For a complete list of Pen & Sword titles please contact
PEN & SWORD BOOKS LIMITED
47 Church Street, Barnsley, South Yorkshire, S70 2AS, England
E-mail: enquiries@pen-and-sword.co.uk
Website: www.pen-and-sword.co.uk

Contents

Introduction and Acknowledgements

The story of the Mitsubishi A6M fighter aircraft of World War II has been told many times, with varying degrees of accuracy. It is essentially a story of myths. Before the outbreak of war in the Pacific in December 1941 both British and American sources, official and unofficial, were essentially united in the myth that their aircraft and their flyers were more than a match for anything that the Japanese could put into combat. More than just a totally unjustifiable belief in their own automatic superiority in production, design and fighting ability was the myth that the Japanese fighting man was basically inferior in every respect to the westerner. This misconception, rooted in racism and arrogance, as well as ignorance, was deep-rooted and slow to change. Such tenets were deeply held and indoctrinated, with otherwise intelligent people such as Winston Churchill and the British chiefs of all three services sharing with their American counterparts both a contempt for their new enemy and a totally false believe in their own invincibility.

Thus you have bizarre statements in pre-war American aviation magazines that the Imperial Japanese Navy's total air component consisted of inferior aircraft carriers equipped with obsolete aeroplanes, themselves flown by incompetent pilots and offered nothing whatsoever for the United States Navy to fear. One typical contributor is Leonard Engel.[1] Among his enlightening revelations to the American public were that the Japanese Navy had '… less than 500 aircraft'; compared to other powers Japanese aircraft were '… the poorest qualitatively …'. Japanese aircraft carriers he stated, '… are inferior to the British. And the British are far inferior to the American'. The carriers *Sōryū* and *Hiryū* could, '… each carry about 30 planes'. The *Kaga* and *Akagi*, carry '30 planes apiece normally, but can handle as many as 50'. He predicted that new carriers (presumably the *Shōkaku* and *Zuikaku*), would, '… not be ready for at least two years'. One final 'prediction' made was that, 'Some day, perhaps, the Japanese will have accumulated enough experience in a mechanical way to catch up, but that day will not come soon.' It proved sooner than Engel thought, just eleven months after this boastful bombast all his bragging was blown asunder. In fact the IJN had ten aircraft carriers in commission with hundreds of modern aircraft embarked flown by veterans of the war in China; the crew of the carrier *Lexington* used to boast being worth at least four Japanese carriers, until, that is, she was sunk by aircraft from one of the least efficient such Japanese ships at the Coral Sea battle; similar bragging was commonplace until Pearl Harbor brought some reality into the situation. Likewise, even five months after the events at Hawaii had demolished, one would have thought, all such long-held illusions, reinforced as it was by the loss of the *Prince of Wales* and *Repulse*, Malaya, the humiliating surrender of a British army in Singapore to a Japanese force about one-third its size, as well as the loss of Burma, Hong Kong, the Dutch East Indies and most of the Philippines.

Another American prophet of complete superiority was Lucien Zacharoff[2] who concluded that Japanese military aircraft were, '... not up to the contemporary standards of efficiency ...' of the United States, Great Britain and the Soviet Union. Among other nuggets of wisdom from this luminary were that Japan '... must depend on foreign types ...' and that the bulk of them anyway were '... ominously obsolete ...' and that they lacked range. In fact the IJN aircraft in general, and not just the A6M, consistently out-ranged US Navy aircraft throughout the entire Pacific War.

The British were no better. When, in April 1942, the Vice Chief of the Naval Staff, one Rear-Admiral Tom Spencer Vaughan Philips, CB, requested that Hawker Hurricanes be sent to Malaya he was mocked by the RAF representative, Air Marshal Sir Wilfred R. Freeman, who lectured him that the Brewster Buffalo was more than adequate to deal with any Japanese aircraft as '... they were not of the latest type'. Tom Philips was later to command the inadequate and ill-fated Force Z, sent east when Churchill, in yet another of his uninformed decisions, overruled Admiralty advice. Frequently accused since of being ignorant in air matters, one cannot help feeling that Admiral Philips was more in tune with reality than the RAF on this particular issue. In August 1941 Premier Winston Churchill, whose knowledge of the Japanese Navy and Air Force was notoriously abysmal,[3] decided to send the Hurricanes, two hundred of them, along with a further two hundred US supplied P-40B Tomahawk fighters to the Soviet Union instead of Malaya.

Yet even as late as April 1942 the British Admiral James Somerville, in command of the Eastern Fleet and reputed to be the most 'air-minded' of British admirals, could still espouse the same nonsense to justify his policy, 'I'm told the Japs are afraid of the dark so I must try and specialize in night attacks.'[4] The battles of Savo Island and Tassafaronga, among others, which saw radar-equipped Allied naval forces destroyed by Japanese units lacking such equipment, put paid to that particular illusion as well.

Professor Arthur Marder opined that the Admiralty was prone to prejudices about Japanese military ability while suffering from inadequate Intelligence assessments;[5] a viewpoint that Antony Best also shared and commented on '... the problems caused by the influence of racial thinking and ethnocentrism'. In downplaying the Japanese ability to both construct and effectively operate military hardware superior to their own, it was always assumed that the Japanese would be inferior in every way. As West concisely put it, 'That British forces might not rise to the exalted heights expected of them seems never to have crossed anyone's mind ...'[6] Similarly, Richard Aldrich noted that there was '... an atmosphere of unreality ...' about the RAF intelligence set-up at Singapore prior to the war.[7] Douglas Ford contends that, 'Britain entered the Pacific War with a misinformed perception of the IJN, as well as an erroneous notion that it possessed sufficient strengths and capabilities to confront the Japanese.'[8] That misconception of the abilities of the Japanese Navy predominated pre-war British Admiralty thinking is also postulated by Professor Wesley Wark, PhD, in his examination.[9] Finally, the American John Dower agreed that, '... it was not so much the success of the Japanese Navy in shrouding the Zero in secrecy that made its "sudden" appearance against the Westerners so shocking in December 1941 as the blindness of the most high-ranking Allied officers, who simply could not conceive of Japan independently designing and manufacturing an aircraft of this caliber.'[10]

However, lest there be bleeding hearts at this evidence of racial stereotyping by the west, it should be made clear that the Japanese were, if anything, even more convinced of their own racial superiority and sure (with more justification) of their military prowess.

And yet, especially in the case of the Mitsubishi A6M Zero fighter aircraft, this combat aircraft had been observed and reported upon at some length and in some detail by knowledgeable commentators of the war in China from 1937. Both British and American (as well as Chinese) military experts had sent in detailed reports on its extraordinary performance and its undoubted abilities. How then, did the appearance of this remarkable aerial fighting machine appear to come as such a total surprise to both British and American aircrews when they first met it? We will examine this extraordinary failure in some detail but it led, almost immediately upon the outbreak of the Pacific War, to a myth on top of a myth. From being a despised and contemptible enemy, the Japanese, and the Zero in particular, became almost immediately the very symbol of a ravaging Japanese military that was rampaging almost at will across vast swathes of the globe and brushing aside all resistance. Now, at a stroke, an assumed impotent enemy became a vastly superior foe, and the Zero fighter became an aircraft to be dreaded as it cleared the skies of what were hitherto considered more than adequate Allied interceptors, the British Hawker Hurricane, Fairey Fulmar and even the Supermarine Spitfire – hero of the Battle of Britain; and also the American P-40, Brewster Buffalo and Grumman F4F Wildcat (known as Martlet to the Royal Navy's Fleet Air Arm). The cult of the *Fuhai no Zero-sen* (' Invincible Zero Fighter'), had gripped the Allies within a few short weeks of combat. One historian wrote how: 'U.S. fighter pilots were apt to go into combat with a distinct inferiority complex. Tales from the Pacific had filtered back to the United States, which attributed to the Zero (and Japanese pilots) a sort of malevolent perfection.'[11]

As always, the truth lies somewhere in between the two extremes of pre- and post- December 1941. In any period of time the development of aircraft proceeds roughly along a steady path of improvement. The development of new, larger and more efficient power plants, both radial and in-line engines; of technical advancements, guns, aerodynamics, methods of construction, advances in techniques and ideas, which from the mid-1930s saw huge strides forward in the efficiency of fighting aircraft, was not confined just to the west, however much they themselves might considered it to be so. These advances applied world-wide, and so in Nazi Germany, in Soviet Russia, Fascist Italy, in France and in Japan, these same strides forward moved forward at the same period, with one design gaining an edge in one country, only for another nation to move the bar a little higher within a few months, before it in turn was overtaken by new advances elsewhere. In those nations whose drive was more dictatorial, this world-wide advance in aviation advancement was government driven, whereas in the western democracies it was far less so and was more independently driven and backed by far smaller arms budgets. So the Spitfire was the match for the Messerschmitt Bf.109, French and Italian fighter designs mirrored each other, Russia, Germany and Italy combat-tested their new aircraft in war condition in Spain; while Russia, America and Japan did the same in China. All moved forward, unevenly, but along the same general lines. The sole exception proved to be the Royal Navy whose aircraft, as a whole, remained an obsolete mixture of inferior types. Long after the US Navy and the Imperial Japanese Navy had moved over to good performance monoplanes to equip their air arms, Britain continued to employ biplanes such as the Swordfish and the Albacore whose performance and ability had hardly improved since the Sopwith Cuckoo of two decades earlier. This was due to inter-war Government parsimony and the crippling effect of the RAF control of all aircraft production, including naval aircraft of which they knew little and cared even less. It was not until as late as 1943, and by the adoption American aircraft, correctly designed for the job, that the British managed to catch up, and by then it was far too late. No such restraints bothered the development of the IJN's naval aircraft programmers, which by 1941 had encompassed not only the arrival of the superlative Zero fighter, but of long-range torpedo- and altitude bombers of great ability also.

The Zero then, was not a totally unique wonder-machine, but part of a logical progression. It was as much a balance between offence and defence, of aggressive intent against defensive capability as any fighter aircraft of the same vintage. The Japanese, had always placed greater emphasis on attack over defence (as they did with every aspect of their martial skills, from the *Banzai* charge, through the design of their heavy cruisers and destroyers, which were also world beaters, to the *Kamikaze* concept of the final days), and had thus opted for a fighter aircraft that was as fast as equivalent British and American machines, but far more agile, and with a range that was beyond the conception of western standards of naval fighter aircraft.

Thus it had these strengths, but, in compensation, and because there was no alternative, these just had to be paid for by weaknesses; lack of armour being the main one. Another was that the assets (large wings and big ailerons) that made the A6M so unbelievably nippy at speeds below 200mph (322 km/h), rapidly fell away at higher speeds due to air pressure, which made those self-same ailerons progressively sluggish and heavy. Also its light weight and high wing lift features tended to make it less efficient in a dive than its American opposite numbers, which were always heavier and grew ever more so, so the tactic of an attack pass from a superior height and a fast dive away was generally adopted for otherwise inferior machines such as the Curtiss P-40 ('Boom and Zoom'). To use one form of analogy, that of the duelling swordsman, the A6M was a rapier; the P-40, (and to a similar extent the F4F), was a cutlass while the Fairey Fulmar was broadsword. How these different concepts played out when they came into contact forms the basis of the first part of our story. But for a crucial period between December 1941 and December 1942, the Mitsubishi A6M fighter was *the* combat aircraft of the Pacific War.

I would like to pay thanks to the many, many people in Japan, America and the United Kingdom who helped me during my researches in all three countries down the decades. Many of these kind and considerate people who gave their time and knowledge unstintingly have now passed on. I remain ever grateful to them all for their assistance and advice and emphasize that the conclusions reached in these pages, although owing much to these contributors, are strictly my own. I also know that in the new-found freedom of the Internet, a reversion has been made to pre-war scepticism about the Zero, with many forums openly deriding the Zero fighter as being inferior to almost any American aircraft it ever met. Such opinions are not likely to be changed by such things as facts of course, so I remain dedicated to trying to present an unbiased account here. Finally, this book, although largely researched from Japanese and American sources, is written for a British readership from a British viewpoint and some of the views expressed may not sit well with other audiences and critics; but facts are facts and for this the author does not apologize in the slightest.

So thanks to: Takashi Doe, Yokohama WW-2 Japanese Military Radio Museum, Yokohama; Ronald M. Bulatoff, Hoover Institution Library and

Archives, Stanford University, California for the Official History of the United States Naval Group China, file in the Milton Miles Papers (Box 5); Caroline Herbet, Churchill Archives Centre, Churchill College, Cambridge for access to the papers of Admiral Sir James Somerville; Jonathan Parshall, co-author of *The Shattered Sword* for views on IJN Fighter Control; Mark R. Pettie, Stamford University, California, author of *Sunburst* and co-author of *Kaigun*, with his information of IJN fighter Control; Lieutenant-Commander Iyozo Fujita, Zero pilot aboard the carrier *Soryū*; Lieutenant Takeshi Maeda, Honorary President *Unabaraki*; Mitsuharu Uehara, Military Historian; Lieutenant-Commander Sadao Seno, JMDF; Captain Masato Shimada; Rear-Admiral Kazuo Takahashi, Chief-of-Staff, Commandant Kure District; Lieutenant-Commander Zenji Abe; Rear-Admiral Taemi Ichikawa, Matsudo City, Communications Officer aboard *Akagi*; Captain Masato Shimada; Rear-Admiral Sadayoshi Matsioka, Superintendant off the Officer Candidate School, Etajima; Commander Sadamu Takahashi, author of *Flying Clouds*; Commander Iyōzō Fujita, Daizawa, Setagaya-ku, Tokyo; Mr and Mrs Shuzo Inaba, Kurre; Tohru Kizu, Editor-in-Chief *Ships of the World*, Tokyo; Lieutenant Takashi Miura; Hitoshi Hasegawa, *Ships of the World*; Rear-Admiral Sadayoshi Matsuoka; Rear-Admiral Hideshi Koyayashi; Miss Misa Matsugi; Vice-Admiral Kazunari Doke, Commandant Kure District; Ensign Kazutaka Abe; Rear-Admiral Katsutoshi Kawano, Director of the Administration Department, Maritime Staff Officer, Etajima who kindly made arrangements via Rear-Admiral Kobayashi for the author's visit to Etajima; Kengo Yamamoto, Hyogo; Captain Hatsuhiko Watanabe; Kunio Kosemoto; Commander Noritaka Kitazawa, Military History Department, National institute for Defense Studies, Tokyo for his unfailing courtesy and assistance during my visits there; Ryunosuke Valenetin Megumi during our meeting in London; Colonel Shogo Hattori; Kunio Kosemoto; Professor Akira Nakamura, Dokkyo University; Nakamise Suzuya, Tokyo; my good friend Tetsukuni Watanabe, his wife and daughter, Nagoya; Seizaburou Hoshino, Sizuoka Prefecture, Etajima; Robert McLean, National Air & Space Museum, Paul E. Gerebet Facility, Suitland, Maryland; Jennifer A. Bryan, PhD, Head, Special Collections and Archives Division, Nimitz Library, US Naval Academy; Barry L. Zerby, Modern Military Records (NWCTM), Texual Archives Services Division, NARA;

Ray Wagner, San Diego Aerospace Museum; Captain N. J. 'Dusty' Kleiss, VS-6; Evelyn M. Cherpak, PhD, Head, Naval Historical Collection, Naval War College, Newport RI for assistance and hospitality during my visits there; John Vernon and Patrick Osborne, Modern Navy Records, Textual Archives Services Division, National Archives, Washington DC during my visits there; Heidi Myers, Reference Librarian, Navy Department Library, Naval Historical Center, for her help during my visits there; Timothy T. Petit, Archivist, Naval Historical Center, History and Archives Division, Operational Archives Branch for his great help and assistance during my visits; Ms Debbie Stockford and Mrs Catherine Rounsfell, Fleet Air Arm Museum, Yeovilton for great help during my visits.

NB In some cases some imperial measurements have been rounded down when they are given as conversions for metric equivalents. For instance, when converting 12 metres the precise imperial conversion would be 39 feet $4^7/_{16}$ inches but this has been rounded down to 39 feet 4 inches as it was felt such preciseness was not required or helpful.

Peter C. Smith
Riseley, Bedfordshire,
November 2013

Chapter 1

The Development of the Imperial Japanese Navy's Fighter Force

Beffore describing the design and combat of the Mitsubishi A6M carrier-borne fighter aircraft of World War II one needs to know just how this aircraft came to be what it was like when she first appeared in the eastern skies. The modern world is very different to that of 1937 and so in order to understand this aircraft's pedigree the origins and history that made her so unique have to be understood. For that a brief background as to why Japan was in China at all, and why a naval aircraft was to dominate land and sea warfare, needs to be outlined.

The origins of the Imperial Japanese Navy's air arm can be established back to 1912 with the foundation of the Commission on Naval Aeronautical Research (*Kaigun Kōkūjutsu Kenkyūkai*) set up under the Technical Development Department. On 19 December Captains Yoshitoshi Tokugawa and Kumazo Hino, conducted the first power flights in a Henri Farman biplane and Grade monoplane respectively. Like its long-time mentor, the Royal Navy, initially much early work was concentrated on airships, but with developments during World War I, emphasis shifted to winged and powered flying machines. Aircraft were purchased from both France and the United States and pilot training commenced also from 1912 onward. From 1914, allied as it was to Great Britain, Japan assisted in the conquest of the German treaty port and base of Tsingtao in November 1914, replacing that power there for eight more years rather than handing it back to China. The Japanese used airships in the siege as well as the seaplane-carrier *Wakamiya* and co-operation between the two navies continued, a flotilla of Japanese destroyers being based at Malta during the war. However, the Japanese Army was equally as strongly pro-German and envisaged the mutually destructive European carnage as an enormous opportunity to exploit the weakness of China while attentions were focused elsewhere. The Japanese duly presented what were known as the 'Twenty-One Demands' to the Chinese Government, which, if implemented, would have given Japan unprecedented control of Chinese internal affairs and commerce and much territory. The Americans also entered the war in 1917 and thus technically became an ally of Japan and, like the British, their initial objections to this take-over were watered-down, with the American Under-Secretary of State, Robert Lansing, stating to Viscount Ishii Kikujirō in a note of 2 November 1917 that America now recognized that, '... territorial propinquity creates special relations between nations and consequently Japan has special interests in China'. This became known as the Lansing-Ishii agreement, which virtually gave Japan *carte blanche* to proceed with her ambitions, while secretly agreeing to extend both nations' influences in China at the expenses of all other powers.

After the Great War ended with Germany's unexpected collapse, Japan benefitted from her involvement on the Allied side by taking over the Mandates of Germany's former Pacific colonies in the Caroline, Mariana and Marshall islands. But these acquisitions did not sate her expansionist plans in China and Manchuria. Meanwhile, Japan still remained allied to Great Britain and Royal Navy influence dominated the expansion of her naval aircraft development. From April 1916 Naval Air Units (*hikōtai*) were established by the Naval Affair Bureau, at Yokosuka and then Kasumigaura. The British experiments with the carriers *Furious* and *Argus* in the latter part of the Great War naturally aroused the interest of the Japanese as did the laying down of the first fully designed aircraft carrier, the *Hermes*. The Americans at this stage were yet to convert the collier *Jupiter* into the carrier *Langley* and lagged far behind the British. The Japanese response was to build the *Hōshō*, and she, due to the malaise that gripped British defence policy post-war, beat the *Hermes* into commission to become the first operational aircraft carrier built as such. The dead hand of RAF control soon stifled the initial British lead and both Japan and America quickly overtook and then left the Royal Navy far behind in naval aircraft development, but in the early 1920s it was still to her ally Britain that Japan looked.

Japanese naval aviators flew from the *Furious* in 1920 and Britain sent an 'unofficial' Naval Air Mission under the Colonel The Master of Sempill, with thirty former RNAS and RAF pilots to Japan between September 1921 and 1922 to train a cadre of naval flyers in the latest techniques. When *Hōshō* commissioned it was again a British flyer, William Jordan, a former RNAS and then test pilot for the Sopwith Company, who, in February 1923, made the first deck landing flying a home-built Mitsubishi aircraft. It was not until 16 March that a Japanese pilot, Lieutenant Shunichi Kira, performed the same feat. Under Herbert Smith former Sopwith flyers such as Jordan, along with Jutland hero Frederick J. Rutland (later to become a spy for Japan), introduced the latest techniques and machines such as the Mitsubishi 1MF3 Type 10 *Kōsen* (carrier fighter). Herbert Smith had been the Chief Aircraft Designer for the British Sopwith Aviation Company. Among the most famous of his many successful warplane designs during World War I had been the Sopwith Pup and Sopwith Camel. When Sopwith's disappeared in the harsh climate of British post-war austerity, Smith was invited to Japan by the Mitsubishi Engine Manufacturing Company, at Nagoya, along with other former Sopwith engineers whose expertise was more prized in Japan than in the UK. This team helped Mitsubishi establish their Aircraft Division and Smith oversaw three major Japanese aircraft designs before retiring and returning home in 1924. This was a single-engined single-seat biplane powered by a 300hp Mitsubishi 8-cylinder water-cooled engine and armed with two forward-firing fixed Type 97 7.7mm light machine guns (LMG), and had a maximum speed of 132mph. Another early Japanese model carrier fighter was the Nakajima A1N1/A1N2 Type 3 fighter, based firmly on the one-off speculative British Gloster Gambet, itself a carrier version of the Gloster Gamecock, and which had first flown on 12 December 1927 and was sent to Japan the following year. The A1N was licence-built, and of similar wood and fabric design but with a 420hp Nakajima Jupiter VI 9-cylinder air-cooled radial engine as power plant, which could attain a top speed of 148mph and also carry two 66lb bombs for dive-bombing. Some 150 were built, the first entering service in 1939. A further advance was the Nakajima A2N1 Type 90 carrier fighter. She was also a single-seater and she was a composite design with an all-metal fuselage construction with metal fabric-covered wings that could attain a maximum speed of 182mph.

British aircraft were the inspiration for early Japanese designers, with the Yokosuka Naval Air Arsenal the first manufacturer of such types quickly joined by Aichi, Mitsubishi and Nakajima. They soon began producing aircraft that were at least the equals of western types. Japan was full of confidence and looked forward to continued expansion of her dominions and power. She had already annexed Korea in 1910 and was looking for further additions to her overseas territories to maintain her expanding population and provide sources for coal and iron to fuel her growth. Two revolutions, one against the Manchu Dynasty in China in 1911 and one for its restoration in 1913, both had the hidden hand of the Japanese behind them who sought to benefit from the destabilization of that state. Now, in 1919, the 'Open Door' policy of access to China was increasingly unacceptable to Japan who sought predominance and the exclusion of all other powers.

Then, in 1921, an unexpected intervention happened on the world stage that eclipsed even the Versailles Treaty; the Americans suddenly called a conference to limit naval shipbuilding and produced a set of ratio figures, in a total arbitrary manner, totally without any consultation whatsoever, and designed to ensure their own domination of the seaways. This followed the vast programme of naval construction initiated by President Wilson designed to elevate the US to be the principal power, based on their own self-image (one not shared by the rest of the world) of 'The leader of the democratic impulse'. This assembly became the generally known as the Washington Naval Conference.

The United States continued to castigate and hector the other delegates during the resulting conference to accept the United States' parity with Great Britain and also assigned tonnage limits on the other world powers.[1] Negotiations were long and acrimonious, especially on the part of Japan who felt that her natural progression to join the leading naval powers and her much-cherished 'Eight-Eight' naval shipbuilding programme were needlessly sacrificed.[2] In contrast, myopic British politicians, headed by Tory politician Arthur J. Balfour, urged on by an all-powerful Treasury Department, meekly caved in to the American demands and abandoned Britain's three hundred-year-old dominance of the sea with hardly a murmur; indeed they wanted to go further so that Beatty, the First Sea Lord, wrote in despair that if things continued '... there would not be a Navy at all'.[3] The Japanese were less accommodating to the *diktat* from President Warren G Harding in the White House and his team backed by demands from Senators from such states as Iowa and Nebraska thousands of miles from any ocean. That the Japanese signed at all was remarkable, as it reduced their total tonnage to just two-thirds of the new American and British limits. While British politicians meekly accepted this ratio, the reception received by the returning Japanese delegates, under Katō Tomosaburō, was dire. Most admirals, the so-called 'Big-Navy' group, and in particular Vice-Admiral Katō Kanji, who had also been a delegate member, were bitterly opposed to the deal, and made no secret of it. Another by-product that favoured the Americans and nobody else was that the Anglo-Japanese alliance, which was due to be renewed that same year, was allowed to lapse. Great Britain therefore lost her naval dominance and her principal naval ally both at the same time – for this outcome Balfour received an earldom! In Japan one effect that the resulting treaty had was that it concentrated the minds of the Japanese Naval Staff on how to offset this deliberate restriction of their ambition, and in the ensuing years they increasingly tended to see the development of their naval air arm as a way of reducing the balance of American dominance. Two of the abandoned capital ships, the battleship *Kaga* and the battle-cruiser *Akagi*, were converted on the stocks to become aircraft carriers.[4]

This switch was further reinforced by the subsequent London Naval Treaty of 1930 in which restriction on tonnages and armament size for cruisers was extended by a limitation on numbers, in roughly the same ratio as for battleships and carriers. This was another blow to Japan, which had sought to build outstanding cruisers to make up for the enforced deficiency in her battle line. Now that expansion was also thwarted the air option increasingly became the attractive option for parity in some fields. In 1924 a brand-new Aviation Research centre was constructed at Kasumigaura to replace one demolished in the Tokyo earthquake, to centralize development, testing and research, although existing facilities at Hirō and a new engine testing centre was opened at Yokosuka. Further development took place here with the building of the new Naval Air Arsenal completed six years later. Once ready this new facility became the focus of the IJN's naval air expansion, allowing both the existing Technical Section and the Aviation Department of the Navy to share design, development, manufacture and flight-testing, via the *Hikō Jikkkenbu* right through to training and tactical application by the Yokosuka *Kōkūtai*, not only of all non-private aircraft types but of the hardware associated with military aircraft as well. Such an integrated facility as the *Kaigun kōkūtai* (re-named as the Naval Air Technical Arsenal – *Kaigun*

Kōkū Gijutsushō – in 1939) was an enormous asset to the Navy and enabled combat experience to be readily assimilated and built into new designs.[5] Compare this seamless progression and total control of all aspects of naval air development with the convoluted and time-wasting process by which the Admiralty had to go cap-in-hand to the Air Ministry with their requests, which the latter had barely concealed contempt for (and a overwhelming aversion to consider any military option other than laying Berlin in ruins), and with a hostile Treasury and pacifist government opposing both. It is little wonder that the Royal Navy's air arm withered while that of the IJN waxed stronger and more powerful each year.

Through this new centralized command the Navy, which contained many air-minded admirals (some of whom, like Vice-Admiral Inoue Shigeyoshi, wanted the entire navy to be solely a land-based aerial armada), was able to channel all Japan's limited resources to achieving two common goals; to cease reliance on foreign designs and to establish air superiority for the fleet. This superiority was not confined to carrier aircraft either; modern long-range bombers, capable of both high-altitude attacks and aerial torpedo attacks, were developed as a fully integrated force rather than as separate entities. This forward-looking policy was named Project Aviation Technology Independence[6] and was carried through with vim and vigour. Private companies were encouraged to compete and from 1932 under the new Prototypes System, under which maximum effort was attained by controlled competition, manufacturers were made to bid in pairs on new designs, outline requirements of which were laid down by the Navy. The best of each competitor's designs were then adopted, but there were no losers for the firm whose design was rejected was permitted to construct their rival's machine, or to provide engines for it, thus keeping both fully engaged and able to maximize output and resources.

Hand-in-hand with these innovations that spurred the indigenous aircraft industry forward and enabled the Japanese to cease to rely on foreign technologies to a large extent, was an expansion of pilot and aircrew training in order to meet a manning requirement for almost one thousand aircraft by 1938.[7]

The development of the bombing arm was consistent with the traditional Japanese approach of attack over defence. This led to the adoption of dive-bombing and torpedo-bombing by the carrier embarked aircraft as well as the long-range bomber, and this tendency somewhat overshadowed the fighter force, which was seen as purely defensive. This was not just a Japanese trait however, the Italian General Giulio Douhet espoused the same philosophy in Europe,[8] while Lord Hugh Trenchard in Britain wedded the whole of the RAF's doctrine to the heavy bomber ethos with Air Marshal Arthur Harris carrying out this theory in bloody detail during the war. American thinking was very much the same with the gimmicky exhibitionism of Billy Mitchell grabbing headlines in a series of very one-sided tests against unmanned, stationary, obsolete warship targets and the predominance of the United States Army Air Corps 'Bomber Mafia' under Harold L. George and John F. Curry at Langley Field. All were to be proved wrong in the years ahead but the Japanese came earlier than most to the realization that the popular mantra 'The bomber will always get through', as propagated by British Prime Minister Stanley Baldwin in 1932, was a typically simplistic political fallacy.

The reason the Japanese were far ahead of the pack in this realization was because in the years between 1918 and 1937 she had continued her expansionist policy in the Far East and had become embroiled in a series of interventions that were, in all but name, wars.

It is typical that, in an oblique apology at the beginning of their book, authors Masatake Okumiya and Jirō Horikoshi stated that Japan had been, on occasions, '... forced into armed conflict with neighbouring countries'. They add that, '... such action may be justified ...', but little or no justification was apparent in the first of such adventures, which they totally ignore, the Liutiaohu Incident, which was nothing less than a plot to take over, through force, the whole of Manchuria. On 18 September 1931, a group of disaffected and militant Kwantung Army officers originated a plan whereby one Lieutenant Kawamoto Suemori planted explosives that blew up the Japanese owned South Manchuria Railway line between Changchun and Lüshun; using this as an excuse, they marched in and took over Mukden, the capital. Here, they put in place a puppet ruler Emperor Kang-de (formerly Puyi of the Quing Dynasty), and created a new subservient state, which they named Manchukuo. At the Liaodong Peninsula in the south (Dairen and the former Port Arthur or Ryojun) Japan ruled directly as the Kwantung

Leased Territory and based their Kwantung Army (*Kantōgun*) there. Thus Japan had gained a firm military foothold on the mainland with Kange-de as a nominal figurehead for a nation that, in reality, the Japanese Army really administered.

In 1932 Japanese naval forces at Shanghai were involved in another incident when, with the beating and murder of Japanese Buddhist priests and anti-Japanese demonstrations as an excuse, an armed force was landed from warships at the port. Unfortunately for them they encountered the Chinese 19th Route Army and had to be hastily reinforced by regular army units sent from Japan. There was much fighting before the matter was settled by negotiation thanks to the British Admiral on the spot, Sir Howard Kelly, acting alone with little support from either his Government at home or the senior Admiral on the spot (an American) who refused to get involved. Meanwhile, the Japanese had annexed Jehol Province into Manchukuo in 1933 and in 1935 another puppet state, the East Hebei Autonomous Council, was set up absorbing the provinces of Chahar and Hebei. This, in effect, almost isolated the Chinese capital of Peking (now Beijing) other than from the south.

Five years later things turned more serious and on 7 July 1937 the so-called Marco Polo (*Lugouqiao*) Bridge incident occurred. Here the Peking (Beijing) to Tianjin railway ran through the town of Wanping, which the Japanese had long set their sights on. This friction point ruptured on the night of 6/7 July when the Japanese Kwantung Army conducted night manoeuvres without notifying their Chinese opposite numbers, who opened fire on the Japanese. The misunderstandings multiplied and fighting broke out on a large scale and the fighting soon spread to Shanghai once more. This began a bitter and costly war between Japan and China that was to last for eight long years. From the Navy's viewpoint the isolation of its garrison in Shanghai led to support from both carrier-based aircraft (the carriers *Hōshō*, *Kaga* and *Ryūjō* were on station) and raids by land-based Mitsubishi G3M2 Navy Type 96 Model 22 bombers (*rikkō*) based on Taihoku, Formosa, and from Ōmua, Kyūshü, the first 'transoceanic' bombing missions directed against the cities of Hangchow, Nanking and Kuang-te. However, in contrast to the Douhet theorists' claims, these bombing raids from both types of Japanese aircraft soon began to suffer very heavy losses when intercepted by fighter aircraft of the Republic of China Air Force. The Chinese airmen were heavily reliant on foreign-built, designed and supplied military aircraft, of which they had around 250 machines in 1937. American-built Boeing P-26C (Peashooter) and Curtiss Hawk II and III fighters, some of which were built at Hangzhou, predominated along with British Gloster Gladiators and, later, Russian Polikarpov I-15 and I-16B 'Donkey' fighters. Among a motley collection of other types were the Italian Fiat CR.30, American Republic P-43 Lancers and a lone Vultee P-66 Vanguard. Both the Soviet Union and America provided 'volunteer' flyers to assist in manning them.

In response to their losses the Japanese hastily replaced their Nakajima Type 90 and 95 biplane fighters, which had proved ineffective, with the still experimental Mitsubishi A5M4 Type 96 in the Second Combined *Kōkū Sentai*, later to be based at Kunda, Shanghai. This little fighter was an all-metal, open cockpit, single-seater monoplane with a fixed undercarriage and powered by either a Mitsubishi 730hp or a Nakajima Kotobuki 41 750hp radial engine, which gave her a top speed of 270mph and a range of 460 miles. She was armed with two 7.7mm Type 89 machine-guns. This feisty little aircraft had been designed by a young Mitsubishi chief designer, a graduate from Tokyo University, named Jirō Hortikoshi. His first design, Prototype 7, had not been a success but he was trusted with the new machine and the Prototype 9 had been completed in January 1935 and was exhaustively flight-tested at the Kagamigahara field and later by the nine pilots of the 'Genda Circus' at Yokosuka. The then Lieutenant Minoru Genda had assembled a group of highly skilled and adept fighter pilots at this period. They put each new model through its paces. At that time the Navy's priority was for high-manoeuvrability, required for the Japanese method of dog-fighting, which itself was terminology based on the Great War's type of aerial combat between opposing fighter aircraft. A modern description is air combat manoeuvring (ACM), or 'turning combat' but the old term is still widely understood and used. In Europe and America in the 1930s this concept was largely abandoned in theory, but World War II and afterwards saw the tactic, if not the name, widely used until the 1990s. The Japanese interpretation, tested and perfected by Petty Officer Mochizuki Isamu of the Yokosuka *Kōkūtai* as early as 1934, was the *hineri-komi* ('in-turning' or in Allied parlance, 'falling-leaf'), manoeuvre, (often reported by Allied survivors who did not understand it as 'acrobatics') by which targeted aircraft that went into an avoiding loop could be brought back into the attacker's gun-sight by carrying out an instant cork-screwing 'inner-loop' before they knew what was happening. One A6M pilot described it this way: 'It was executed near the top of a loop by applying cross control (aileron: right, rudder: left) for a short moment. But I have never used it on actual combat, because the plane would be slowed down at the top of a loop, making the plane an easy prey for other enemy fighters.'[9] Attaining such an individual skill set by a combination of intensive training and an aircraft that was agile to the *n*th degree, perfectly suited to the Japanese pseudo-*Samurai* warrior duelling ethic, was based on a flexible, loose three-plane formation (*shōtai*), something that, hitherto, had best been obtained from a biplane configuration and so Hortikoshi's monoplane prototype was something of a watershed. Having already exceeded the Navy's requirement for a high top speed, the Genda team tested the Prototype 9 against a range of foreign designs, including the British Hawker Nimrod, German Heinkel He.112, American Severesky 2PA and French Dewoitine D510, as well as the existing Nakajima Type 95. The new aircraft, a product of the *Mitsubishi Jūkōgyō Kakbushiki-Kaisha* (Mitsubishi Heavy Industries Company) outperformed them all save the latter as expected, but when climbs and dives were incorporated as part of the tests even the Type 95 was outshone. As the Type 96 the new Mitsubishi was officially still under consideration but the urgent needs of the China front overcame caution and the carrier *Kaga* returned to her home port of Sasebo and exchanged her old aircraft for this newcomer. They soon saw combat.

Among the outstandingly skilled fighter pilots serving with this unit were Lieutenant-Commander Motoharu Okamura, Lieutenant-Commander Minoru Genda himself, Lieutenant Ryoji Nomura and Lieutenant Mochifumi Nangō. One of the group, Petty Officer Isamua Mochizuki, further developed this *hineri-komi* technique, thus ensuring a fighter aircraft could turn a potentially deadly situation, with a more manoeuvrable enemy aircraft on its tail, into a killing advantage by pulling sharply up into a loop, and, by utilizing a hard left rudder and shifting the control column to the starboard, would side-slip out of the arc prior to reach the top and thereby roll quickly and easily into a spot astern of the opponent in a perfect firing position.[10] The A5M not only had greater speed, climb rate and range than its opponent therefore, but skilled pilots and superior tactics. This combination proved conclusive in the aerial fighting that followed, along with superior numbers (the Japanese outnumbered the Chinese and their foreign 'advisors' by three-to-one at this period) and was later also to prove equally deadly to western opponents during the air combats of 1941–42.

Japan's air ascendency commenced with a devastating assault on 19 September 1937 when Chinese fighters intercepting a carrier-borne dive-bomber attack and, expecting the usual easy pickings, were annihilated by the Japanese escort of twelve A5Ms, which shot down a dozen Chinese machines without loss to themselves. When another raid met Chinese fighters in the same area the next day the Chinese fled without offering any kind of a fight. This established a precedent causing the Army commander to admit that the Navy flyers were as good as his own Army flyers were useless and that the latter might as well be handed over to the former. On 2 December the A5Ms knocked down no fewer than ten Russian I-16Bs without loss and Nanking duly fell to the Japanese by the end of 1937. Meanwhile, aerial fighting moved elsewhere with fierce battles over Nan-ch'ang on two occasions in December when the Chinese lost fifty-four aircraft. The sturdiness of the Mitsubishi design was demonstrated when Petty Officer Kanichi Kashimura's aircraft lost one third of his port wing when his second victim plummeted into it and sheered this chunk off. Notwithstanding, Kashimura managed to nurse his little fighter safely home. However, a new phase was opened because just to reach this new fighting zone required the Japanese fighters to land and re-fuel at Kuangte *en route* as the zone was beyond the reach of even the Type 96. To counter the new tactics a fighter with an even greater range was obviously a requirement for the Navy.

The Japanese, with intermittent and half-hearted attempts at negotiation, rejected by the Chinese and elements of their own Army and Government alike, continued to extend their operations even deeper into China, with a new offensive directed toward Hankow to where the Chinese Government had once again retreated. The arrival of Soviet Union aircraft and pilots had helped stem the one-sided nature of the air war for a while and on 29 April 1938 a hard-fought aerial duel took place over the city. Wild claims and counter-claims were subsequently made by both sides.[11] Whatever the truth, Hankow went the way of Nanking in October and the Nationalist Government of Chiang Kai-shek, pulled back yet further west up the

Yangtze again, this time to the mountain stronghold city of Chungking, on the Upper Yangtze. Air raids duly commenced against this place along with many other Chinese cities from Canton in the south, to Lan-chou in the north-west through which Soviet aid was flowing and Ta't'ung in the north. In these raids the A5M was impotent as even with wing tanks she could not reach such targets. Unescorted bombers once more began to suffer at the hands of Chinese and Russian fighters and so it continued into 1940. But history was to repeat itself, and once more a breakthrough in Japanese fighter design, even more revolutionary than the introduction of the Type 96, was to turn the tide in Japan's favour.

The re-equipped and confident Japanese Navy flyers now went about establishing air superiority in the skies over the Chinese capital Nanking toward which the army of General Yasooi Okamura steadily was advancing from June 1938 onward. In October 1938 during the battle of Wuhan the Chinese Air Force was all but eclipsed and withdrawn from combat to re-organize.

In addition to long-range bombing missions the IJN flyers operated close-support missions from Hankow with both dive-bombers and attack bombers but the Type 96 fighters found relatively little employment during 1939. The Japanese Army Air Force aircraft remained relatively inferior but, with German assistance, the Chinese anti-aircraft artillery increased in efficiency. With the introduction of Russian flyers and aircraft, mainly I-15 and I-16 fighters, a resurgence of Chinese fighter defence also began to be once more experienced, with the A5Ms lacking the range once more to provide aerial defence of the G3Ms bombers now joined by the improved Mitsubishi G4M1.[12]

It was clear that a repeat of the earlier situation had been brought about and the Japanese response was the same, the early introduction of a brand-new fighter aircraft. That such a fighter was available at this time was due to two factors, the first being the far-sighted specification laid down by the Navy's aeronautical planners in calling for a world-beating design, and the second being the skill and perseverance of the Mitsubishi design team in attaining this objective. The whole scheme was truly original and breathtaking in concept. All over the world it was 'accepted' that naval aircraft must be inferior to land-based machines. The IJN's Aviation Department, with the six years' experience of actual combat in China as their matrix, dared to think otherwise.

The preliminary outlines presented by Lieutenant-Commander Hideo Sawai May 1937 of what was termed the Prototype 12 or 12-*Shi*[13] experimental (*shisaku*) fighter aircraft were revolutionary. But further modifications were incorporated as the latest lessons from China were analysed and these came as a complete surprise to the Mitsubishi and Nakajima design teams when the final Planning Requirement was issued on 5 October 1937.

The overriding requirement laid down for the new aircraft still remained the same, an essential ability to perform – that would ensure the superiority of this fighter over any foreign-built opponent. The Japanese penchant for out-duelling one's opponent had been the mantra of IJN pilots throughout, and was to remain so. Although this technique had been largely rejected by the other major military air arms since the Great War, Japan remained firmly wedded to this fundamental credo. Everything else was subjected to this ability to out-turn and out-manoeuvre the enemy. Fair enough, this had been the basis of the Type 96, and the 12-*Shi* was to at least equal, and preferable excel that aircraft's ability, but now the Navy was demanding more, much, much more. Just how much was revealed once a study was made of the detailed requirements called for by the specification.

The new fighter was to have long range in order to provide the long-range bombers full escort and protection on their missions far into the hinterland of China. But Prototype 12 was still, first-and-foremost, a naval plane and had to operate from carrier decks and be stowed in the ships' hangar spaces. The *Akagi* and *Kaga* were large vessels, reflecting their origins, but the new breed of Japanese aircraft carriers were of smaller tonnages and dimensions, and thus space was at a premium.[14] The limitation placed on the new fighters dimension reflected these carrier space restrictions in that the wing-span had to be *less* than 12m (39ft 4in). Likewise the length of carrier decks deemed a short take-off length and the new fighter's limitations in this respect were pegged at less than 70m (229ft 8in) into a wind over deck of 39.37ft/sec (12 m/sec) and with a more generous allowance of 175m (574.2ft) for land operations with no head wind. In a similar manner a landing speed for carrier decks of lower than 58 knots (107km/h) was demanded.

The speed of the Type 96 fighter had proved inadequate once the new foreign aircraft had been introduced in the China war. With the Soviet Polikarpov I-16 *Ishak* fighters capable of top speeds of 326mph (525km/h), the Type 96's best performance of 279.62mph (450 km/h) was deemed insufficient. The new fighter needed to attain a top speed that exceeded 310.69mph (500 km/h) at an altitude of 13,123ft (4,000m).[15] For the aerial combat advantages envisaged the Navy planners specified a climb rate of 9,842ft (3,000m) height attainable within 3½ minutes. Altitude fighting required that the new aircraft be fitted with an oxygen inhaler.

Once engaged with the enemy the new fighter would require additional punch to knock down the recently introduced all-metal aircraft of its potential foes. Machine-guns were still deemed essential, but extra hitting power was increasingly seen as vital and so, in addition to a pair of 7.7mm such weapons, the 12-*Shi* model was to carry two 20-mm Type 99 Model 1, Mk 3, *Dai Nihon* recoil cannon firing ball, incendiary or high-explosive shells at 450rpm for the first time. This meant additional weight for two sets of 102.294lb (46.4kg), 55 inches long, plus supporting members and the weight of the two thirty-round drum magazines, as did other essential aircraft-carrier operational needs, a Type 96 *Ku* Model-1 radio set to maintain communication between formations, and also the essential Type 1 *Ku* Model 3 radio direction-finding outfit to help airborne aircraft re-locate their parent ship. The latter equipment was the standard issue set for most IJN aircraft and had been combat tested by the A5M4. It was known as the *Kruesi*, Geoffrey Kruesi of Dayton, Ohio being its originator as it was a direct copy of the Fairchild Aero Compass, which Fairchild Aircraft's Aerial Camera Division was manufacturing in New York and had an American manufactured Eclipse generator. The Fairchild Company's logo was found on both #3041 at Fort Kamehameha, Pearl Harbor in 1941 and on #4593 that crash-landed near Dutch Harbor in 1942. They were also equipped with a Toyo Electric Corporation crystal-controlled voice or continuous-wave (CW) radio, the Aleutian Zero's aircraft set being tuned to a 4145 KC frequency.

The vexed question of the reliability of the radio sets fitted in the A6M provoke heated responses and, as with everything about the aircraft, the common fallacy, still being promulgated today, that the Zero pilots simply tore them out and threw them away as they were both useless and weighty. We shall examine this widespread belief in detail later.

Both carrier operations and land-based long-range operations shared the common requirements of range and endurance. In these factors, the 12-*Shi* was to prove outstanding. The range requirement was 1,161 miles (1,870km) but by fitting an external drop-tank under the fuselage this could be extended to a remarkable 1,932 miles (3,110km). Endurance was to be 1.2 to 1.5 hours at 9,842ft (3,000m) utilizing the normal fuel capacity, extending to two hours with the drop-tank, while it was hoped that by fine-tuning an economical aspiration of between six to eight hours' flying time could be attained. Additionally, there was even a requirement to carry a pair of 132lb (60kg bombs) in overload condition. The weight of the first prototype when put together, still in a fully complete state, had been 3,452.21lb (1,565.9kg), but a later weighing with full a complement of parts and fuel, came out at 3,570.5lb (1,620kg).

One area of aeronautical expertise in which Japan still lagged behind the more industrialized nations was that of aircraft engine design and construction. This was to be the greatest hurdle of all to overcome for, in demanding all these desirable qualities the Navy was asking that the designers achieve all these advances with a strictly limited range of power plants, none of which exceeded a modest 1,100hp.

Available to the designers of the 12-*Shi* at this period were just three home-produced twin-row, 14-cylinder, air-cooled radial aircraft engines. Two of these were Mitsubishi products, the first the 875hp *Zuisei* 13 engine, the alternative the more potent 1070hp *Kinsei* 64. An alternative to this pair was their rival firm's Nakajima 950hp *Sakae* 12. This increased horsepower was achieved with only a 1.3in (3.2cm) increase in diameter and just under 9lb (4kg) increase in weight over the *Zuisei*. To opt for a rival engine was not a choice Mitsubishi would happily make but it still had to fulfil the demanding specification the Navy was insisting upon. It was a tough ask from a relatively young industry.

The very experienced Nakajima team studied the requirement for three months and then, after a meeting with the naval representatives, as we shall see, decided that it was simply not achievable.[16] They dropped out of the competition leaving the Mitsubishi team as sole contenders. Initially, Dr Jiro Horikoshi's team had the same reaction. The 12-*Shi* project at that stage appeared destined to be stillborn.

Chapter 2

Striving for the Impossible

M itsubishi's Chief Designer, Horikoshi, had wide experience of the military fighter field, having worked at cutting-edge aeronautical companies in Germany, the United Kingdom and the United States, in addition to which he could draw on his own personal experience of having designed the most successful Type 96, which was still the principal Japanese interceptor. In the latter aircraft he had the advantage of on-going military combat against the latest foreign types against which to evaluate his ideas for the new aircraft that the Navy demanded. Continual information from the front line was fed in and the Type 96 was constantly being modified and amended in the light of this war experience. Nobody in the world, therefore, was better placed to tackle the task, than Horikoshi and his team. He espoused the view, which was generally held to be correct for an era of rapid change, that no matter how innovative a fighter aircraft design was, it would be outmoded by rapid progress; his estimate was this process would only take four years even in times of peace when there were no pressures from the front, but that this would reduce to a mere two years under the hothouse of war conditions. It was an excellent estimation for indeed two years was to prove almost exactly the period of time that the future A6M was to totally dominate the Pacific air war without serious challenge. With the China 'Incident' raging on without any end it sight, it was under war conditions that the new Prototype 12 was to be finalized.

Horikoshi has recorded how he initially concentrated on the power plant for the new fighter; this being the area that he knew would most restrict his airframe design as the choices were so limited.[1] Initially then the choice that confronted Horikoshi was a straight choice between his own company's *Kinsei* Type 46 engine and the *Zuisei* Type 13. The Model 14 *Zuisei* ('Holy Star') was developed in 1931 as a 14-cylinder, supercharged, air-cooled, double-row radial with various marks, typically rated at 1,080hp (805kW),

2,700rpm for take-off. It weighed 1,190lb (540kg). The *Kinsei* (Venus) was a 1934 developed Navy engine also a 14-cylinder, air-cooled, double-row radial, with a dozen marks, rated at 1,075hp (802kW) at 2,500 rpm at 5,560ft (2,000m). It had a weight of 1,202lb (545kg).[2]

To choose the *Kinsei* would give the design an immediate power boost, but being larger it was therefore heavier and took up more space, which impacted the size of the airframe, wing and tail size and fuel considerations. This would result in an estimated 6,614lb (3,000kg) aircraft, entirely unsuitable to the Navy's specification. To opt for the smaller *Zuisei* would reduce these dimensions and give a smaller, lighter aircraft, a more acceptable 3,527lb (1,600kg) weight, far more suitable for carrier operations and closer to existing Navy fighters and would also increase mobility. Eventually the weight factor won and Horikoshi accepted the loss of power that would result from this choice. Dr Den-ichiro Inouse set up a special design sub-team to deal with the problems of propulsion, which were far from settled yet. Lack of power was to ever dog the A6M's otherwise brilliant career, more so later when increases in performance were constantly required to counter newer Allied types as the Pacific War progressed.

Having made that decision Horikoshi then made outline sketches that incorporated his thinking about streamlining, which meant a fully retractable landing gear for low drag,[3] but more weight, a new low-wing planform with a straight taper and narrow tip replacing the currently fashionable elliptical shape with matching horizontal tail. The wing format was crucial as it had to be thick enough to accommodate port and starboard integral fuel tanks and also the 20mm cannon. The 7.7mm machine-guns were housed in the engine cowling and were based on a British Vickers design being licence-built, each LMG having a 680rpg capacity and an effective range of about 600 yards (548.64m). Being so close together limited their effectiveness as to their cone of fire, however, and there were vibration problems. The low wing loading was essential in ensuring the design's superior turn radius was achieved and was aided by the large ailerons. The actual upper surface of the wing formed the cockpit floor giving the aircraft considerable integral strength and also aided ease of construction and maintenance. Horikoshi consulted with his team. Sadahiko Kato was assigned design of the retractable undercarriage and stowage; to Yohimi Hatakenaka was given the task of planning the 20mm cannon mountings and Yohitoshi Sone was allocated to sort out the wing dimensions and structure. Having decided on these basics with his team, during the last months of 1937 Horikoshi wrestled with how to fit in all the Navy's requirements to this outline design. He was then only just recovering from stress through overwork and the problems seemed insurmountable.

On 17 January 1938 a joint Navy/Company meeting was held at Yokosuka Naval Aeronautical Establishment with representatives of both Nakajima and Mitsubishi, the latter including the Project Head, Jyoji Hattori, as well as Jiro Horikoshi, Yoshitoshi Sone and Sadahiko Kato on the one hand, and the Navy representatives, all under the auspices of Vice-Admiral Koichi Hanajima, the director. Present were Lieutenant-Commander Misaro Wada, Head of the Fighter Section, and a score of leading naval aviation experts, including leading fighter aces from the China front line, including Lieutenant-Commander Minoru Genda who was serving on the Aviation Staff with the Second Combined _Kōkū Sentai_. The latter gave graphic descriptions of the air fighting then underway while the senior officer emphasized the probable future direction and extension of the war, the deterioration of the international situation[4] and the urgent need for the new fighter. When asked for designer opinions Horikoshi requested that at least one or more of the extreme requirements be withdrawn, but was met with a steely response – there was to be _no_ compromise on the Navy's part and this he was forced to accept. Genda himself, many years later, admitted that even he had reservations about how '... the impossible, incompatible, requirements ...' could be met.

As we have seen the result of this conference was that Nakajima threw in the towel, but the reaction of Mitsubishi was sombre determination. A five-section design team, covering computing, structure, propulsion, armament and landing gear, was immediately established under Hattori and Horikoshi to push forward with Prototype 12. The latter spent the next ten months agonizing about how to get the lowest weights and the best performance from his outline design. In that period more than 3,000 detailed drawings were made, checked, modified and approved. The engine for the prototype being agreed upon, he applied himself to the propeller and decided that, as with most things associated with this aircraft, a radical approach was required. It was decided to adopt a constant-speed unit, whereby instead of having fixed pitch propellers automatically adjustable ones were used that lowered the blade angle at low speed and increased it as speed rose, changing the pitch by way of a governor to meet the continually changing speeds encountered in operations, and in fighter combat conditions in particular. This was one area were Japan was deficient and Horikoshi revealed that the Navy '… pressured industry to import engineering know-how from the United States'. This was done and as a result, although the early A6M had a two-bladed variable-speed propeller, when these aircraft later suffered from vibration problems in service, subsequent marks used the three-bladed variable-pitch metal Hamilton Standard Constant Speed propeller, which was built under licence by the Osaka-based Sumitomo Metals.

Dr Isamu Igarashi and Engineer Yasuyuki Ozeki of this same corporation had developed a new lighter-weight but higher-strength zinc aluminium alloy (T-7178), which was dubbed Extra Super Duralumin (ESD) and patented in 1936. It was a decade ahead of western practice, although, again, many American historians claim that Japan merely copied US materials. It was, in truth a development of a German invention used in the construction of frames for Zeppelin Airships in World War I. One of these airships was shot down near London and a Japanese military liaison officer stationed there sent a fragment from the wreckage back to Japan for it to be analysed.[5] After receiving Navy approval, Horikoshi eagerly incorporated this metallurgical advance into his design, not for 'skinning' but principally for the main wing sparring and internal forgings.[6] The designer estimated he saved over 66lb (30kg) of weight with this material.

This innovation was a blessing to the A6M designers when weight considerations were paramount throughout every stage and aspect of the project and a constant headache for the Mitsubishi team. Again normal usage had to be thrown aside and even the 1932 established Summary of Airplane Planning went by the board, with Horikoshi opting for a stress safety multiple of 1.6 times the overall aircraft's maximum load weight with certain members constructed as 'slender' units instead of 'stubby' units, rather than the 1.8 factor laid down as standard. Where it did not affect strength detrimentally, widespread use of 'meat trimming' was practised, whereby surplus material was bored out of solid fitments. The use of flush riveting on the semi-monocoque structure combined minimum weight with a aerodynamic airflow, which along with the fully enclosed cockpit and retractable undercarriage, folding inward from a wide base, and even the tail-wheel retracted into a recess under the tail-plane, all made agility in the air machine. This hydraulic tail-wheel retraction gear was prevented from providing egress to dust and debris from land-based operations, with the provision of a canvas cover. Both the Mitsubishi- and the Nakajima-built A6Ms utilized the same design for this cover, which was in two parts to allow free movement of the wheel. Whereas the Type 11s, being land based were rated as 'Base Defence Fighters' the Type 21s were pure and simple carrier-based fighters. With these aircraft destined principally for sea service all were in-built designed to be fitted with a 'stinger' tail hook, located just ahead of the tail-wheel.

The A6M1,[7] due to its lightness, although an incomparable mount in turning combat, was notoriously slow into a dive, and this aroused much criticism post-war from armchair warriors warring from behind their PCs. They accused the designer of an oversight here. In fact, Horikoshi examined this in detail when designing the wing form and area. He wrote:

> ... I decided to provide an ample wing area with a wing span of almost twelve meters, the maximum allowable according to both our experience and foreign data. This permitted me to achieve the Navy's requirements with respect to maneuvering, turning radius, landing and takeoff performance, but it reduced the aircraft's performance with respect to diving, level flight speed, and lateral maneuverability, because of the increased drag and weight of a larger wing. On balance, I decided to proceed with this plan, since turning radius and takeoff performance had a higher priority.

He planned to compensate for the speed issue through the maximum elimination of drag factors, as described above. The A6M's clean lines were an indication of his care. The old maxim that an aircraft looked right then it flew right, applied. The wings had a slight dihedral but the cigar-like fuselage was unmarred save for the for oil cooler air-scoop. In planform the leading edge of the wing tapered more than the trailing edge, while the pilot's view was excellent with a greenhouse style canopy with sliding access that sat above the fuselage giving all-round vision. Behind the (unprotected) pilot's seat was the Direction Finding Antenna loop to enable him to 'home-in' on his parent aircraft carrier in the wastes of the Pacific and he also had a radio compass to further aid ocean navigation. The pilot's fresh air intake was via an elliptical intake located at the starboard wing root, but from airframe #227 onward it was changed to become a smaller square aperture for ease of construction. The carrier-borne A6M pilots were also equipped with both parachutes and life rafts.

Two more controversial features were the large vertical and horizontal tails, which tapered to a point to aid airflow; these added extra weight but were considered essential to give lateral and longitudinal stability. A lengthened fuselage also assisted pilot control when firing the 20mm cannon. The square cannon apertures in either wing were overlarge to minimize blast damage and had curved corners, but the subsequent drag effect resulted in them being reduced in size and made circular, becoming flush with the leading edges of the wing from airframe #326 onward and they were retrofitted on some earlier aircraft. On the credit side the innovative 'wash out', a subtle downward twist to the tapered wings leading-edge extremities, was carried over from the Type 96 design to reduce stall at high angles of attack.

The incorporation of the wings into the fuselage structure and constructing them as one overall unit rather than in outboard and inboard sections, gave added strength here in compensation. Here Horikoshi acknowledged that although he had considered using it earlier, he was following Nakajima's lead here with their Type 97, Ki-27 fighter design.[8] The most glaring omissions to western minds was the omission of armour protection for the pilot and self-sealing fuel tanks, but neither factor had been asked for by the combat pilots themselves, nor in the Navy's specification. It ran against their offensively orientated mind set. However, the war was to show that these increased the A6M's vulnerability, although even Allied aircraft *with* self-sealing tanks frequently failed to survive the experience of taking cannon shells into them. In fact the Mitsubishi team did give serious consideration to fitting such tanks in the wings, but rejected it because the existing aluminium tanks could hold more fuel. To give the Prototype the extra range demanded a streamlined low-drag auxiliary fuel tank to be attached below the fuselage as had been done with the Curtiss Hawk III and was first used in combat by the Luftwaffe's *Kondor Legion* during the Spanish Civil War.

Even with these radical measures Horikoshi and the Prototype team, under Naokazu Yui, still, in March 1938, lacked confidence that they could meet the original Navy specifications. The team returned to Yokosuka once more on 13 April and when Horikoshi revealed his continual worries about which aspect, fighting agility, speed or range, should take priority, it resulted in a fierce argument between Naval Aviation representatives, Lieutenant-Commander Minoru Genda arguing for the former to be stressed, while Lieutenant-Commander Takeo Shibata was equally as vehement for the latter attribute to be emphasized, arguing that combat fighting could be improved by training but speed and range could not. There seemed no possible compromise in the two viewpoints and Horikoshi reached the conclusion that only by adopting a much improved power plant and bringing in the adoption of the constant-speed propeller could he even begin to please both requirements.

The full-scale wooden mock-up was already completed at the Oye-cho Minatoku, Nagoya plant, as per normal practice in those days, with dummy engine and guns emplaced. This was duly inspected by a Navy team under Captain (later Rear-Admiral) Sunichi Kira, and included the irascible Shibata; the design was criticized for its size with a further 100 amendments being recommended. With that, work commenced on the first two actual Prototype 12s themselves. Further theoretical criticisms of the design were received from front-line aviators in China, which led to yet more heart-searching. The 20mm cannon were criticized for their low muzzle-velocity, their limited magazine capacity and low hitting rate. Also criticized was, in an apparent *volte-face*, the long-range and, again, the physical size of the new fighter. Lieutenant-Commander Eiichi Iwaya, controller of fighter production at the Tokyo Naval Aeronautical Headquarters, consulted with Horikoshi and the latter worked hard on an alternative design to meet these requests, but, fortunately, no more was heard of it and work on the Prototype 12 continued unchanged. The first test airframe was duly delivered (in two segments) by rail to the Aeronautical Establishment to be expended in a series of trials to destruction. Known as the Naval Experimental 12-*Shi* Carrier Fighter, this aircraft was to revolutionize air warfare being the first carrier-based fighter to totally out-perform all her land-based opponents. Until the advent of the A6M it was an article of faith among air forces that naval aircraft would always be inferior, due to the demands of ship-born operations in the case of the United States and Japanese navies, and total neglect by their RAF masters in the case of the British FAA. The A6M turned this 'given' on its head.

Under the auspices of Dr Kiyoshi Matsudaira and Engineer Tsugumaro Imanaka, the results of the vibration tests were pronounced as very good as were the wind tunnel and flutter tests figures with stress tests to follow. The only modifications insisted upon at this stage were that the tail should be re-positioned further aft; with a small ventral fin added to the Prototypes in the interim. Meanwhile, the completion of the first Prototype led to its own inspection on 17 March 1939. Done on site by a Navy Inspector, the principal concern for Horikoshi was, as always, the weight factor. The aircraft had already been criticized purely on size, but weight was crucial. In fact, the aircraft came in at 3,452.2lb (1,566kg) against the original estimate of 3,382lb (1,534kg), but this extra 342lb (55kg) could be explained away by the excess weight of the engine, propeller and landing gear, all of which had been sourced by the Navy itself, and therefore the Mitsubishi team were thus fully exonerated. Horikoshi revealed that when it came to the first Prototype's initial flight from Kawasaki's Kagamigahara, Gifu Prefecture, on 23 March 1939, the weight came out at 3,571lb (1,620kg), an excess of 190lb (86kg), but with the same unavoidable deductions applied the Navy still considered this satisfactory. On 1 April 1939 the Prototype A6M1 Type 0 carrier fighter made its first official test flight.

Some indication as to why westerners believed that no such aircraft could possibly be designed and built, let alone operated by a nation such as Japan, (her acknowledged military and naval humiliation of both China and Tsarist Russia just a few decades earlier, notwithstanding), can be gleaned by the mode of transportation of this high-tech machine from plant to the closest flight test ground. Disassembled into two sections, the transportation was conducted by ox-cart over unpaved roads! The A6M was to retain this detachable rear fuselage feature in order to facilitate transport but also to simplify maintenance. It was found that this useful function had the drawback of entailing damage to the glazed rear segment of the cockpit canopy on occasions. To overcome this, a totally metallic after segment was substituted from airframe #47 onward. The date of the first test flight was 1 April 1939 and Kumataro Takenaka ensured all was ready before being joined by many of the design and construction teams. Two test pilots were on standby for this flight, Harumi Aratani, a graduate of Tokyo Engineering University who had undergone Navy flight training, and the more experienced Katsuzo Shima, a retired Navy Petty Officer with a long track record of successful flight testing at the Aeronautical Establishment. In the end Shima was selected for the initial ground testing and brief 'jump' aerial flight. On conclusion Shima expressed satisfaction with the control surfaces, but dissatisfaction with the machine's braking system. Further flights with the undercarriage down were carried out by both test pilots duly over the next twelve days, overseen by Commander Satoshi Imada and Lieutenant-Commander Hiroyoshi Nishizawa. Vibration was experienced in the climb, level flight and gliding with the engine shut down. This problem remained in subsequent flight testing with the undercarriage fully retracted; this was found to be due to resonance and a change from a two-bladed propeller to a three-bladed one in tests conducted on 17/18 April reduced this vibration by 50 per cent. A second difficulty involved the elevators, which proved to be over-efficient at higher speeds. This Horikoshi solved by a major re-design aimed at reducing the stiffness in the control system and introducing more springiness, while at the same time reducing the weight of the control cables without sacrificing strength. Extensive wind tunnel testing revealed the validity of this solution, which was adopted forthwith.[9] On 25 April the aircraft was laden to a weight of 5,139lb (2,331kg), the planned regular operations norm, and flight tested. The recorded speed was 304.47mph (490km/h), which Yoshimura stated was less its true speed by about 11.75mph (18km/h) due to a faulty Pitot tube placement.[10] If true then the planned-for speed of 316.68mph (500km/h) was actually exceeded that day, a highly satisfactory result.

As part of the solution, the Navy had granted permission for the *Zuisei* engine fitted in the first two A6M1 aircraft with a Nakajima *Sakae* Type 12, Navy designation NK1C, for the third test model. The *Sakae* ('Prosperity') was a 950hp, double-row, 14-cylinder, air-cooled radial engine licence-built from the French Gnome-Rhone 14k. With this power plant the aircraft was expected to easily meet and exceed the original IJN *12-Shi* specifications

Meanwhile, with the first Prototype there still remained issues with the stiffness of the ailerons, however, and the Navy pressured Mitsubishi to solve these problems quickly. After adjustments to the control system flight testing by four different test pilots, Harumi Aratani, Seiichi Maki, Chujiro Nakano and Katuzo Shima, on 6 July, improvements to the elevators were shown, but the trials continued. On 23 and 24 August and again 10 September, yet further flight tests were conducted at Kagamigahara and, after minor tweaking, the condition was deemed satisfactory. Speeds of 316.28mph (509km/h) were recorded at 11,811ft (3,600m) altitude. The two A6M1 aircraft (Serials #201 and #202) remained the only ones of their type.

The arrival of the *Sakae* engine was accompanied by other modifications and ultimately brought about a change of designation to A6M2. The new prototype machine was duly fully successfully flight-tested at Kagamigahara field on 5 June in front of Vice-Admiral Koichi Hanajima by test pilots Aratani and Shima. Further tweaking of the new control system, and the replacement of the first engine with a more reliable one of the same type, followed and on 6 and 7 July Navy test pilots Lieutenant-Commander Chujiro Nakano and Lieutenant Seiichi Maki joined the flight testing. As a result all further attempts at using the two-bladed propeller were abandoned. A total of forty-seven test flights were carried out at this time, followed by further official tests on 23/24 August and a final Acceptance Flight was concluded on 13 September. Total flight-testing for the Zero was therefore only 43 hours and 26 minutes over 119 flights which, considering the revolutionary aspect of the aircraft, was quite impressive. Service testing of various aspects continued under the auspices of Lieutenant Mambeye Shimokawa of the Yokosuka *Kōkūtai*. Thus, after ground tests and 215 flight tests, the Prototype 12-*Shi* was formally handed over on 14 September.

Demands from the China front continued to be received and continued to be the same conflicting pulls between manoeuvrability and range, with the latter now predominating as the Chinese Air Force had unilaterally withdrawn from engaging regular fighter combat at this time. Still, the overriding call was for the new fighter to reach the front as urgently as possible. The Naval Aeronautics Headquarters reacted to this by initiating a plan to introduce at least some preliminary A6Ms into the combat zone ahead of schedule. The tests of the second Prototype 12 followed at Kagamigahara on 25 September and at Yokosuka from 18 October.

On 18 and 19 January 1940 the third Prototype was flight-tested with the *Sakae*-12 engine. As predicted, results were highly satisfactory, and testing continued at Yokosuka from 25 January onward. Three more aircraft followed, each with minor changes, many involving the introduction of the constant-speed propeller.

However, plans for early introduction into service were threatened when, on 11 March 1940, the second prototype, carrying out a series of dives to test the constant speed propeller's variable pitch operation, with experienced test pilot Masumi Okuyama of the Establishment, had apparently disintegrated in mid-air over Oppama field. According to eyewitness reports there was an explosion at an altitude of 16,460.5 to 1,312ft (500–400m), which blew the wing off, the engine and propeller separated and the fuselage disintegrated. Although Okuyama successfully baled out at 1,312ft to 984ft (300–400m) he became separated from his parachute and fatally plunged into the shallow waters just off the coast. On the conclusion of the prolonged Naval Aeronautical Engineering Establishment (as it had now become) trials and testing, the Navy concluded that the mass balance weight (mbw – which was an adjustable attachment to the control surface of an aircraft in an effort to eliminate or reduce flutter) attached to the elevators had become fatally weakened by repeated operational shocks and had sheared off, causing uncontrollable elevator flutter and, in turn, terminal vibration through the airframe. Measures were taken to redesign and strengthen this area, but it was to result in an inevitable delay to the operational use of the aircraft, which was postponed to July by which time the name *Reisen* had started to come into general usage in Japan itself, while Zero was beginning to be accepted elsewhere.

Chapter 3

Trial and Error

In the official designation in Japan of the A6M, the letter A designated it was a carrier fighter, the letter M indicated it was a Mitsubishi design, and the figure 6 meant it was the sixth such type designed by that company. A second figure was added after this indicating the production series. Thus the A6M1 was the prototype indicator. The designation Type 'O' was an abbreviation of the Japanese year in which it appeared, which in the case of the A6M was the Japanese Year 2600. It was not until 31 July 1940 that the official designation The Type Zero Carrier-Based Fighter, Model 11 was formally adopted and Mitsubishi was notified of this fact. This was quickly modified into everyday usage as the 'Type 00', which in turn became simplified to 'Zero' around the world, although other Japanese aircraft had been accepted in this same year. Each version of the aircraft was also allocated a Model Serial, the first being Model 11 and this aircraft, sixty-six of which were initially produced, had fixed elliptical wing-tips. An adaption to enable the A6M to fit the new carrier's lifts and hangars was the adoption of folding wing-tips and this became the Model 21, arguably the most famous Model of many that subsequently followed. The Japanese also referred to this aircraft as the *Rei-sen*, which was a composite word amalgamating *rei* (Zero) with the abbreviation of the Japanese for fighter, *Sentoki*, which became shortened to *sen*. Common usage both at home and abroad settled, after various alternatives such as Navy-O, Double-OO and so on, to Zero. Another option was *Reisen Kanjukisen* (Celebration) marking the 2,600th anniversary of Emperor Jimmu's reign. When later allocated a name under the Allied code system devised in July 1942 by Captain Frank T. McCoy's Air Technical Intelligence Unit (ATIU) at Hangar 7, Eagle Farm airfield, Brisbane, the A6M was designated as the 'Zeke'.[1] Other units referred to them as the 'Ben' and others as the 'Ray' for short periods. Later a variant, the Zeke 32, received the separate name of *Hap*, later changed to *Hamp* for a while due, it was rumoured, to the strong and indignant objections of General Henry H. 'Hap' Arnold, Chief of the USAAF, himself; while a floatplane fighter variant received the code-name *Rufe*. But whether the *Reisen*, Zeke or Navy-O, she was to achieve world-wide immortality as the Zero.

Many foreign observers at the time (indeed many current American die-hards), amazed at the performance of the A6M fighter, totally refused to accept that this aircraft was the result of Japanese thinking and originality. Even today some websites contain such claims; even the Grumman F6F Hellcat is touted as a contender on one forum even though it appeared five or six years later than the A6M and was specifically designed to counter it! Aside from such nonsense however, serious allegations have been made down the years.

Even decades after end of the war Americans doggedly maintain that Horikoshi copied features from American aircraft of the period, even vastly inferior ones! Their mind-set remain firmly fixed in an outdated and never very accurate cultural assessment, which even Japan's post-war technical dominance failed to expunge. Examples abound but we can look at a few.

Over four decades on from the war's termination Air Force journalist Gary Boyd repeated a twenty-year-old claim originally made by another author in a British magazine[2] that Horikoshi merely copied the best features of the Vought V-143 fighter. This prototype had been rejected by the United States Army Air Service (USAAS)[3] but the Mitsubishi Company bought it and shipped it back to Japan for detailed analysis around the same time that Horikoshi was beginning his design work for the A6M.[4] The allegation has more recently been regurgitated yet again.[5]

Originally a 1935 Northrop concept, the 3A, this single-seater, low-wing, monoplane fighter with enclosed cockpit and retractable undercarriage, was developed from the XFT carrier prototype, which Vought took over in 1936, when she became re-designated as the V-141. The USAAC rejected her in favour of the Seversky P-35. Re-modified as the V-143 with a 750hp (551.62kW) Pratt & Whitney R-1535-A5G radial engine, she was again rejected, this time by Argentina, Turkey, Norway, Sweden and Yugoslavia. The re-engined aircraft was otherwise modified but once more rejected by the USAAC in June 1937. The aircraft was demonstrated to a certain

Captain (later Rear-Admiral) Misao Wada of the engineering division of the IJN at Hartford, Connecticut, on 26 April by well-known Test Pilot Edmund T. Allen. They asked whether it could be fitted with the Swedish Oerlikon FF (under licences as the '*Aerlikan*' Type 'E' or Type 99-1) 20mm wing cannon (oddly, the current IJN terminology of the day termed these weapons machine-guns). The fixed wing-mounted cannon were supplied from 60-round drum magazines firing 72RB rounds at 490rpm, with a muzzle velocity of 1,970ft/sec (600m/sec).[6] The weight of each projectile was 129 grams and the weight of each gun was 50.7lb (23kg).[7] These new weapons were to be produced by a new arms manufacturer established by a group of retired admirals, the Dai Nihon Heiki KK.

In July 1937 the aircraft was finally sold to Mitsubishi for $175,000 and they duly tested as Navy Experimental Fighter Type AXVI for the IJN, and they, in turn, rejected it as being inferior to current Navy type fighters! And that was that. However, in 1946 an American newspaper columnist, one Drew Pearson, ran a story on the sale and how, during an inspection of an A6M shot down over Honolulu during the Pearl Harbor assault, Vought's President, Eugene E. Wilson, had told Admiral Chester W. Nimitz, Commander-in-Chief, Pacific Fleet, '… that's a Vought-Northrop fighter I tried to sell the Navy …'. Further fuel to the fire came from Vought's Chief Engineer Fred N. Dickerman, who stated, '… the Zero was just a copy of an airplane that Northrop originally designed and built'. In fact, the only thing comparable between the two designs appears to have been the landing gear retraction system.

Another much-touted American contender for the Zero's origin has been the Hughes 1B Racer – a product of the febrile and erratic genius of Howard Hughes. Designed for Hughes by Richard Palmer, the H-1 was indeed a groundbreaker, a cantilever monoplane incorporating many revolutionary construction techniques, such as flush riveting to leave a smooth aluminium skin with no drag and similarly both the main undercarriage and the tail skid were fully retractable to aid the same result.[8] As a low-wing monoplane in the age of biplanes the H-1 found no favour with the USAAC, being too much ahead of its time. Despite its powerful 700hp (522kW) Pratt & Whitney R-1535 two-row 14-cylinder radial being tuned to emit more than 1,000hp (750kW), thus giving her a maximum speed of 352mph (566km/h) when she broke the world landplane speed record in 1935, no military orders resulted. With new wings the H-1 also smashed the non-stop transcontinental speed record in 1937.

Hughes himself kick-started this myth post-war when he stated that Mitsubishi filched large parts of his design, claiming that it was obvious to everybody that on examination of the two aircraft the Japanese Zero fighter was substantially a copy of the Hughes H-1 Racer. Hughes, who was actually defending himself from hostile press accusations of actually designing the Zero for the Japanese, said:

> The Japanese Zero was a shock of the utmost magnitude to the United States because it had been thought up to that time that the Japanese were far inferior mechanically. I should say in point of aircraft design and mechanical aptitude, to the United States and nobody expected the Japanese to have an airplane that would be at all competitive. Well, in any event, when one of these Japanese Zeroes was finally captured and studied and analyzed it was quite apparent to everyone that it had been copied from the Hughes plane …

A certain Al Ludwick had stated that Japanese generals had made a detailed inspection of the H-1 in New Jersey pre-war, at least according to Bill Utley, who acted as the Hughes Corporations publicity officer. This unsubstantiated story (the Japanese Army Air Force had no input whatsoever into Japanese Navy aviation), was given wide publicity and is still repeated, but in an exclusive interview with one aviation writer, Horikoshi himself totally denied that the H-1 had any influence on his design.[9] He stated later that with regard to the A6M nothing came directly from any foreign design. Fortunately, the National Air & Space Museum houses both the H-1, donated to the Smithsonian in 1975, and an example of a salvaged A6M from Saipan, so anyone with an interest can visit and compare for themselves the validity or otherwise of both Hughes' claim and Horikoshi's denial.

In 1980 Paul R. Matt answered the origins of the Zero theorist's puerile speculations in this manner: 'And that poor Mitsubishi OO Zero … it was the copy of so many aircraft it's a wonder it ever flew incorporating so many foreign parts. The Hughes Racer did not escape the lookalike contest. The myth is so out of step that no further comment is necessary.' Alas Paul, another four decades down the line, and the Internet abounds with 'the conspiracy of copying' devotees repeating the same old legends.[10]

Perhaps the closest foreign aircraft in appearance was the Gloster F.5/34, designed by H. P. Folland, two prototypes of which were built in response to an Air Ministry requirement for a fighter that could, ironically enough, operate in the hot climates of the Far East! When the first machine appeared (K5604) in December 1937 the resemblance was uncanny, being a all-metal cantilever, low-wing monoplane powered by a 9-cylinder Mercury IX air-cooled radial engine of 840hp (625kW). The wingspan was 38ft 2in (11.63m), shorter than the A6M, overall length 32ft (9.97m) longer than the Japanese machine. The powerful gun armament consisted of no fewer than eight 0.303in (7.7mm) calibre Brownings. She was credited with a speed of 316mph (508km/h or 275 knots). A second aircraft (K8089) appeared in May 1938 but no further development took place and the two machines became test beds until around 1941. Although Gloster had previously done work with Nakajima, there is no truth at all in the persistent stories that this aircraft had any connections at all with the A6M design.

Chapter 4

Into Action

1940 was the year of transition for the Japanese Navy's fighter force, with 153 A5M4s being produced against 98 of the new A6M2s. The figures are very modest for both types considering the combat involvement in China but they make reflective reading. In the first four months of the year just one A6M2 per month appeared compared with A5M4 figures of 20, 19, 17 and 14 respectively. In the next three months A5M4 production remained steady at fourteen machines per month, while in May four of the new fighters were produced, with three in June and nine in July. August saw A6M2 production exceed A5M4 numbers for the first time, but only six of the latter and eight of the former appeared. September was similar with just five A5M4s against nine A6M2s. The last three months saw a continuation of the trend with the A5M4 tailing off to eleven, nine and ten only while the A6M2 totals were nineteen, twenty-three and nineteen respectively for October, November and December.[1]

Meanwhile, knowledge of the new Navy fighter had long circulated among the veterans at the front over the three years of development and their demands for its earliest introduction led, as we have seen, to the despatch of fifteen preproduction *Rei-sens*. There was strong opposition from many in the Navy against this move, which was felt to be highly premature. Although impressed by the aircraft's performance many felt that further flying experience was necessary as minor problems were still being experienced. Even top-notch pilots needed to get accustomed to such a powerful new machine before being pitched into combat. Teams of highly qualified pilots were being assembled and were undergoing intense training and these had encountered difficulties. Problems were experienced during the firing of the 20mm cannon, already suspect by the China Group as we have seen, when they tended to jam at high acceleration. The fault was found to be inadequate clearance in the cartridge ejector tube, which had to be modified.

Such a blockage might very well have proved fatal if encountered in actual aerial combat. A different problem occurred on 25 June when Lieutenant-Commander Manbeye Shimokawa's group of six aircraft was conducting climb and altitude testing. One aircraft had a sudden oil pressure malfunction at 25,590.6ft (7,800m) altitude and a second reached 33,793ft (10,300m) before suffering engine difficulties. Analysis of the problems found that due to the A6M's good, if not exceptional, climb rate, fuel cooled extremely rapidly and vaporized, chocking the pipe. The solution was found to be the use of a newly introduced aviation fuel with a 92-octane rating. Another fuel-related problem concerned the new streamlined long-range ventral drop tank. This was designed for quick-release when combat was imminent but in practice it sometimes refused to detach unless the aircraft's speed was below 205mph (330km/h). Fortunately this unintentional retention was found not to impair the A6M's actual aerial performance unduly when it occurred. Finally, cylinder overheating problems were encountered during dog-fighting practice or when climbing under full-power. This glitch was unresolved when the units were suddenly ordered to China.

Despite these teething problems the urgency from the front was such that these aircraft flew out with their picked, but still not yet fully familiar, pilots, in two groups, six under the command of an experienced combat pilot from the carrier *Sōryū*, Lieutenant Tamotsu Yokoyama of the Omura *Kōkutai*, and nine under Lieutenant Saburo Sugindo of the Yokosuka *Kōkutai*. Initially these A6Ms were allocated to operate under the 12 *Rengo Kōkūtai* (Joint Naval Air Corps) commanded by Captain Kiichiro Hasegawa, based at Hankow on July 21 —which was ten days *before* the IJN officially accepted the A6M2 into service. Overall command was vested in Admiral Shigetarō Shimada of the China Air Area Fleet. The move also necessitated the despatch of ten newly trained A6M ground servicing teams, plus specialist technicians to work on the faults while in the field; these included armament specialist Sotoji Inzei, engine specialist Lieutenant Osamu Nagano and Lieutenant Shoichi Takayama to oversee airframe problems.[2]

Under the IJN organization each *Daitai* (unit) comprised a base unit with between eighteen and twenty-seven operational aircraft and up to twelve reserve machines. The entire A6M complement of a carrier division was termed the *Kōkū-sentai*. Each type of aircraft, fighter, dive-bomber, torpedo-bomber, had its own *hikōtai* (squadron) with a *hikōtaichō* (squadron leader) under overall command of a rear-admiral, and was composed of *hikōtai* (squadrons) under the command of a lieutenant (j.g) or warrant officer. Each had a *fukuchō* (executive officer or XO). Normally nine aircraft comprised a *chūtai* (division), which normally had nine aircraft on strength plus three reserves. There were usually three sub-divisions, *shōtai*, with three aircraft apiece, usually deployed in inverted 'V' formation and the leading aircraft stepped-down a little, described by one RAF pilot as a '... the loose trailing formation ...'. Later, from 1944 onward, a different formation was adopted following American practice and became based on the two-plane *buntai*. The *shōtai* became four-plane formations and chūtai eight with the *daitai* reduced to sixteen, while the *hikōtai* became uniform and adopted a two-or three-numerical designation.[3]

In fact the initial fifteen Model 11 A6M2s[4] that were sent over to China for combat evaluation, were hand-made pre-production prototypes. Immediately upon arrival at Hankow there were high expectations among veterans of air fighting conditions over China, chiefly Rear-Admiral Takijirō Ōnishi, 2 *Rengo Kōkūtai* 2 Joint Air Corps) commander and Rear-Admiral Tamon Yamaguchi, 1 *Rengo Kōkūtai* (1 Joint Air Corps) that they could go straight into action. Both men were 'fire-eaters' who wished to get stuck into the enemy, but Yokoyama had to tactfully disabuse his two superiors and explain that the Zero was not quite ready. Even so he was under considerable and constant pressure to get his units into battle. A suitable 'fix' was found for the cylinder overheating problem and meanwhile nine further A6Ms flew in under Lieutenant Saburo Shindo and were similarly modified. The Zero was finally ready for action.

Although pronounced fit to fight, actually achieving any combat contact with an increasingly reluctant Chinese enemy was itself a frustrating experience as they once again stubbornly refuse to engage. Whether forewarned by spies at Hankow or not, the Chinese policy was to avoid all air action. The first mission of the A6M took place on 19 August and saw Lieutenant Yokoyama lead twelve of them as escort for fifty-four Mitsubishi G3M *Rikko* Navy bombers[5] for a bombing attack on Chungking. For the A6M this mission, involving as it did a round-trip of over 1,118 miles (1,800km) by a single-engined aircraft was a validation of its long-range credentials. The hitherto immunity of distant enemy targets abruptly ceased with the arrival of the Zero. Thirty enemy fighters were reported in the air and waiting for them; however, whether or not the Chinese had been forewarned, they once more refused the bait and absolutely no aerial opposition was encountered over the target. The bombers discharged at will with no reaction and all returned to base unscratched. The same lack of reaction was encountered the following day when Lieutenant Shindo carried a similar escort mission of G3M bombers to the same target. All the A6Ms could do was make a strafing attack on Chonmachow airfield on their journey back to base.

The Navy was about to terminate the bulk of its involvement in China, planning to withdraw all its aircraft save a few selected units and this inability to draw up the Chinese defenders and administer a drubbing before they left was frustrating. It therefore was decided to leave the special group of Zeros and a group of bombers to continue operations for a further period. The Japanese tried again on 12 September, with Lieutenant Yokoyma leading twelve A6Ms escorting twenty-seven bombers this time. Accompanying this force was a Tachikawa Ki-36 Type 98 Direct Cooperation Reconnaissance aircraft. A monoplane (later codenamed 'Ida'), this machine had a service ceiling of 26,740ft (8140.4m) and she circled the Chungking area at high altitude and took aerial photographs while the attack was underway. Once again no air combat resulted but the Japanese were able to analyse that thirty-two Chinese fighter aircraft identified on the ground prior the attack, took off and sought sanctuary in the mountains during the raid. Once the Japanese aircraft had withdrawn these fighters re-appeared and after a brief sortie landed once more.

Accordingly, Yokoyama and Shindo laid a simple trap to surprise these reluctant warriors into battle. On 13 September yet another air raid was mounted against Chungking and thirteen A6Ms participated in two groups, commanded respectively by Lieutenant Saburo Shindo in person and Lieutenant (j.g.) Ayao Shirane. The formation was again observed from on high by the Tachikawa Ki-36. The fighters stationed themselves above and behind the bombers during the actual attack and, as before, departed in the same formation on completion of the bombing run. However, the reconnaissance aircraft maintained a watch above the city and was duly rewarded when Chinese aircraft were once more seen returning to the area from their south-westerly loitering point. The scout immediately radioed this information to Shindo, and the thirteen A6Ms reversed course once more taking up a watching position to the north of the city, an area of the sky in which they were obscured from the approaching Chinese, which were deployed in nine sections each of three fighters, twenty-seven machines in total. The enemy were identified as Soviet-built and supplied Polikarpov I-15 and I-16 fighters.

Unwittingly then the Chinese Air Force had seemingly obligingly played to the A6M's strengths and paid the penalty. The A6Ms had the advantage of altitude and surprise and attacked immediately before the enemy could flee once more. Within the space of ten minutes every one of the Chinese fighters were destroyed without loss to the Japanese. In addition to their speed, which enabled the Japanese aircraft to easily overtake the fleeing enemy, Horikoshi was told that the smashing power of the 20mm cannon was decisive; as he later explained, '... if the shells hit the wing root, they destroyed the entire wing. This is understandable if one remembers that the wing of an aircraft is under heavy load when it is going at high speed, and under such circumstances the wing will come off very easily when hit.' Those not destroyed in the one-sided dog-fight were wrecked by crashing after three of their pilots prematurely baled out, while two others went in trying to evade combat.[6] Two more were torched on the ground at Baishiyei field. The only damaged received by the Japanese aircraft was that one, piloted by Ensign Yoshio Oki, was hit in the fuel tank, which failed to release, but did not explode, and three others who had trivial damage.

So pleased was the Navy at the magnificent debut that what were considered to be three main contributors, the Mitsubishi design team, the Dai-Nihon Heiki (Japanese Weapons Company) for the 20mm cannon and Nakajima Aircraft for the *Sakae* engine, were summoned directly to Tokyo on 14 September for a special commendation ceremony at the Navy Ministry itself overseen by Vice-Admiral Teijiro Toyata, Chief of Naval Aeronautics. However, in order to conceal the performance of the new fighter from potential enemies the terms Zero or Navy Type O were, for the time being, censored from the press who referred to the victorious fighters and their crews by the euphemism 'Sea Hawks'.

Clearly the A6M had proved a great success and rapid expansion was ordered. In common with the usual existing IJN practice at this time the Navy extended the production to include the rival Nakajima Company. Mitsubishi was paid for the design and then transferred all the necessary documentation over from Nagoya to Nakasaki's Koizumi plant. This ensured a smooth transition and production was thus almost seamless, with the first Koizumi Zero being accepted as early as September 1941.

None of the subsequent aerial fighting exceeded this stunning debut, but the operational qualities of the A6M impressed both friend and foe alike and from then on the Japanese dominated the air war in China, while the Chinese found fewer and fewer sanctuaries. The next mission they were involved in was mounted on 16 September, and again the target was Chungking, but they could only find a single enemy aircraft, which was summarily dispatched. The skies were clear and it was plain that even longer-range sorties would be necessary to flush their foes out of hiding. Accordingly, on 4 October, eight A6Ms in two groups of four, under Lieutenants Shirane and Yokoyama, flew cover for twenty-seven G3M bombers against Chengtu, Szechwan Province. The flight involved a refuelling stop at Ichang. Only one enemy fighter was encountered near the target and this was promptly destroyed by Petty Officer Matsuo Hagiri. The fighters went to Taipingsi airfield where they located and destroyed five I-16Bs and a Soviet Tupolev SB-2 medium bomber before machine-gunning and destroying nineteen aircraft on the ground, damaging four more and many of the airfield facilities. Not content with this, and to show their contempt for the enemy, four A6M pilots, Warrant Officer Ichirō Higashiyama and Petty Officers Matsuo Hagiri, Masataka Nakaishi and Hideo Oishi, deliberately landed their aircraft on the runway. Their plan was to leave their aircraft engines running and by hand, personally destroy remaining enemy machines. This was a foolhardy and quite dangerous idea, typical of the aggressive mindset of the Japanese of course, but could have left four of Japanese most secret fighter aircraft at the mercy of the enemy. Strong defensive fire from the Chinese troops guarding the airfield forced this mad scheme to be aborted promptly but all four got away safely. Subsequently two I-16s and a Soviet-supplied Tupolev SB twin-engined bomber were destroyed. Only two A6Ms received slight damage and the unit received yet another special commendation for the mission.

On 5 October a raid was made on Chengtu's Fenghuangshan airfield with just seven A6Ms under Lieutenant Fusata Lida; ten aircraft were destroyed along with fourteen decoys.

Meanwhile, from 5 September Japan's southern expansion had continued when the pro-Nazi Vichy Regime in French Indo-China agreed to permit Japanese forces to move into French air bases in the Saigon area, Thu Dau Moi, Soc Tranaga, Phu Quoc and others. Into these bases flew one *Hikōtai* of the 12 *Rengo Kōkūtai* (12 Joint Air Corps) A6Ms to conduct long-range escort missions. Their first success was during an attack on Kunming when seven A6Ms and nine A5Ms escorted Aichi D3A1 dive-bombers (later code-named 'Val'). During an aerial melee there thirteen Chinese aircraft were shot down. A similar mission against Siangyun on 12 December saw seven A6Ms involved and they destroyed twenty-two Chinese aircraft caught on the ground, while on 8 October to 31 December 1940, they flew a total of twenty-two sorties but only managed to find and destroy two enemy aircraft.

Meanwhile the IJN recalled all its G3M bombers back to Japan leaving just the remaining thirty A6Ms at Hankow to continue to fly missions against the familiar targets of Chunking and Chengtu. No enemy were flushed on 10 October, but on the 26th of that month eight A6Ms caught and shot down ten Chinese aircraft over Chengtu, while on 30 December eight Zeros made a fourth attack over that cities airfields, strafing Fenghuangshan, Taipingssu, Shuanglin and Wenchiang, during which thirty-two enemy planes were destroyed as well as wrecking ground facilities, all without loss, although a pair of A6Ms were slightly damaged by flak.

By the end of 1940 the A6M's combat record was impressive. Not a single Zero had been lost, and just thirteen slightly damaged, mainly by ground fire, while in return they had mounted 153 sorties, and achieved 212 'kills' both aerial and on the ground. When aerial fighting resumed targets remained scarce but, on 14 March, again over Chengtu, the A6Ms led by Yokoyama managed to intercept a strong Chinese squadron and destroyed two dozen of them, with three probables. The G3M bombers returned in May along with the new Mitsubishi G4M (late code-named 'Betty') and the A6M's resumed long-range escort missions once more.

On 20 May thirty Zeros yet again strafed installations and parked aircraft at Shuanaglin and Taipingssu fields at Chengtu. Here the A6Ms' incredible good fortune finally ran out and they suffered their first casualty. The aircraft of Petty Officer Eichi Kimura was heavily hit by ground fire and it crashed, killing the pilot. Three other Zeros suffered damage on this day, an indication that the German-trained and controlled flak gunners were getting their eyes in. Kimura's aircraft wreckage was located and examined and a fairly accurate report on its armament and other details was compiled by the Chinese. This information was subsequently passed on to Singapore via Hong Kong and thence forwarded to London. As we have recorded the British Air Attaché at Chungking also sent details of the estimated performance figures for the machine, which he stated was 'Good, by any standard', which the Combined Air Intelligence Bureau also forwarded but it failed to make much impression. The RAF's Air Vice-Marshal Conway Walter Heath Pulford stated on 15 October 1941 to assembled pressmen that the 'Navy O' fighter was '… on a par with our Buffalo …'.[7]

Attacks continued, 22 May seeing nineteen A6Ms deployed against Chentgtu, where they shot down a pair of Chinese machines and burnt ten more on the deck, but they suffered five of their numbers hit by anti-aircraft fire in return. On 26 May nine A6Ms hit Nancheng where they engaged twenty Chinese machines and shot down five of them without loss to themselves before strafing and destroying another eighteen aircraft on the ground. On 27 May twenty A6Ms were over Lanchow but the Chinese refused combat, although a pair were torched on the runway. It was back to Chungking once more on 7 June when four Zeros shot down one of a pair of Chinese fighters. Another large group, totalling twenty A6Ms again sortied against Lanchow but encountered no aerial opposition, but again fierce flak damaged two of their number.

On 22 June nine Zeros were over Chengtu again, where they found a few targets on the ground, which they strafed. At the same time a further six had better fortune when they engaged six Chinese fighters over Kanyuan, and shot down half of them without loss. Seven further A6Ms raided Tienshui with seven aircraft and destroyed a solitary enemy plane there, while on 27 June it was the turn of Ipin, where six A6Ms destroyed two and damaged five other Chinese aircraft.

The second combat loss of a Zero occurred on 23 June. She was part of a three-plane escort for a pair of Type Mitsubishi C5M2 Type 98 Command

Reconnaissance aircraft (later code-named 'Babs') at low-altitude in the area of Lanchow and Yuncheng. This group was bracketed by extremely accurate anti-aircraft barrage and the mount of Kichiro Kobayashi was heavily hit and crashed, killing the pilot.

Not until 11 August did the A6Ms manage to bring the enemy to battle once more; this time the engagement took place above Chengtu. Seven of the new G4M bombers were under escort of sixteen Zeros this day when the Chinese decided at last to offer resistance. While defensive fire from the bombers claimed two enemy fighters, the Zeros' 20mm cannon destroyed three more before the fighters disengaged, without loss to the Japanese force. Seven further enemy machines were destroyed on the ground and nine damaged to varying degrees.

Finally the A6M's range was tested as never before with a raid planned against Sung-p'an (Songpan, Sichuan Province). Due to its remote location and barred by mountain ranges, this city had only been attack once before. The plan was for five of the best Zero pilots to mount the operation being led through the difficult approaches by a pair of Tachikawa Ki-36 98 reconnaissance aircraft. The mission was mounted on 31 August, but the weather conditions were too intense and all seven aircraft were forced to abort. This proved to be the final Zero sortie of the 'China Incident' for now the war clouds were lowering over the Pacific and the Navy was withdrawing its eagles to their eyries in readiness for more serious opposition.

The operations of 1941 had seen the A6M conduct 354 sorties and they had destroyed forty-four Chinese aircraft in aerial combat and damaged sixty-two more. All this cost the Zero just two of their number, both destroyed by flak, while twenty-six had minor damage.

The final commander of the A6M detachment in China had been Ayao Shirane and the unit had built up a fine record of expertise and skill during its time in China, among the recognized outstanding pilots were Koshiro Yamashita with five confirmed kills; Kihei Fujiwara and Yoshio Ohki each with four kills; Tsutomu Iwai and Toraichi Takatsuka both with three kills; Saburo Kitabatake, Masayuki Mitsumasa, Kazuki Mikami and Hatsuyama Yamaya all with two kills apiece, and Masaharu Miramoto, Ayao Shirane and Toshiyuki Sueda, each with a single kill to their credit. By this time Stalin had ordered the Russian 'volunteers' back home, leaving the skies to the Japanese until the much later arrival of the American Volunteer Group (AVG or 'Flying Tigers') equipped with Curtiss P-40B Warhawks.

At this period Mitsubishi was producing about one A6M each day at Kagamigahara, which were then flown to Yokosuka but as reports from the front came in minor changes were being incorporated all the time to tweak and improve the aircraft. As a result the strengthening of the rear wing spar was deemed desirable and this was carried out on the twenty-second A6M2 onward when the fin and rudders were enhanced. Minor amendments included the shifting of the engine exhaust tubes back from the fourth to the fifth cowl flap from airframe #35 onward. The oil cooler and carburettor intake remained combined as in the Model 11 for the initial trio of the new model, used solely as trial aircraft but subsequent to those three airframes the cooler and carburettor were separate and each had it own individual air intake. From the sixty-seventh aircraft the 'pinched' shape of the chin scoop changed to a full depth intake. Another problem was the re-occurrence of complaints, first encountered with the initial Prototype, of the heaviness of the ailerons at certain speeds and in certain configurations. The 'fix' here was invented by Technical Establishment's Lieutenant Isao Takayama who introduced balance tabs on the trailing aileron edges, which kicked in once the undercarriage was fully retracted. This modification was carried out from the sixty-second production aircraft. With the move back to the Pacific and carrier operations once more predominating, the question of stowage aboard the new carriers, the deck elevators (lifts in Royal Navy parlance), which were of smaller dimensions, arose. The precise wingspan of the A6M was 39ft $4^7/_{16}$in (12m) so Hirotsugu Hirayama helped to resolve this difficulty by re-designing the wing-tips so that they folded vertically upward about $19^{11}/_{16}$in (0.5m) inboard. This modification was introduced on the sixty-fifth production aircraft and resulted in a new designation, changing from land to carrier-based function from the Model 11 to the Model 21. Another change was the result of combat experience in China, where pilots had been complaining, with increasing vehemence, about the heaviness at higher speeds of the controls. The Navy's answer was to introduce a trailing-edge aileron balance tab linked to the landing gear retraction mechanism, which reduced the problem. This was introduced on the 127th aircraft. Further aileron flutter problems resulted, which was rectified by modification of the tab balance on the 192nd aircraft.

January 1941 had witnessed the annual competition between the fighter aircraft of the Imperial Army and Navy. The A6M, piloted alternately by Lieutenant Yoshitomi and Lieutenant Manbeye Shimokawa, had been entered against the Army types Nakajima-built Ki-27 ('Nate'), Ki-43 (''Oscar') and Ki-44 ('Tojo'). In the all-important consideration the (on-paper) superior Ki-44 was totally outclassed by the Zero. The top speed recorded by the A6M during the competition was 329mph (530km/h). All military aircraft of this period had an emergency over-boost capability (also termed war emergency power), which enabled the horse power available to be increased a few vital minutes of combat taking the speed up to around 345mph and, of course, the aircraft were all stripped down. The Japanese sometimes boosted for as long as ten minutes, but the *official* speed for the A6M2 was listed as 317mph (510.16km/h or 275 knots). Comparisons with the German-built Heinkel He-100 fighter, three examples of the D-O variant having been imported by the Navy as the AX*Hei*, which had briefly having held the world speed record of 394.15mph (634.73km/h), although much faster in level flight, only emphasized the A6M's superiority, especially in range and reliability.[8]

With regard to design, the steady improvement and progression of the Model 11 A6M received another nasty shock when, on 17 April 1941, a second A6M suffered a similar fate to the earlier accident, the aircraft breaking up in mid-air during a dive. Once again this resulted in the death of the pilot, another very experienced Navy flyer, Lieutenant Manbeye Shimokawa, who was the chief of the Fighter Division with the Yokosuka *Kōkūtai*. This accident naturally led to another detailed enquiry. It was established that the previous day another test pilot, Lieutenant (j.g.) Yasushi Nikaido, serving aboard the carrier *Kaga*, was conducting his flight training schedule in a Zero fitted with the new balance tabs, at Kisarazu airfield, Chiba. He reported first seeing skin wrinkling during tight turns. When in a 50-degree dive from an 11,482ft (3,500m) altitude he noted the same problem commencing at 6,561ft (2,000m). As his speed hit 373mph (600km/h) he started to pull out of the dive when the aircraft was shaken and he temporarily blacked out. On almost immediate recovery he found himself flying straight and level at 186.4mph (300km/h) but that the upper surfaces of both his wings had shed large areas of their skinning and also that both ailerons had disappeared while his leading-edge Pitot tube[9] was bent and buckled. He managed to land safely and made his report, the details of which were immediately transmitted to Yokosuka.

The report was read by Shimokawa who determined to repeat the test using two A6Ms at hand, both machines also returned from the *Kaga* for examination having suffered similar wrinkling, one fitted with the new balance tab and one without. This was done the next day and Lieutenant-Commander Setsuzo Yoshitomi instructed Shimokawa to cease the test immediately wrinkling was observed. Shimokawa first flew the aircraft, which did not have the balance tab fitted, diving at the same angle and from the same height and reaching a terminal speed of 640km/h without any serious problems. Next he repeated the exercise in the machine fitted with the tab, again without anything untoward occurring. He then conducted a second test, commencing the dive from 13,123ft (4,000m) this time and increasing his dive angle to 60 degrees. On commencement of the pull-out, sheeting from the port wing shed off and then the whole tail section detached and the remainder of the doomed aircraft went straight into the sea, Shimokawa going down with her.

The Navy investigation that immediately followed, under Engineer Kiyoshi Matsudaira, initially came to the conclusion that failure to re-calibrate stress for the wing, aileron and control system at the time the tabs had been added resulted in unacceptable force being exerted on the aileron's trailing edge. However, this initial verdict conclusion was later reversed following more detailed examinations. Matsudaira announced the team's final conclusion on 13 June. Careful vibration and stiffness testing and subsequent adjustments had reduced the speed threshold of wing flutter from 466mph (750km/h) to 391mph (630km/h) on a Zero not fitted with the balance tabs. This was further reduced to only 373mph (600km/h) when balance tabs were fitted. This problem was described as the 'Aileron Rotational Wing Torsional Compound Flutter' effect.

The solution in the case of the A6M was a mixture of 'fixes'; the outer wing skinning was made thicker, with deeper countersinking to enable strong rivets; longitudinal stringers were added to increase torsional resistance; a mass balance was introduced on the opposite side of the balance tab; and finally, as a temporary measure, the diving speed of the Zero was reduced to 670km/h and similar restrictions were retrospectively applied to all aircraft. As a result no further accidents of this nature ever took place. From airframe #227 onward the mass balances were once more deleted and replaced with a more aerodynamically acceptable device inbuilt to the leading edge of the aileron.

What were the A6M's main pluses and minuses? On the plus side, being designed for such close-in air fighting it was manoeuvrable in the extreme, especially at moderate (270mph – 434.52km/h) speeds, although this asset fell away at higher velocities; its great reach, an asset in China that was also to prove equally so in reaching the Philippines in December 1941 and in the long-drawn missions down to Guadalcanal a year later; and while its 20mm cannon gave it some edge there were limitations to their value, as we have seen. One asset the Japanese did have an abundance of initially was that their pilots were combat-experienced and highly skilled. They were not trained in deflection shooting as were their opposite numbers in the US Navy, but then again, nor were the vast majority of their opponents. What the A6M lacked was any decisive speed advantage in level flight over many of its opponents at its critical altitude;[10] a maximum of 332mph (534km/h) at 14,930ft (4,500m) as listed by Robert Jackson and Paul Gunston for the A6M2, was nothing extra-special,[11] while Okumiya and Horikoshi list a more modest 328mph,[12] which was similar to her main foe, the US Navy Grumman F4F Wildcat.[13] Being a lightly constructed machine the A6M lacked the edge in dives over its heavier and more armoured opponents. Its most fatal flaw was its vulnerability, lacking self-sealing fuel tanks and armour protection.

Chapter 5

None so Blind

Much has been made of the 'failure' of British and American Air Intelligence to forewarn the Allies of what they might face from the new Japanese Navy fighter. Just what was known of the A6M pre-December 1941 then? Actually a considerable dossier of descriptions, eyewitness accounts, reports and other data flowed into Allied hands between 1937 and 1941. Some eighteen months prior to Pearl Harbor reports began to be received by Western Intelligence Agencies about the new Japanese fighter. Initial response was often disbelief but, contrary to accepted myth, many of these details were distributed to the front-line units, though only few at the sharp end seem to have absorbed them thoroughly.

Let us examine some of them, first the Americans.

The Assistant US Naval Attaché was James M. 'Jimmie' McHugh who had served in China with the American Legations at Peking and Shanghai, on-and-off for twenty years and was present in that post from 1937 when the Chinese Incident developed into a full-scale war. He became fluent in Mandarin and, as a major, was assigned his post on 30 October 1937.[1] He had close personal contacts with *Generalissimo* Chiang Kai Shek and the power behind the throne herself, Madame Chiang (Soong May-ling) and was close to Chiang's political advisor, W. H. Donald. He remained in China until August 1940 and learned much and when brought home to Quantico that month was almost immediately sent back to China once more. As a lieutenant-colonel he became the full naval representative at the Chinese Government and fulfilled his brief to report back all he saw and learnt. One historian noted how, 'McHugh had always been fearless in making reports whenever he felt the good of the United States was concerned.'[2]

McHugh had filed not but two reports on the A6M to the ONI (Office of Naval Intelligence) pre-war, the first in December 1940 and a second in June 1941. The first report was built on the Chinese interrogation of a Japanese

Navy pilot captured after his A6M was shot down by AA fire. Herein the speed, rate of climb and armament were accurately described. The second report was amplification with information gleaned from another A6M shot down near Chengdu City, north of Chongqing, on 20 May 1941, along with a carefully detailed analysis and drawings of what was described as a 'Sea Fighter 0-1, Model 1'. The sketches were not totally accurate because the AA shells had blown off the aircraft's tail and this section had to be guessed at (the Chinese filled it in by copying a Nakajima Ki-43 *Hayabusa*) and was misleading. Other data, obtained by careful measurement supplemented by interrogations, was revealing and shows exactly what was known of the A6M at least eighteen months *prior* to Pearl Harbor. The engine was described as an air-cooled, two row 14-cylinder 840-hp *Kinsei* X. The aircraft's wingspan was 39.36ft (12m), length 28.40ft (8.65m), and the height 9.02ft (2.75m) with a surface area of $256ft^2$ ($23.76m^2$). The weights were given as 3,705lb (1,684.3kg) unladen; 5,126lb (2,334.6kg) gross; 5,739lb (2,608kg) with an outer tank. The maximum level flying speed with (5m turbo pressure HP 9025) was given as 314mph (505km/h), or with maximum rated HP 840 at 305mph (491km/h). The cruising speed with drop tank was 267mph (430km/h), and with the drop tank 261mph (420km/h). Maximum altitude was recorded as 13,120ft (4,000m). The cruising range was listed as 698 miles (1,120km) or 1,207 miles (1,940km) with the drop tank. The climbing rate at sea level was 3,022ft/min (921m/min) and the time to climb to 13,120ft (4,000m) was 4.3 minutes. The fighter's ceiling was listed as 35,860ft (10,930m). Landing speeds with flaps deployed were, normal loading, 62.7mph (101km/h) or overloaded 65.5mph (103.3km/h). The take-off distance with normal loading was 364 ft (111m) or in overload condition 421ft (128m). Armament was listed as two 7.7mm fixed machine-guns, with 600 rounds and two 20mm fixed machine-guns (*sic*), with 60 rounds.[3]

Nor was this the only detailed report on the A6M to arrive on the ONI's desk in Washington at this time. Another was filed by Major Ronald Boone, USMC, in July/August 1941, three or four months before the attack on Pearl Harbor, with very similar details and probably from the same source. This report also contained very accurate details of this aircraft's speed, climb rate and range, although it was way out in its estimation of the manoeuvrability of the fighter. Far from being suppressed Boone's report was, in fact, distributed to the fleet in the US Navy's Fleet Air Tactical Bulletin dated 22 September 1941, distributed by the Navy's Bureau of Aeronautics (*BuAer*). In this format it was available to be read and studied by front-line service personnel. Indeed it was read by many, including by one Lieutenant-Commander John S. Thach, the commanding officer of VF-3, at that time based at San Diego. From it he worked his famous 'Beam Defense Position' tactic that much later Lieutenant-Commander James H. Flatley of VF-10 assigned the title of the 'Thach Weave', which he used at the Midway battle. This unofficial manoeuvre proved to be a tactic far more celebrated in print and discussion than ever used in combat as it required special conditions for it to be applied, and only a few pilots managed to learn it, with even fewer having the opportunity to actually put it into practice, no matter how 'celebrated' it later became by some historians. It was, moreover, first-and-foremost a defensive a tactic designed to preserve the F4F when they should have been concentrating on the enemy bombers. However, that fact does not invalidate Thach's reaction to information that he received and it shows that *some* Navy front-line pilots took note of the information dissembled to them, even if many did not.[4]

The last pre-war US Naval Air Attaché Lieutenant (j.g.) Stephen Jurika, Jr, had submitted two reports pre-war. That dated 9 November 1940, concerned what he termed the 'Mitsubishi Type Zero 1940 Fighter', an identification that he based on Chinese reports of a 'Type 100' airframe. He described the machine as a twin-engined aircraft based on the Dutch Fokker D-23.[5] What he was in fact describing appears to have been the Japanese Army Type 100 fast bomber, the Mitsubishi Ki-46 (later allocated the Allied code name 'Dinah').

A second report, dated 7 April 1941, concerned his attendance at a public donation ceremony (termed *Hokoku* by the Navy, *Aikoku* by the Army) at Hanada airfield in January 1941 where he had apparently actually been permitted to sit in the cockpit of what he described as on a new 'Type Zero Zero' fighter aircraft, which was, in his estimation, a '... new version of the old Type 97 – the Ki-27 - singer seat fighter with retractable wheels and increased power'. He noted it had two 'droppable' auxiliary wing tanks emplaced.[6] Among the side plates there he is alleged to have found the aircraft nameplate, written in English with other details such as design clues, landing gear operation and the composition of the airframe and wings. He made a mental note of some figures, from which he concluded that the A6M weighed about half as much as the contemporary American Navy F4F Wildcat fighter, but the engines' horsepower was approximately the same. He reasoned that this ratio would mean that the Japanese fighter would therefore have better speed, climb rate and manoeuvring than her American opposite number. One account stated: 'About three months after he submitted his report, ONI chided him that he should be more careful in reporting the characteristics and estimated weight of Japanese aircraft.'[7] In other words, he was entirely disbelieved.

This may because his reports were so confusing. He could not have sat in the cockpit of a A6M during a *Hokoku* ceremony because the first public presentation of that aircraft,[8] actually took place in November 1941, not January.

This was the mountain of reports than reached the Navy. But the United States Army was also receiving equally disturbing information from China. These were famously the reports submitted over the same pre-war period by Claire Lee Chennault. It is a fact, even if a fact that is more ignored than admitted, that the Curtiss P-40B Tomahawks of the American Volunteer Group (AVG) at no time were ever engaged with the Japanese Navy's A6M over China. The aircraft that tangled with Chennault's mercenaries were Japanese Army aircraft, notably the Oscar. Chennault's initial reports on the A6M, notably one dated 12 December 1940 directed to no less than General George Caslett Marshall, Jr, Chief of Staff of the US Army, were based almost solely on interrogations of surviving Chinese pilots who had duelled with the A6M and survived the experience, and were made long before the AVG was much more than a gleam in Chennault's eye, let alone the 'Flying Tigers' of American newspaper headlines.[9] He had been in China since May 1937, ever since he was 'retired' (or rather pressurized out) from the Army Air Service, where he had been overseeing the training of Chinese fighter pilots. At this later date Chennault was beginning to make his case in the US to aid and assist the Chinese Air Force, which was in dire straits. That this was so was, as we have seen, largely due to the introduction of the A6M and this Chennault made clear to Marshall.

Later, Chennault appeared to have much the same detailed and insider access to the Chinese data from the same shot down and largely intact A6M fighters that his Marine Corps fellow countrymen did, and he also dutifully filed back the information to his former colleagues. Again, far from dismissing such information out of hand as often alleged, Marshall had the good sense to recognize sound intelligence straight from the horse's mouth so to speak, and at a subsequent meeting propagated Chennault's information. Whereas Chennault might still be regarded as *persona non grata* in the ranks of the still predominant heavy bomber clique, at least his news got a hearing. In February 1941 Marshall also sent direct warning to Major-General Walter Campbell Short, in charge of the USAAC units based at Hawaii, of what he might have to face should the growing tensions in the Far East terminate in conflict between Japan and the United States. Again much of the information was accurate, although Marshall credited the A6M with rather higher top speed than she was capable of, and with armour protection and self-sealing fuel tanks, while he did not emphasize the remarkable agility of the Japanese machine. Tellingly Marshall told Short that although the number of his Pursuit squadrons had been tripled and beefed up with new aircraft, which improved both numbers and quality, 'When compared to the performance of the present carrier based Japanese plane the deficiencies are only too evident. Incidentally, the new Japanese plane is rated at 322 miles an hour, with a very rapid climb, with leak-proof tanks[10] and armor, and with two 20mm machine guns [*sic*] and two .30 caliber guns.'[11] Marshall also sent the same details to General George Grunert, who commanded the Philippine Department in 1941. Whether Grunert took this information on board seriously or not was negated by General Douglas MacArthur who shortly afterwards had been dug out of retirement and appointed in command in the Philippines, and who promptly abolished Grunert's command and sent him packing back to the States.

Post-war Chennault, re-instated as an Army Air Force Lieutenant-General, was alleged (again by Burton) to have claimed some of the material he had sent to Washington DC had been rejected as unrealistic by US analysts and destroyed. However, this does not appear to have been the case in every instance, for, just like the Navy, the USAAS published a series of information manuals that gave known details of the A6M well in advance of actual hostilities. In March 1941, the Army issued an updated edition of their Identification series featuring known Japanese aircraft. The A6M had a fairly detailed, although not fully comprehensive, entry under the heading 'Fighter 100'. It described the new machine as a single-seater monoplane with hooded cockpit and retractable landing gear. Armament was correctly identified as being two 20mm cannon wing guns and two fixed machine-guns whose calibre was not listed. The power plant was given as a single 14-cylinder, twin-row, radial, which was air-cooled, but the manufacturer and type was not listed. The rate of climb was listed as 'Fast', with a maximum ceiling of 10,000 metres or 6.2 miles, with a maximum endurance of 6 to 8 hours with a belly tank containing 150 gallons while total fuel capacity was given as 1,200 litres or 324 gallons. They noted that a radio telephone was fitted. This was pretty good information, although the accompanying notes let the whole accuracy down. While commenting that the fighter '... can operate from carrier', which one would assume was a basic given for any naval fighter, the originator added that the aircraft '... avoids use of acrobatics'.[12] Never was an assessment more inaccurate. In fact after a brief period of warfare in which they experienced the A6M's superior turn and climb, the most appropriate slogan adopted by western aviators was 'Never dogfight a Zero!' Some of these major errors were repeated and enhanced in a subsequent edition, which appeared a year later, when the war had been underway for three months and more factual information should have been available from combat reports from US forces. Here the A6M is mentioned as a Zero (albeit as 'Nagoya Zero') but listed solely in the Japanese Army section; one wonders just how the author figured a land-based fighter managed to reach Pearl Harbor!

Not that the British Intelligence Service in the Far East or the RAF's way of dealing with it, was notable. Their cause was not embellished by the fact that one of their own, Captain Patrick Heenan, a New Zealand-born sympathizer of the Irish Republican Army terrorist campaigns, serving with Air Intelligence Liaison Section, was a Japanese spy who supplied them with detailed information of RAF strength and dispositions both prior and during the Malayan campaign.[13] Nor was the view from London an enlightened one, being largely racial. While discussing the possibility of a Japanese attack on British colonies in the Far East as early as May 1941 the British

Joint Intelligence Committee (JIC) dismissed reports of the large numbers of both shore and carrier-based aircraft the Japanese had readily available. These numbers, far exceeding any British military aviation strengths in that region, were discounted because, '... the operational value of the Japanese Air Force is probably akin to that of the Italians'.[14] Such a view equated with Winston Churchill's equally ignorant remarks that the Japanese were '... the Wops [a derogatory term for the Italians] of the East'.[15]

The British had also been in receipt of Claire Chennault's reports on the new Japanese fighter but they made even less use of it than their American counterparts and for mostly the same reasons. The first report was received from Chennault by the British Air Liaison Officer (ALO) based at Hong Kong as early as October 1940, over a year before war broke out in the Pacific.[16] On 6 February 1941, Wing-Commander James Warburton, RAF, the British Air Attaché (AA) at Chungking, received detailed information from the Chinese Air Force on a fierce aerial battle that had involved thirty-one Chinese-piloted I-15-3 fighters against twelve A6Ms. The results of this encounter saw twelve of the Chinese fighters shot down against a claimed loss of four of the Japanese machines (in fact, no A6M was lost). Again, rather than take heed that the new Japanese fighter was a formidable opponent, Warburton's subsequent report, as well as the Air Intelligence Division (AID) summary of the battle, stressed the inefficiency of the Chinese pilots rather than the potency of their opponents.[17]

Even when the Intelligence Officers managed to obtained detailed information on the A6M their findings and information were not always well received or passed on down the line to the fighting aircrews in the obsolete Brewster Buffalo and Hawker Hurricane fighters. Post-war Air Commodore Stanley Jackson Marchbank, who served on the Air Staff HQ Far East between 1938 and 1943, informed Sir George Neville Maltby at the Foreign Office on 21 September 1954, that all such details were kept at Air HQ and were not passed down to the RAF squadrons themselves![18] The men at the top later blamed lack of Intelligence, the former C-in-C Far East, Air Chief Marshal Sir Robert Brooke-Popham, under interrogation post-war on why the information received about the A6M was not handled more efficiently merely commented that, '... what we lacked was a good secret service established years before'.[19]

However, Brooke-Popham cannot be allowed to get away with that because he early on revealed that he knew a great deal about the A6M (after all Chennault had several times met with him and advised him about this aircraft), enough about it to give him great concern even before the battle commenced. In his dispatch he was to record, 'What we were particularly on the look-out for was any indication of the movements of long distance bombers or of the Zero-type fighters with detachable petrol tanks.' This remark, a group of American specialists noted, was '... a statement which suggests a concern felt about the Zero that was not evident when, only a few weeks before, in Australia, he had vouched for the superiority of the Buffalo; and a reminder, perhaps, that campaign dispatches are written after the fighting'.[20]

As far as the British and Australians in Malaya, the British and AVG in Burma, the British in India and the Chinese at this period of the war, most of this concern about the A6M was academic anyway. Despite the scores, if not hundreds, of descriptions of Allied aircraft being outflown and outfought by the Mitsubishi A6M Zero, the fact is that hardly any true Navy Zero fighters took part in any of these operations.[21] What all these Allies were being outfought and outflown by was not the A6M but the Japanese Army Air Force Nakajima Ki-27 ('Nate') and Ki-43 ('Oscar') fighters, persistently misidentified (both then and since) as the 'Zero'. Looking ahead briefly, we can see that the real and true combat strengths of the Japanese in all this theatres of war during 1941–42 were as follows:

Malaya

1 *Sentai* – 42 Ki-27Bs; 11 *Sentai* – 39 Ki-27Bs, 59 *Sentai* – 24 Ki-43b/c aircraft, 64 *Sentai* – 35 Ki-43b/c aircraft and 77 *Sentai* – 27 Ki-27Bs; a total of 167 Army fighters. Attached to the Japanese Navy 22 *Kōkū Sentai*'s *Genzan*, *Mihoro* and *Kanoya* bombers units, based near Saigon, were eighteen A6Ms, operational of 22 *Kokutai* based at Soc Tang. During the famous mission of 10 December 1941 when the new battleship *Prince of Wales* and the old unmodernized battle-cruiser *Repulse* were both sunk, some of these A6Ms were belatedly dispatched to provide fighter protection to the bomber forces, but they arrived too late to take part in the action. Allied Brewster F2A Buffalo fighters also arrived too late to participate, but there was no contact between the two sets of fighters.[22]

Singapore

1 *Sentai* – 42 Ki-27Bs, 11 *Sentai* – 39 Ki-27Bs, 47 Independent *chūtai* – 9 Ki-44 pre-production fighters, 59 *Sentai* – 24 Ki-43 1c aircraft, 64 *Sentai* – 35 Ki-43 1c all Army fighters, plus 22 *Kōkū Sentai*'s Fighter Group, 26 A6M2 Model 21s; a total of 145 Army fighters and 26 Navy fighters.

Sumatra

59 *Sentai* – 24 Ki-43 1c aircraft, 64 *Sentai* – 35 Ki-43 1c Army fighters, plus carrier *Ryūjō* with 9 A5M4 fighters embarked for a total of 59 Army and 9 Navy fighters, none of them A6Ms.

Burma

On 25 December 1941 Japanese fighter forces in Burma were 64 *Sentai* – 10 Ki-43s, 77 *Sentai* – 32 Ki-27s, a total of 42 Army fighters. By 22 January Major Yoshioka Hiroshi's 77 *Sentai* had been reduced to 25 Ki-27s, but had been reinforced by 50 *Sentai* (Major Makinō Yasuo) with 31 Ki-27s. Due to bomber losses Lieutenant General Michio Sugawara, commanding the 3 *Hikoshidan*, ordered the 64 *Sentai* with 18 Ki-43s to Raheng and part of the 47 Independent *chūtai* equipped with Nakajima Ki-44 *Shoki* (codenamed 'Tojo') Tojos to Don Muang, a transfer that cost the 47th three fighters *en route* with only four machines arriving safely, the majority of the unit being diverted to Singapore and the Dutch East Indies. By 20 March further reinforcements in the shape of 1 *Sentai* with 15 Ki-27s and 11 *Sentai* with 14 Ki-27s had arrived on station, being freed up by the fall of Singapore.[23]

The only time the Navy A6M was anywhere remotely near the air fighting in Burma at this period of the war, was when eighteen of them were detached briefly from the 22nd *Genzan Kōkū Sentai* and moved to newly captured RAF Mingaladon air base[24] on 30 March in order to provide a land-based back-up reserve to Vice-Admiral Nagumo's *Kidō Butai*'s planned excursion into the Indian Ocean but more so should air cover be required for that associated raid into the Bay of Bengal by Vice-Admiral Jisaburo Ozawa's raiding force between 4 April and 10 April. This latter attack on shipping off the eastern coast of India by the carrier *Ryūjō*, five heavy and one light cruiser and eight destroyers netted a total of 92,000 tons of British shipping without loss to themselves. Eighteen Mitsubishi G3M bombers (codenamed 'Nell') from the Mingaladon base attacked Calcutta (now known as Kolkata) and Akyab (now known as Sittwe) on 5 April sinking the Indian Navy Sloop *Indus* at the latter port. The A6Ms flew escort missions for these attacks but encountered no aerial opposition.

In short, the impact of the A6M on the Allies was that this fighter was seen and reported everywhere, even when none of them were ever present.

In sharp contrast to the above areas of 'phantom' A6M combat, it was the air battles over the Philippines and Java that saw the involvement of those A6Ms that were not with the *Kidō Butai* carriers attacking Pearl Harbor and Wake Island. Here they did indeed prove a decisive factor.

The Philippines

3 *Kōkūtai* – 45 A6M2 Model 21s, *Tainan Kaiguan Kōkūtai* – 45 A6M2 Model 21s, and carrier *Ryūjō* – 9 A5M4 fighters with the Army following up after the Luzon landings with 24 *Sentai* – Ki-27Bs and 50 *Sentai* – 36 Ki-27Bs, both second-string Army fighters; for a total of 90 A6M2s and 9 other Navy fighters plus 60 Army fighters.

Java

11 *Sentai* – 39 Ki-27Bs, 59 *Sentai* – 24 Ki-43 1c aircraft and 64 *Sentai* – 35 Ki-43 1c aircraft, all Army fighters; plus 3 *Kōkūtai* – 45 A6M Model 21s and the 22 *Kōkū Sentai* Fighter Group – 26 A6M Model 21s. A total of 98 Army fighters and 71 Navy A6Ms.

It must be borne in mind that the figures for each unit as above, are, of course, the *initial deployment* numbers, with losses being replenished as they were taken. The actual full strength complements of the A6M in both Formosa-based units 3 *Kōkūtai* and Tainan *Kōkūtai* were seventy-two aircraft, plus eighteen reserve machines for a total of 180+ aircraft. However, even bearing that in mind, none of these figures indicate an overwhelming Japanese numerical superiority in fighter aircraft. The Japanese aerial dominance was achieved on a shoe-string, no wonder they subsequently developed contempt for their enemies as a consequence.

The most pungent summary of the western attitudes to the Japanese and the A6M aircraft in particular, were made by historian Hedley Paul Willmott. His final comments on the impact the A6M made deserve to be quoted in full as they encapsulate perfectly why they were so devastating:

Western observers in Japan and China, and the French in Indo-China, had reported the appearance of an exceptionally maneuverable fighter with great powers of endurance. Photographs and sketches had been made available to Western governments and services. The American pilots with the Chinese Air Force had even devised tactics to try to take advantage of some of the aircraft's known weaknesses, not that these tactics had achieved very much. In the period September 1940 to August 31 1941 thirty A6Ms had destroyed 266 confirmed Chinese aircraft. Such information was ignored. Western agencies chose to consider that Japanese fighter and pilots were, *ipso facto*, inferior to those of the West. The revelation of the quality of the Zero-*sen* was possibly the most psychologically damaging catastrophe to befall the Allies; Westerners simply could not understand that the Japanese could equal or surpass their own best efforts in various fields at certain times. At this time there were widely believed stories that German pilots flew Japanese aircraft; anything was done to deny the Japanese credit, to nurture the belief in white supremacy.[25] Some post-war historians have aided the confusion by referring to both the A6M and the Ki-43 as the 'Zero-type fighter' The RAF and AVG reports are full of eyewitness accounts of duels with 'Navy O's' and similar, made by professional pilots, but they were almost all totally delusional.[26]

There were stories that the designs of the Zero-*sen* had been drawn up but rejected by a Western power – normally given as the United States, but this varied. Nothing was further from the truth. In these ways were the Japanese aided even by their enemies. The failure to take the Japanese seriously before the war, the refusal to recognize that in the situation in which she found herself in late 1941 Japan was forced to go to war, and the inability to see the high quality of Japanese equipment and professionalism all combined to create for the Allies a situation that, in a matter of days after the start of hostilities, was pregnant with disaster.[27]

Chapter 6

Preliminaries to War

While Japan was still poised on the brink of all-out war, several diverse strands of the A6M story were being initiated on the design table and in the air.

Float-fighter

Although heavily extended in the China Incident air fighting, in 1940 the defensive needs of her far-flung Mandated territories[1] were essential should war with the United States provoke their attack under their long-established War Plan Orange. Officially Japan was forbidden to construct warlike facilities on these territories and where no air bases existed a float-fighter was considered the ideal solution. It was therefore long recognized by the IJN that a float-fighter (*Suisen* or hydro-fighter) of high performance was a requirement that needed fulfilling. Design work had been initiated on just such an aircraft, the Kawanishi N1K1 *Kyōfū* (Powerful Wind) single-seater, (later code-named 'Rex'), which eventually morphed into the powerful land-based NIK-J *Shiden* (later code-named 'George'). However, to fill the gap until the new aircraft arrived a more immediate stop-gap solution was proposed under the 15-*Shi* programme of 1940, which was promulgated by the Navy in February 1941.

The Navy charged the Nakajima Company, which had far greater capacity than Mitsubishi at this period, to adapt the A6M Model 11 accordingly. A design team under Chief Engineer Shinobu Mitsutake and designer Atsushi Tajima produced a solution, the single-seater *Suisen-2*. The existing airframe was therefore simply modified, the whole of the undercarriage and landing gear, tail wheel and carrier deck landing hook were done away with and faired over smoothly. A huge streamlined single cantilever main float (pontoon), which doubled as an 81-gallon fuel tank, was affixed to the lower body by means of a massive 'V' shaped main strut, with the two outrigger floats extending vertically downward from the outer wing undersurfaces each on their own slim strut for balance. To aid balance the vertical tail was lengthened and extended the full height with the rudder extended downwards, while a thin stabilizing fin was attached ventrally. The internal fuel tank capacity was 156 gallons giving her a range of 1,107 miles (1,782km). She had an empty weight of 4,235lb (1,912kg) and a loaded weight of 5,423lb (2,460kg) with the 950hp Nakajima NK1C Series *Sakae*-12 radial. Armament remained the same but she also had two hard points to carry a single 132lb (60kg) bomb under either wing for anti-submarine patrol work. Not surprisingly, performance fell off by roughly 20 per cent with the extra weight but she compared well with foreign types such as the French Loire 210.

The first A6M2-N flew on 8 December 1941, and after prolonged trials was accepted the following July, equipping the Yokohama *Kōkūtai*. Many of the first batch were shipped straight out to Tulagi in the Solomon Islands, where a surprise strafing raid by fifteen F4Fs from the carrier *Wasp* destroyed the majority of them on 7 August during the US 'Watchtower' landings and the beginning of the Guadalcanal operations. A total of 327 A6M-Ns were eventually constructed and saw wide-ranging service.

A6M3 Model 32

There was a perceived need for the A6M to achieve better performance at higher altitudes and this led to the introduction of the 1,130hp (831.11kW) *Sakae* 21 radial engine equipped with a two-speed supercharger. To aid performance further slightly elongated propeller blades were fitted and because the new engine had a down-draft carburettor this led to a modification of the engine cowling, the most noticeable feature being that the air-cooler intake scoop was shifted from below to above the enlarged Sumitomo (licence-built Hamilton Standard) constant- speed, three bladed type spinner with a diameter of 10 ft (3.05m).[2] The bigger engine cowl meant that the fronts of the two 7.7 machine-guns were enclosed and had to fire through slots rather than along troughs. The 30rpg capacity of the 20mm was long recognized as inadequate and early in 1943 this was increased to a 100rpg drum; at the same time a hinged cover was fitted for the expended rounds chutes. There were obvious weight penalties for the heavier engine and extra ammunition stowage. The fuel capacity was reduced by twenty-one gallons as the engine mounting had to be shifted 185mm towards the stern leading to smaller oil and fuel tank capacity; in compensation the wing-root tank was increased from 100 US gallons (380 litres) to 110 US gallons (420 litres) by reducing the rib height in that area. In a belated attempt to put right this much-criticized lack of reach from serial number 3191 onward the wing tank capacity was increased by 2.2 gallons (10 litres). To hopefully further increase agility at high altitudes the folding wing-tips were totally eliminated, the ends being merely faired over straight across, which pared down the overall wingspan from 39ft 5in (12m) to 36ft 2in (11m) and produced a distinctive new 'clipped' wing-form.

Flight tests for the new Model 32 were conducted from June 1941 but were extremely disappointing. In fact the modifications appeared to have produced an inferior aircraft in most respects. The maximum speed showed about 7mph (11.27km/h) improvement, the roll rate was quicker as was the diving speed and, although higher altitudes were attainable, the climb rate suffered. Fuel consumption of the larger engine at cruise speed equalled the smaller power plant but at full power it increased considerably, reducing the aircraft's range, a big factor with pilots operating from Rabaul at extreme distances. The Model 22 outranged her by about one hundred nautical miles. Other downsides were that the famed turning radius actually increased, which did not impress *Rei-sen* pilots one little bit when it first entered *Hikōtai* service with 2 *Kōkūtai* at Rabaul in 1942, especially when, soon after the embroilment in the Solomons campaign a long reach became an absolutely essential requirement.

Only 343 Model 32s, in range 3001 to 3343, were built. The model was to be allocated the Allied codename 'Hap' (quickly changed to 'Hamp' when Arnold expressed his distaste for the original tongue-in-cheek choice). They were built at the Mitsubishi factory before the run was terminated. The A6M3-K was the designation of those that were made-over into training aircraft. Another designation mentioned occasionally was the A6M4 (*-shi*). Apparently a single experimental Model 32 was fitted with a special test turbo-supercharger, and this would have been the designation had it gone into production, which it did not.

Sōjü'in (pilot) training

The A6M was a superlative aircraft with which to wage war in 1941, but complementing this machine was the fact that the IJN was able to provide equally outstanding pilots to fly it. When they hit Pearl Harbor and the Philippines the A6M pilots had under their belts an average of 800 hours of flying time, much of it in the hard combat environment of China. The most junior of the A6M flyers had at least 600 hours of flight operation behind them and some of the senior pilots had clocked up 1,500 hours. None of their opponents, save for a handful of former Battle of Britain and Desert warfare RAF and RAAF veterans in the skies over Singapore, could come anywhere remotely close to them in terms of experience.[3] Little wonder then that the combination of a superior fighter aircraft and highly experienced pilots swept aside all Allied opposition with almost casual ease in the opening months of the Pacific War.

Despite the size of the IJN's air arm, training was organized to produce the very best from the system, an elite force that would overcome numbers with skill and aggression. The same qualities and ground plan was applied to all arms of the Navy – this resulted in them building the biggest battleships with the biggest guns – the *Yamato* and *Musashi* were more than twice the tonnage of Allied battleships then building and armed with 18.1-inch guns; Japanese heavy cruisers were larger, faster than the Allied ships of the same type and equipped with heavy long-range 24-inch torpedoes (which American post-war writers gave the retrospective title 'Long Lance', although they were never known as such by the Japanese themselves) as well as 8-inch gun batteries; their destroyers were a decade ahead of Allied types of the same type and also equipped with this superb weapon as well as dual-purpose 5-inch guns, and their submarines had enormous range, some capable of carrying seaplanes and were also intensively trained. The A6M was another part of this attitude, and the training reflected it. Quality was sought rather than quantity. Indeed, so strict and severe were the qualifications criteria applied to new naval aviator recruits that only a fraction were able to qualify to the exacting standards insisted upon. This limited new intakes to as low as one hundred only, with no redress or second chances. Even skilled applicants were rejected, which, in the years after 1942, would have been welcomed with open arms. This produced an outstanding elite, but did not lend itself to a long campaign.

Initially induction to qualification was over a period varying from seven to nine months during which many potential *Sōjū'in* were eliminated and rejected, especially from enlisted applicants. Not until 1940 was this duration extended as by that time it had become apparent that many more would soon be required. The course followed the usual practices of most nations with a six-month period of Primary training with the *Dai-Jūni Kōkū Kantai* (11 Combined Air Flotilla).

Initial flight training was carried out with the Yokosuka K2Y biplane trainer, which later was replaced by the Kyushu K9W (a licence-built version of the German Bücker Bü 131, later codenamed 'Cypress'). Officer cadets would clock up to sixty hours while enlisted men had a lower target level of forty-five hours or so. Those that made it past this stage went on to Intermediate training in the K5Y (later code-named 'Willow'), which was of four to six months' duration and involved up to one hundred flying hours. If a candidate made it past this hurdle and graduated he would be assessed for fighter, dive- or torpedo/attack or reconnaissance potential according to his perceived skill sets and temperaments. Accordingly, a three or four month Operational training period ensued in the selected type of aircraft. On conclusion of this and with about 400 hours of flying time for officer cadets and 250+ hours for enlisted men, they would qualify.

Unlike the American armed services, but following the lead of their Royal Navy peers, the greater majority, almost 90 per cent, of IJN pilots inducted under the *Sōjū Renshūsei* (*Sōren* – Pilot Trainee System) were NCOs (Non-commissioned Officers), petty officers, warrant officers and former naval ratings. It not being considered a requirement for flyers to be leaders, these latter tended to be gunnery, torpedo or navigation specialists. The actual nature of the Pacific War as it subsequently developed, and the very heavy losses in flying personnel, came too late to alleviate this acute lack when urgently required at front-line bases. These were either taken from volunteers from a regular surface fleet already suitably indoctrinated having served a minimum of one year on a conventional warship, of which an incredibly small number were finally taken, or inducted civilians in the fifteen-to-seventeen age group – both groups having to sit an examination that would pass them into the *Hikō Yoka Renshūsei* (*Yokaren* – Flight Reserve Enlisted Trainee System). A small selection of university graduates were also accepted under the *Kōkū Yobi Gakusei* (Student Aviation Reserve) selection process who, if they qualified, became *Yobi Shōi* (Reserve Ensigns) to be trained up by the Yokosuka *Kōkūtai* (later the *Kasumigaura*). Once qualified they would continue their studies or find employment until required. In the same way anyone who already held a civilian flying licence from the Ehime and Nagasaki flying schools, could follow the same route to become *Yobi Renshūsei* (Drafted Reserve trainees) but very few fighter pilots came from that source. As with all these schemes a huge expansion followed the outbreak of war with the sudden enormous increase in demand. The tiny proportion of pre-war Officer Air candidates was to have severe repercussions from 1943 onward as combat losses meant that few survivors had the necessary rank (lieutenant-commanders and commanders) to serve as fighter unit leaders.

As in all arms of the Japanese services discipline was harsh and strictly administered. It was deliberately no career for the faint-hearted and brutality was rife.[4] Physical punishment was frequent for even the most minor mistakes, and group punishments were also common as an aid to instil team reliance and mutual responsibility. Suicide in the event of failure, or some sort of self-immolation to atone for error, was quite usual.

Once selected as having the basic attributes to make a potential fighter pilot, the candidate left Basic Aviation Training and entered Joint Aviation Training by being posted to a combat unit to have his skills finely honed. The fighter pilot candidate would study and practise the current methods being used in the field with formation flying and learn the skill of working in the close-ordered three-aircraft *shōtai* grouping, gunnery including target practice, close-range aerial combat practice, carrier-deck landings and take-off procedures, and navigation. This assimilation required constant attention to detail, and it could be a year of such hard work, during which many fell by the wayside, before their commanding officers would consider them ready to actually take part in the aerial battles over China.

Here, after a year flying from shore bases on combat missions, most flyers could expect to be sent back to their carriers for sea duty, and then back ashore once more in rotation to round off their knowledge and expertise but this proved not always to be the case. Once the Pacific War got underway the needs for the best pilots to be active with the *Kido Butai* spearhead, which was perpetually short of pilots, experienced or otherwise, to maintain its non-stop series of offensive operations, soon overrode any such considerations. This of course meant that some carrier pilots just had to serve until wounded and hospitalized, if they were not killed first. Even the new carriers *Shōkakū* and *Zuikaku* made so many demands on limited pilot resources that 11 *Kōkū-kantai* was just about stripped of all its training cadres to man them, and this was right at the onset of war. The two ships, having so many fresh pilots aboard, were regarded poorly in comparison with the older carriers with more established aircrews embarked, a reputation they never succeeded in shrugging off.[5]

Two Zeros captured in China

With regards the standard model by 1941 the IJN could count on a force of around 400 A6M2s. Just prior to the outbreak of the Pacific War, in November 1941, not one but *two* A6Ms, one of them almost totally intact, fell into Chinese hands. The Japanese had come to an agreement with the Vichy-French administrators that allowed them to occupy several strategically important airfields and were moving in the G3M bombers of the 22 *Koku Sentai* (both the *Genzan* and *Mihoro Kaigun Kōkūtai*), along with G4M bombers of the *Kanoya Kōkūtai*. To provide long-range fighter protection for this force (soon to be instrumental in sinking the British capital ships *Prince of Wales* and *Repulse*) a special fighter unit was established on 22 November, the 22 *Kōkü Sentai Shireibu Fuzoku Sentokitai* (22 Air Flotilla Headquarters Attached Fighter Section) under Commander Yutaka Yamada. The A6Ms to form this unit were drawn from the 3 *Kaigun Kōkūtai* (thirteen), led by Lieutenant Tadatsune Tokaji, and the *Tainan Kōkūtai* (fourteen), led by Lieutenant Kikuichi Inano. There were also twelve Mitsubishi A5M4 fighters and six Mitsubishi C5M1 reconnaissance aircraft. In order to assist the A6Ms transferring to the newly acquired French air base of Soc Trang 150 miles south of Saigon from their home base of Tainan, Taiwan, all these fighters had their radios removed to lighten them for the long haul south, although their antennas were retained, presumably with the aim of re-installing the ditched equipment at a later date. Even with this slight lessening of the weight, the aircraft were scheduled to make a refuelling stop at Hainan Island.

The A6Ms commenced their transfer flight in two groups on 26 and 27 November and the bulk arrived safely on 1 December. However, two were found to be missing. Somewhere *over* Hainan they had run into foggy conditions and two of the fighters, piloted by Petty Officer 1st Class Shimezoh Inoue (V-172) and Petty Officer 2nd Class Taka-aki Suimohigashi (V-174), had become separated from the main group. They apparently overflew Hainan Island itself and, low on fuel, made landfall close to Teitsan (Qian Shan) on the south-east of the Luichow Peninsula. Here both aircraft put down on the beach but Shimohigashi's aircraft was damaged in the process.[6] Both pilots were captured by the Chinese and executed while the two A6Ms were salvaged. The damaged machine was hacked up and removed in chunks but Inoue's aircraft was taken out almost complete and transported to Liuchow and slowly restored by a team under a former German AVG mechanic Gerhard Neuman, and repainted in Chinese livery. Neuman wrote that it was obvious that this aircraft, '... had not been mass-produced' but was custom-built.[7] It was too late to influence events elsewhere but in July 1942 it was inspected there by Major-General Nathan F. Twining, USAAF, and Chennault sent two AVG airmen, plus a reporter and cameraman, to restore it to a flyable state, whereupon Colonel John R Alison, commander of the 75th Fighter Squadron flew it back up to Kweilin where it was flight tested by 23rd Fighter Group before being transferred to Karachi where it was crated and shipped, finally arriving at Wright Field, Ohio, for further flight testing there and at Elgin AFB in American colours.

Final moves

With the decision to go to war rather than *kow-tow* to the various American *diktats*, with its resulting loss of face and Empire, unacceptable to the proud Japanese, the IJN decided on a bold course of pre-emptive action that saw their forces striking the bemused Allies from Malaya in the west, through the Philippines in the south, at Hong Kong, and, the boldest stroke of all, against the American Fleet at Pearl Harbor. This strike was an updated re-run of the attack by destroyers on the Russian fleet at Port Arthur at the commencement of that earlier conflict but with the new long-range naval air power substituting for the destroyers and torpedo-boats employed on that occasion. The aim was the same for both operations, to put out of action the main enemy battle force and buy time. In 1941 that time was to be used to gain the oil-, minerals- and rubber-rich territories of the colonial possessions in the region, and exclude such powers, including the United States, from the area. It was believed that by thus attaining a secure source of resources and securing a barrier of distant island bases, the Imperial Navy could counter any counter-attacks until the Allies grew war weary. It was a colossal gamble but the alternative was, to the Japanese, beyond contemplation, a fact of which the United States and Great Britain were very well aware when they turned the screw.

The Japanese Navy had been experimenting with operating their carriers together as one powerful unit instead of separate forces, and this combining of their total air strength into one well-drilled and integrated fighting unit, came as a shock to her enemies who still organized their carriers far less intensively. Allied aircraft carriers either operated alone or in penny-packets of two or three at the most, with each carrier interpreting its operating procedures individually.[8] The *Kidō Butai* ('Attacking' or 'Striking' Force – there were many striking forces of course, but by popular usage the term has come to represent this particular force down the decades) commanded by Vice-Admiral Chūichi Nagumo, was a grouping of six of their most powerful carriers into one massive co-ordinate bloc of power, and proved revolutionary. It was this force that sailed secretly and headed for Pearl Harbor, Oahu, Hawaii, which was the main United States naval base in the Pacific.

Chapter 7

Forging a Legend

The dice were cast and the final decision was made and the pre-arranged signal to initiate the attack on the main American naval base at Pearl Harbor, was sent to Admiral Nagumo: '*Nitaka-yama Nobore*' ('Climb Mount Nitaka').[1]

Pearl Harbor

The six Nagumo force carriers at 0550 hours on 7 December 1941 were some 220 miles north of Oahu. On a bearing of 10° they turned their noses into the wind and increased their speed ready for launching. The attack was to be made in two waves, the first being 183 aircraft strong. The A6Ms were split between each wave plus maintaining a Combat Air Patrol (CAP) over the force at all times from a combined retained pool of forty-eight Zeros.

The *Kaga* contributed a nine-strong A6M2 *hikotai* to the first wave, under Lieutenant Shiga. The *Sōryū* sent off nine A6Ms in the first wave under Lieutenant Suganami. The *Hiryū* sent out just six Zeros in the first wave, led by Lieutenant Okajima. *Shōkaku* also dispatched six A6Ms under Lieutenant Kaneko in the first wave. The *Zuikaku* contributed six more A6Ms under Lieutenant Sato in the first wave. They attacked the Marine Corps Air Station at Kaneohe Bay. From a total of thirty-six PBY Catalina seaplanes based there, no fewer than twenty-seven were destroyed and a further six damaged to varying degrees. The first Aichi D3A dive-bomber tipped over at 0755 to commence the attack.

The opening move of the Pacific War was but a few hours old when the A6M2s took one of their first combat losses of the Pacific War. Ironically, that loss was not due to US reaction but to the over-zealousness of one Zero flyer, which brought about his own demise. The *Akagi* had contributed the No. 1 Fighter Strike Unit comprising a *hikotai* of nine A6M2s divided into three *shotai* of three planes each. No. 1 *Shotai* was Lieutenant-Commander Shigeru Itaya, who was in overall command of the 1st Wave fighter aircraft, with Petty Officers 1st Class Takashi Hirano and Shinatsugu Iwama. No. 2 *Shotai* consisted of Lieutenant Masanobu Ibusuki, with Petty Officer 1st Class Yoshio Iwashiro and Seaman 1st Class Toichiro Hanyu. No. 3 *Shotai* comprised Warrant Officer Suekichi Osanai, Petty Officer 2nd Class Masao Yaguchi and Seaman 1st Class Mitsuyoshi Takasuka.

The Zeros made landfall close to Kahuku Point, north-eastern Oahu. The first aircraft encountered was a civilian trainer they overtook close to Nuuanu Pali Pass, which they quickly dispatched before moving to the south-west toward Hickham Field. At 0800 local time they were beginning to line up their attack when a flight of Boeing B-17 Flying Fortresses of 38 Reconnaissance Squadron, *en route* to Pearl Harbor from Hamilton Field, California, stumbled into their view flying along the south coast. Itaya's leading *shotai* immediately commenced a run on one of these aircraft, which he mistook for a transport aircraft, followed by the rest of the group in line astern. The B-17 was heavily and continually hit and began to burn; the pilot attempted to land the crippled bomber as Itaya's fighters passed overhead before turning to strafe the airfield at low level. The B-17 crew members, eight of whom were wounded, were running for shelter and one was killed by strafing, while the bomber itself was shot up burned out. One attacker, Petty Officer Hirano, made a very low pass machine-gunning as he went and misjudged his height. His propeller blade tips scraped the runway, twisting them out of shape, and his bulky belly tank was wrenched off. Out of control the A6M (AI-154) veered upward south-west toward Fort Kamehameha with her pilot struggling to keep her engine running before entering a terminal stall and diving through the palm trees, which broke the Zero up and slewed her into the forts Ordnance Machine Shop, instantly killing Hirano as well as four US soldiers and injuring others from a group standing on the ramp gaping at the oncoming aircraft out in the open. The wreckage was later moved to the Hawaiian Air Depot hangar at Hickham for analysis.

The second wave arrived over Oahu seventy-five minutes after the first. *Akagi* contributed a further nine A6Ms to the second wave under Lieutenant Saburo Shindo, another China veteran, while nine more helped maintain the Combat Air Patrol over the force. The *Kaga* contributed a nine-strong

A6M2 *hikotai* to the second wave, under Lieutenant Yasushi Nikaido. The *Sōryū* dispatched nine A6Ms in the second wave under China veteran twenty-seven-year-old Lieutenant (j.g.) Fusata Iida. They engaged the few American P-40s that managed to get airborne and quickly destroyed them all, and then turned their attentions to Kaneohe Bay Marine air base. After their strafing attack the section re-assembled and it was then noticed that the aircraft of Lieutenant Iida was streaming aviation fuel, which eyewitness Sub-Lieutenant Iyozo Fujita assumed was from a hit from a small-calibre weapon and not serious. However, Iida was seen to close his cockpit canopy deliberately, and went into a vertical dive toward the runway. Fujita later related:

> Thinking that he was going to make another strafing run on the field, I immediately began a wingover to follow his plane down. I realised abruptly, however, that Lieutenant Iida was flying in a most unusual manner, quite different from his usual tactics. I watched his plane as it dived in its vertical, inverted position until it exploded on the ground between the Kanoeohe airfield hangars.[2]

Fujita himself was involved in some of the little aerial fighting over Pearl Harbor, and at 0915 was claimed shot down by Lieutenant Lew Sanders flying a P-36, but, although taking mechanical damage, Fujita remained airborne and soon afterwards he shot down a P-36 flown by Second Lieutenant Gordon Stirling. Nursing his damaged engine and escorted by two wingmen, he managed to reach the *Sōryū* where he landed safely at 1145. Lieutenant Masaji Suganami's section conducted three separate strafing runs against Wheeler Field in between attacks by D3A dive-bombing strikes, and then moved over to Ewa Field and repeated the process. The *Hiryū* also flew off a full nine-plane section in the second wave, under Lieutenant Sumio Nōno.

The IJN lost a total of nine A6Ms during the Pearl Harbor attack. The casualties in the first wave were Petty Officer 1st Class Takashi Hirano from *Akagi*, Petty Officer 2nd Class Seinoshin Sano from *Kaga* and Petty Officer Toru Haneda also from *Kaga*. The second waves A6Ms losses were Lieutenant Fusata Iida, Petty Officer 1st Class Shun-Ichi Atsuma and Petty Officer 2nd Class Saburo Ishii – all these three from the same *hiko shotai* from *Sōryū*. Also lost were Petty Officer 1st Class Shigenori Nishikaichi from *Hiryū*, Warrant Officer Ippei Goto from the *Kaga* and Petty Officer 1st Class Tomio Inenaga, also from the *Kaga*.

The fate of Shigenori Nishikaichi was particularly poignant. His aircraft was damaged during a dogfight with Curtiss P-36 Mohawk fighters from 46 Squadron, 15 Pursuit Group, USAAC, over Diamond Head, and as he headed back north toward the safety of the *Hiryū*'s deck his fuel was draining away. Nishikaichi knew as he passed the most north-westerly of the Hawaii Island chain that he would not make it back and decided in desperation to make an emergency landing. An island had already been pre-selected for just such an emergency and the Japanese had thought it totally uninhabited. A submarine was tasked to rescue any such stranded aviators from the north beach. However, contrary to Japanese belief Ni'ihau Island *did* have a resident native population, albeit a tiny one. It was a privately owned island run since 1864 by the New Zealand Robinson family, whose then head, Alymer, kept outsiders well away to preserve the wildlife, habitat and language (it became nicknamed 'The Forbidden Isle') and employed the Ni'ihauan islanders to help with the ranch. There were no telephones or electricity on the island and of course nobody had the remotest idea of the momentous events even then taking place 150 miles to the south-east of them. The A6M2 was on her last legs and so, after two passes to seek a suitable landing spot, Nishikaichi put her down in a flattish field, near a small house. Unfortunately, on the final few feet of his approach he flew into an unnoticed wire fence, which flipped his aircraft up and he ended up nose-down and briefly out for the count.

His crash had been observed by Howell Kaleohano and he, naturally, ran to assist the dazed occupant out of the aircraft cockpit, also carefully confiscating his revolver and flight documents. Nishikaichi's English was rudimentary and other neighbours, Yoshio Harada, and his wife, Irene, were summoned. From a Japanese immigrant family, Harada was Hawaii-born and bred and thus fluent in both languages and Nishikaichi told them of the attack, hoping to play on their family heritage and loyalties and get his weapon and map back and enlist their help to reach the rescue beach. They fed him and even entertained him and when the news of the attack came over the radio they kept him interred then took him to Ki'i Landing for the US officials to collect him. They never came as all sailings had been banned in the panic following the assault. Eventually, after six days, Harada decided to help and stole a shotgun. After attempts to communicate with the submarine via the A6M2's radio had failed, in desperation on the night of the 12th the two men entered the township and took several residents hostage. Eventually one Ben Kanahele, despite being shot twice, and his wife, wrestled with Nishikaichi and killed him, while Harada turned the shotgun on himself and committed suicide. Nishikaichi's body was buried on the island for a time, then at the end of 1942 removed from the main island, ultimately being returned to Japan for family re-internment. His A6M2 (B11-120) survived him and parts of it are on exhibit at the Ford Island Pacific Aviation Museum.

The American air strength in Hawaii was considerable, totalling 223 US Army aircraft, but proved mainly ineffective. The main fields were Hickam, Wheeler and Bellows, with the Navy Luke Field on Ford Island and the Marine base at Ewa, which were all heavily hit, the Marine flyers having eight F4F3 fighters torched on the deck. The full list of aircraft casualties was that the US Navy lost 92 destroyed and 31 damaged, whereas the US Army lost 77 and had 128 damaged. The American fighter losses included five P-40Cs, thirty-seven P-40Bs, and four P-36As, while bomber losses included four B-17Ds, twelve B-18As, and two A-20As.

The US Navy carriers *Enterprise* and *Lexington* were absent that day; fortunately for them for they were the primary targets of the Japanese dive-bombers, but that did not prevent them suffering losses. On the 7th the *Enterprise* under Vice-Admiral William F 'Bull' Halsey was returning from ferrying twelve Marine F4F Wildcat fighter aircraft to Wake Island. As customary she started to fly off her aircraft to Ford ahead of her arrival, some eighteen Douglas SBD Dauntless dive-bombers being the first dispatched and launching from 0618 onward. They arrived over Pearl at 0835 and five of them were immediately shot down by the A6Ms, with Petty Officer 1st Class Isao Doikawa claiming to have destroyed three and Petty Officer 3rd Class Shinichi Suzuki claiming another two. In fact, the A6Ms are credited with destroying four while another SBD was damaged by fire from an Aichi D3A and another was destroyed by US anti-aircraft fire.[3] The earliest US Navy losses, however, had been inflicted on the Consolidated PBY Catalina flying boats at Ford, twelve of which belonging to VP-22 were targeted by D3As of which seven were destroyed and the remainder damaged. From a total of sixty-one PBYs only eleven survived the assault intact, many being lost to strafing A6Ms as we have seen.[4]

The Philippines, 1941

On 7 December 1941 the Far East Air Force (FEAF) of American and Allied air forces in the Philippines had at their disposal, 227 combat aircraft, of which 175 were fighters, but of these only the 107 Curtiss P-40E Kittyhawks and P-40B Tomahawks were considered modern. Among older types included the Seversky P-35 and the Boeing P-26, known as the Peashooter. There were seventy-four bombers of which thirty-five were Boeing B-17C/D four-engined Flying Fortresses. The island of Luzon with, at its south-west end the capital, Manila, with the Bataan peninsula across Manila Bay shielding the Navy base of Subic Bay, was the most important target. Under General Douglas MacArthur, elevated to command from retirement, the major defence of the island was to be undertaken by the Army Air Service and to defending its principal bases of Clark, Iba and Nichols Fields he assigned his main priority. The Japanese were equally sure of the importance of quickly gaining control of the air before their invasion forces became engaged ashore, and had mustered considerable air forces at Chiai, Taichung, Tainan, Takao and Tungkan airfields in Formosa (Taiwan) in readiness. Of course, had the time zones not been so different, they would have wished to made simultaneous air attacks on both Pearl Harbor and the Luzon airfields. Pearl being five hours, twenty minutes ahead of Luzon, they had to accept the fact that their aircraft strikes against the latter would probably meet a fully alerted enemy. Nonetheless they were not deterred by this potentially dangerous situation. All their six main fleet carriers were locked up in the Pearl Harbor strike of course, while the Imperial Army Air Force's 5th Air Army's bombers could hit the target in the northern part of the island but lacked sufficient range to reach central and southern Luzon. This left the IJN long-range bombers of Vice-Admiral Nishizo Tsukahara's 11th *Kōkū-kantai* to carry out the mission. This was no problem for, as we have seen, they had been conducting such operations for five years in China.

With a strong American fighter force waiting for them, it was clear that the extended range of the A6M was the ace-in-the-hole the Japanese relied on to accompany and protect their bombers, as before. What all the planning in the world could not do for either side was predict the weather. The morning of 8 December found most of the Formosa airfields shrouded in thick fog, which grounded them, although some forty-three Army bombers made raids on northern Luzon targets.

The Americans, also, with their advance warning, had the option of pre-empting the Japanese moves, by sending the B-17s to blast the Formosa airfields, albeit without fighter cover of their own, but the USAAS had long scorned such protection as superfluous and were confident of their heavy bombers' ability to not only fight their way through but also to deliver precision attacks. They were to be repeatedly disabused of these tenets of belief before the war was many weeks old. They also deluded themselves that that their own bases were safe from attack from Japanese forces, despite the obvious examples of the numerous Japanese long-range strikes over China in the years 1937–41. There was a plan to attack Formosa with everything they had ('Rainbow 5') or, alternatively, flying their aircraft away for safety, either option being available to them.[5] Accordingly the USAAS , like Brer Rabbit, sat tight and said (or rather did) nothing. Major-General Lewis Brereton twice requested permission from Chief of Staff Lieutenant General Richard Kerens Sutherland, to initiate the air attack operation, but MacArthur, who kept a firm grip on all his subordinates, failed to issue the necessary order until 1120 local time, far too late.[6] After the war MacArthur was to deny any knowledge at all of such a request. Indeed he stated that Brereton, '… never recommended an attack on Formosa to me …' adding that the Japanese fighters came from aircraft carriers, which was totally untrue. The original Japanese plan had envisaged that the light carriers *Ryūjō*, *Taiyō* (the converted merchant ship *Kasuga-Maru* and *not* the much larger and much later built *Taihō* as Saburo Sakai has it) and *Zuihō* be used in this manner, considering a return flight of a over 1,200 miles plus aerial combat in between, would be impossible, being an even longer mission than those conducted in China. However, none of these small carriers had ever operated the A6M before and their capacity was small. However, under constant pressure from their unit leaders, Captain Masahisa Saito and Captain Yoshio Kamei, the elite A6M pilots of the Tainan and Takao (Kaohsung) based flyers, including Commander Motoharu Okamua, Yasuna Kozono, Commander Takeo Shibata, and Lieutenant Hideki Shingo, and veterans of the Sino Japanese conflict such as Lieutenant Tamotsu Yokoyama and Petty Officer Saburō Sakai, undertook an intense series of exercises, which stretched the range of the A6M from six to seven hours in the air to ten to twelve, with mass formation flights. The Zero carried 183 gallons of fuel and constant practice eked the average fuel consumption out from 35 gallons per hour to just eighteen, Saburō Sakai himself attaining under 17 gallons. Saburō Sakai explained just how this was achieved:

> To conserve fuel, we cruised at only 115 knots (59 mps) at 12,000 (4267.2m) feet altitude. Under normal full-power conditions, the Zero was capable of 275 knots and, when over-boosted for short emergencies, could reach its maximum speed of about 300 knots. On our long-range flights we lowered propeller revolutions to somewhere between 1,700 and 1,850 revs per minute, and throttled the air control valve to its leanest mixture. This furnished us the absolute minimum of power and speed, and we hung on the fringe of losing engine power at any time and stalling.[7]

This remarkable feat was duly reported to Vice-Admiral Fushizo Tsukahara, 11 *Kōkū-kantai*, who was thus able to dispense with all three light carriers completely. They were used in ferry and subsidiary operations. The *Taiyō* conveyed Type 96 fighters to Palau and *Zuihō* carried A6Ms to 11 *Kōkū-kantai* from Japan to Davao in February, while *Ryūjō* covered the landings at Davao and Legaspi with her A5M4 'Claudes'.

A few defensive air patrols were mounted by P-40s and P-35As, but although some B-17s were got aloft for their own safety for a spell, many remained static, not even taking the elementary defensive tactic of dispersal, but lined up wing-tip-to-wing-tip, in row upon row on their runways, although fully fuelled. Within a short while, '... the greatest concentration of heavy-bombers in the world' as General Marshall had recently boasted, were being destroyed. It was Pearl Harbor all over again, but with absolutely no excuse of surprise. Meanwhile the fog lifted in Formosa and eighty-four

A6Ms, thirty -four from the Tainan *Kōkūtai* led by Lieutenant Shingo and fifty from 3 *Kōkūtai* under Lieutenant Tamotsu Hideki Yokoyama, escorting 108 G3M and G4M bombers, finally took off and headed south.

The Japanese executioners, having spent a frantic few hours waiting for the mist to disperse on their home fields and thinking that each minute that ticked by meant an increased period of readiness for the foes, were delighted when, on arrival over their targets at the delayed time of 1215 hours, they found that their victim had considerately placed his own neck upon the block. Again, as at Pearl, the asset of radar warning was wasted when communication was lost. The Japanese thus, and to their amazement, achieved total surprise. They were hardly likely to waste such an opportunity. They swept aside American fighters, wiping out a flight of eight P-40Es of 3 Pursuit Squadron caught preparing for touch-down at Iba airfield, and clashed with the P-35As found at De Carmen field, eliminating half and then setting about the rest. At Clarke the bombing had been intense and deadly accurate. What few aircraft survived this annihilating bomber assault were finished off by a force of thirty-four ground-strafing A6Ms.[8] At the end of the afternoon a total of fifty-six P-40 and P-35 fighters had been destroyed, along with eighteen B-17s and twenty-six other types, with many, many more damaged to varying degrees, most of them still sitting on the deck, along with base facilities, while the Japanese suffered the loss of just seven A6Ms.[9] It was a stunning victory.[10]

About the only fighter unit untouched at the end of day one, was the Philippine Army Air Corps (PAAC) 6 Pursuit Squadron equipped with twelve P-26 Peashooters and based at Zablan Field. Four of these obsolescent machines (they had first flown as long ago as 1932 and had a top speed of 234mph) were flown to Clark Field and flew reconnaissance missions for the next days over Lingayen Gulf. At 1130 local time on 10 December the unit was surprised at lunch by a force of strafing A6Ms. Four aircraft managed to get airborne, piloted by Captain Villamor and Lieutenants Geronimo Aclan, Alberto Aranzaso, Jose Gozar and Godofredo Juliano, and engaged in a brief skirmish over Pasig before the Zeros, low on fuel, withdrew leaving half the Philippine unit destroyed. The survivors moved to Batangas Field the following day. Here, at 1100 local time on 11 December four machines were scrambled away to intercept a force of twenty-seven bombers at 8,000ft but had difficulty catching them. They were immediately jumped by their Zero escorts who they had failed to notice but claimed to have shot down at least one of them. However, Batangas Field was heavily bombed as was Maniquis where 10 Bombardment Squadron lost its old Martin B-10s plus ten miscellaneous types on the ground.

Meanwhile the Zero sweeps continued, the Tainan group contributing twenty-seven fighters against Clark Field while the Kaohsiung Wing went for Nichols. Tainan A6Ms found no targets remaining at the wasteland that was Clark Field, and flew cover instead over the Vigan invasion force and here Saki destroyed the B-17 of Captain Colin P. Kelly, Jr, that same day.

The Japanese maintained the tempo of their air assault over the following days, indeed increasing it slightly, and, by 13 December had virtually destroyed MacArthur's air power and, on the 10th an air attack, one of ten the base suffered, totally gutted the Cavite Navy Yard (Sangley Naval Base) itself, blowing up the torpedo arsenal for the entire Asiatic Fleet, power supplies and office buildings, as well as sinking the submarine *Sealion* (SS-195) and damaging her sister *Seadragon* (SS-194) and other units. Subsidiary movements included the dispatch of 3 *Kōkūtai* A6Ms to Palau with G3M bombers to cover the landings at Davao, on the southern coast of Mindanao, on 20 December.

A notable achievement of the A6M in this brief aerial campaign came on 25 December. A Japanese invasion force was put ashore on Jolo Island to seize its strategic airfield. The Tainan Group with its long-range expertise sent twenty-four A6Ms to provide air cover for this operation and they exceeded all their previous achievements. One post-war account summarized this mission thus: 'This involved a mass non-stop formation flight of twelve hundred nautical miles. This flight of the single-seat fighters was unprecedented in aviation history.'[11]

The Japanese invasion was already well established with little loss, and their follow-up supply convoys could pretty well come and go as they wished. MacArthur retreated to Bataan where he held out, fruitlessly, for some months but the rest of the Philippines had gone the same way as Hong Kong, Borneo, Malaya, Singapore and soon to follow, Burma and the Dutch East Indies.

The Formosan A6Ms were quickly moved south to provide the same level of air supremacy as the Japanese moved methodically and easily through the colonial possessions of the British and Dutch Empires to the south. Each step of the conquest was taken under the umbrella of fighter cover, airfields were consolidated and then the next step took place. At sea the Japanese Navy proved equally able to crush or brush aside anything the Allied Navies of American, Britain and Holland could muster, and with equal ease they swept the waters of every fragment of organized opposition just as the A6M swept the skies. There was suddenly a great awakening in the west.[12] There proved much for them to ponder in the weeks that followed.

The fall of Singapore

On 18 December the Japanese deployed eleven fighters escorting twenty-six bombers against Singapore. They shot down fifteen defending fighters for the loss of just two of their own fighters. Two days later the Japanese dispatched fifty-two bombers escorted by nine fighters, with Singapore again the target, the A6Ms shooting down twelve Allied aircraft again for the loss of two of their own. On the ground the Allied troops had continually fallen back and ceded the Malayan airfields without much resistance and the Japanese were able to move their A6Ms over the South China Sea and occupy these vital bases for themselves. On 26 December nineteen A6Ms of the 22 *Kōkū Sentai* left Soc Trang and flew into Kota Bharu.

On 14 January 1942 fourteen A6Ms conducted a fighter sweep over Singapore after their bomber force of fifty aircraft had aborted their mission, the Zeros briefly tangling with Brewster Buffaloes of Nos 243 and 488 Squadrons, without loss to either side. The following day three A6Ms escorted twenty-seven G4Ms in an attack on Tengah airfield, their assigned target of a British aircraft-carrier reported anchored in Keppel Harbour proving illusionary! The trio of Japanese fighters strafed the airfield afterward with no results. On the way back one A6M, piloted by Hiroshi Suyama, was lost.

Twelve A6Ms escorted twenty-four G3Ms in an attack on Seletar airfield on 16 January without casualties and on 17 January eight A6Ms strafed Tengah airfield damaging three Bristol Blenheim IV bombers, two Blackburn

Sharks and a Fairey Swordfish that were among many caught on the ground, without suffering any damage in return. On 18 January eleven A6Ms escorted twenty-six G4Ms and were once more in a fight with Buffaloes from Nos 243 and 488 Squadrons. For the first and last ever time the Buffalo had the advantage of surprise and height and at least one A6M, piloted by Yoshihiro Salirana, was lost while one British fighter was damaged beyond repair. It was a rare little defeat for the Japanese.

On 20 January eighteen A6Ms escorted eighteen G3Ms in an attack on Singapore City but they were not engaged as the Hawker Hurricanes tangled with Army bombers instead, losing several of their number in the process. On 21 January nine A6Ms escorted twenty-five G3Ms and twenty-seven G4Ms to bomb Keppel Harbour. Two days later nine A6Ms escorted twenty-five G3Ms to attack Kallang airfield. They were intercepted by Hawker Hurricanes from 232 Squadron and destroyed five of them, damaging two more for the loss of two Zeros.

On 27 January nineteen A6Ms escorted twenty-four G4Ms for another bombing of Kallang, which proved very successful. Four of No. 488 Squadron's Hurricanes were destroyed, three severely damaged and three slightly damaged. Almost all No. 243 Squadron's Buffaloes were wiped out, as well as two Bristol Blenheim bombers, while the airfield's infrastructure was shattered. The pattern was repeated on 29 January when eighteen A6Ms escorted twenty-six G3Ms for an attack on Seletar airfield and the following day Singapore was again attacked with A6Ms providing the escort.

When the island was humiliatingly surrendered on 15 February 1942, 138,708 Allied troops laid down their arms to General Yamashita's 30,000 soldiers, the last three Hurricanes and a lone Buffalo having flown to safety some days before. The whole Singapore campaign had cost the Japanese Navy five A6Ms, along with just four G3Ms and a single C5M.

The Dutch overwhelmed

Having examined the farce of Singapore's air defence, we must go back in time to see how Britain's fellow European ally, the Netherlands, fared against similar opposition.

Although, the third major European colonial power in the East, Holland itself, like France, had rapidly fallen to the combination of Hitler's Panzers and Stuka dive-bombers, her Queen and Government had been rescued by the Royal Navy and brought back to England where they remained resolute allies. Unlike the French Vichy regime, which quickly turned to outright collaboration with the former foes and ceded bases to Germany's Axis partner, Japan, in Indo-China, the Dutch determined to fight for their eastern possessions. They had little with which to do so and relied heavily on what assistance could be obtained from the crumbling forces of America, Australia and Great Britain.

The Japanese were not to allow them much respite. Already nine A6Ms under Lieutenant Kikuichi Inano had flown from Saigon into the airfield at Miri, Sarawak, which had been captured without a fight on 16 December, and began flying air cover the supply convoys unloading there. On Christmas Eve they also protected G3Ms Singkawang II airfield in south-west Borneo and carried out strafing attacks. On Boxing Day the 3*Ku* sent six A6Ms under Lieutenant Toshitada Kawazoe against Menado on the north-eastern tip of the Celebes (now known as Sulawesi) where they surprised and destroyed four or five Dutch Dornier Do 24s and one KNILM Sikorsky S-43B flying boat. On the 28th the 3 *Kōkutai* sent another seven A6Ms from Davao under Lieutenant Kawazoe against Tarakan where they became engaged with Dutch Brewster Buffalos of the I-VlG-V, four of which were lost along with a pair of Ryan STM training aircraft, while a single Zero was damaged. Four further A6Ms were in a second raid by G3M on the same target later that day, while five more from Miri intercepted three Dutch Martin 139[13] bombers attacking their airfield, destroying two of them and badly damaging the third. Thereafter Dutch air resistance in that area faded away.

The Tainan *Kōkutai* moved bases to the newly occupied Jolo airfield, in the Sulu Islands, south-west of Mindanao, in groups, the first of which was completed on 30 December and the last on 7 January, totalling twenty-seven A6Ms. Thence it was a comparatively short move 270 miles down the island chain to Tarakan, on the north-east coast of Borneo. Here conditions were extremely bad and the fighters were hard-pressed to maintain patrols to cover the Balikpapan invasion force. When eight B-17s attacked on the 4th they made the usual highly exaggerated claims of ships sunk and damaged, but only scored a single hit, one bomb striking the No. 2 turret of the heavy cruiser *Myōkō* but causing only superficial damage; five A6Ms failed to intercept them. In addition two A6Ms had slithered off the makeshift runway and been written off. Saburo Saki recalled how much of a shoe-string operation it was, writing:

> … in the early months of 1942 23 had less than seventy Zeros available for the entire vast area of the East Indies. And since a good number of the fighter planes were always undergoing combat repairs and a thorough overhaul after 150 hours of flight, we average thirty fighter planes at any given time for combat action.

Despite this they were dominant and on 5th January Saki nailed his second B-17 over Balikpapan. On 11 and 12 January, to capture the Langoan airfield, the Japanese dropped paratroops and followed up with seaborne landings and ten A6Ms of 3 *Kōkūtai* gave air cover while at Tarakan an attack by three B-17s was met by three A6Ms from Jolo, resulting in damage to one machine on each side but no losses. The next day 3 *Kōkūtai* Zeros destroyed four Australian Lockheed Hudson bombers from a force of seven over Menado. On 13 January three A6Ms destroyed three Dutch Glen Martin 139s over Tarakan and, joined by three Zeros, shot down a further two out of three Dutchmen. A strong force of eighteen A6Ms working from Menado made a surprise assault on the Dutch airbase on Ambon Island off the south-west coast of Seram in the Molucca archipelago, on 15 January. Here they engaged and destroyed two Dutch Brewster Buffalo fighters and strafed one Hudson and destroyed a pair of American Consolidated Catalina PBY flying boats without loss to themselves. A second attack was made the following day when one A6M was shot down by another PBY. The same day the newly captured field at Tarakan was occupied by nine A6Ms from Jolo and by 19 January no fewer than fifty-one A6Ms had concentrated at Manado.

The *Kidō Butai* now took a hand and mounted an attack on the Australian base at Rabaul on the 20th to soften it up prior to its occupation. Vice-Admiral Nagumo led four big carriers, *Akagi*, *Kaga*, *Shōkaku* and *Zuikaku*, along with their escorting battleships, cruisers and destroyers. There were two RAAF airfields at Lakunai and Vunakanau to guard the harbour and

No. 24 Squadron RAAF had nothing to defend them and the shipping in Simpson Harbour with save seven Commonwealth A-20 Wirraway trainers acting as makeshift fighter planes. The fleet's A6Ms brushed them aside, instantly shooting down four of them while so damaging two of the others that they were forced crash-land and were written off. They also damaged a lone Lockheed Hudson. Only two Wirraways were left fit to fight and they were hastily evacuated to safety. Next day the *Shōkaku* and *Zuikaku*'s A6Ms escorted diversionary raids on Lae, Madang, Salamaua and Wau in New Guinea while *Akagi* and *Kaga* aircraft hit Kavieng, New Ireland. On the 22nd they destroyed two Australian artillery positions and both ports were then occupied by Japanese invasion forces while A6Ms escorted Aichi D3A dive-bombers against Port Moresby on New Guinea's southern coast. The Dutch East Indies were just about isolated from all sides with these moves.

On 24 January both Balikpapan, west Borneo, and Kendari, west Celebes, were invaded and the A6Ms were kept busy providing cover for both operations repelling desperate attacks by Allied aircraft, including B-17s and Dutch Glenn Martin 169s, and clashed with Dutch Brewster Buffalo fighters. One of the A6Ms, piloted by Tainan 2 *Shotai*'s Warrant Officer Yoshimitsu Harada was shot down by anti-aircraft while conducting a strafing run, killing the pilot. The wreckage of his Zero was later surveyed by Dutch pilots, probably the closest they had ever got to the A6M without risk of death. During the afternoon two more Dutch F2As and three Glen Martin bombers were destroyed while one Zero was forced to ditch. The following day the Dutch lost a further Glenn Martin and three more were badly damaged from the ten that remained, in return Otojiro Sakaguchi's A6M was destroyed but he parachuted to safety. In intercepting seven B-17s later two A6Ms were lost; five of the American bombers were damaged, two crashing on the way home. While 3 *Kōkūtai* with thirty-five A6Ms shifted base from Menado to Kendari the carriers *Hiryū* and *Sōryū* sent in another attack on Ambon and later landed eighteen of their A6Ms ashore in readiness for the occupation of Amboina and Ceram.

On 4 February a flight of A6Ms moved base to Balikpapan airfield itself and were later joined by the rest of the group. To cover their invasion convoys A6Ms of the 22nd Flotilla operated from Kahang field, located between Kluang and Mersing. On 14 February the Allies made concentrated efforts to bomb these Japanese ships in the Banka Strait, but took heavy losses, as, for example, when several formations of Australian Lockheed Hudson twin-engined bombers from Nos 1, 8 and 62 *Hikōtai* totalling sixteen machines, of which seven were lost and two more crash-landed, A62 pilots Kozaburo Yasui and Keisaku Yoshimura claiming four of them. Despite this Palembang was taken and its airfields occupied and by the next day the southern tip of Sumatra, with Bali falling five days later and Timor the next day leaving Java isolated. Allied fighter aircraft, Brewster 339s, Curtiss Hawks, Curtiss-Wright CW-21Bs, Hawker Hurricanes and Curtiss P-40Es with mixed units of American, Australian and Dutch defenders had been reported concentrating at Djombanagh, Soerabaya at the island eastern end. This was not without hazard and fourteen from a flight of forty P-40s were lost during the transfer north from Darwin via Koepang to Madura Island airfield, near Djombanagh. Meanwhile the Japanese were busy reinforcing their fight strength in the area ready for the final assault and conducting offensive sweeps. On 2 February seventeen Zeros from Balikpapan made a long-range sweep over eastern Java and strafed the Dutch Maospati airfield, Soerabaya, finding few worthwhile targets, but Lieutenant Jun-ichi Sasai, with wingmen Susumu Ishihara and Shizuyoshi Nishiyama from the covering A6Ms did succeed in shooting down one of a number of Brewsters, while, during the initial approach Yoshisuke Arita and Yoshio Motoyoshi had also destroyed a B-18 bomber over Sedajce, killing US radar specialist Colonel William H. Murphy and his staff, Major Straubel, CO of 7 Bomb Group as well as both pilots. Madang, Madioen and Soerabaya naval bases were heavily attacked the following day with a total of seventy-two G3Ms escorted by seventeen A6Ms under Lieutenant Hideki Shingo and twenty-seven under Lieutenant Tamotsu Yokoyama respectively. Over the target 3 *Kōkutai* had a field day massacring the Dutch fighters for the loss of three of their own and Tainan A6Ms achieved equal success, burning five B-17s on the ground at Singosari, Malang, and another in the air by Yoshiri Hidaka as well as a Consolidated Y-40 flying boat destroyed by Saburo Nozawa. The A6Ms then tangled with Dutch Hawks and CW-21Bs shooting down seven of them while four more were forced to crash-land. They then strafed the seaplane base destroying three Dornier 24s, three Dornier Wals three Fokker C-XIs and two Fokker T-IVs. The Tainan A6Ms attacked nine B-17s and destroyed one of them. Finally two P-40s out of six were shot down by 3 *Kōkūtai* for the loss of Hatsumasa Yamaya, Sho-ichi Shji and Masaru Morita, while Kyoji Kobayashi of the Tainan Zeros was also killed.

This resounding victory was repeated two days later when, on 5 February, twenty-seven A6Ms of the Tainan group sortied against Soerabaya again, followed by eleven from the 3 *Kōkūtai*, while a third section of ten A6Ms of 3 *Kōkūtai* headed for Depassar, Bali. One Dutch CW-21B and two Hawks were shot down, a B-17 badly damaged, and three more flying boats, three Dutch Do24s, two Dutch Catalina Ys and two American PBYs were destroyed by strafing. At Bali ten American P-40Es came off worst when they mixed it with ten 3 *Kōkūtai* A6Ms losing seven of their number destroyed and three damaged. The battles continued in this vein, with on 8 February a force of nine B-17s attacking Kendari, Celebes, being met by nine Tainan A6Ms who immediately shot down two of them and damaged all the others. It was not totally one-sided, AA fire at Makassar claiming the life of one of the leading A6M China veterans, Masayuki Nakase of 3 *Kōkūtai*, with eighteen confirmed kills on his belt.

Darwin negated

The *Kidō Butai* under Vice-Admiral Chūichi Nagumo meanwhile took a hand in proceedings on 19 February when the carriers *Akagi*, *Kaga*, *Hiryū* and *Sōryū*, escorted by two battleships, three cruisers and nine destroyers steered by Halmahera and Ambon and entered the Banda Sea. On the morning of 19th, these carriers despatched a strong force of bombers (seventy-one Aichi D3A2 dive-bombers and eighty-one Nakajima B5N2 attack bombers in two separate groups). The bombers were escorted by fifty-four A6Ms, and these comprised nine *Akagi* fighters led by Lieutenant-Commander Shigeru Itaya, nine *Kaga* Zeros under Lieutenant Yasushi Nikaido, nine *Hiryū* fighters led by Lieutenant Sumio Nono and nine *Sōryū* fighters under Lieutenant Iyozo Fujita. This whole mass of aircraft was to strike at Port Darwin, the Allied main supply base for Java. In co-operation the 21 and 23 land-based *Kōkū Sentai* contributed a further fifty-four Mitsubishi G4M2 bombers.

The Allied air power at Darwin comprised ten American P-40Es, fourteen Australian Commonwealth Wirraways, seventeen Lockheed Hudson bombers, several Consolidated PBY Catalina flying boats and some minor units. Of these five P-40Es were on patrol, while half the Wirraways were inoperational and the rest never got airborne. It seemed as if nothing whatsoever had been taken on board even now from all the earlier lessons from Pearl Harbor, Malaya, the Philippines and the Netherlands East Indies. Two radioed warnings from coast watchers north of Darwin were ignored by the Allied HQ and even when one of the Zeros, piloted by Yoshikazu Nagahama shot down a Consolidated PBY Catalina flying-boat over the American supply ship *Florence D*, no warnings were issued or any other defensive measures taken. Thus the whole port was caught totally flat-footed. Even the patrolling P-40Es were totally surprised when the same Nagahama, along ahead of the main Japanese force, dived down on them from above. The A6M pilot lost no time in shooting down three of the startled Americans and damaging the other two in the space of a few minutes.

The first wave of Japanese bombers then arrived while the rest of the A6Ms then made a low-level strafing run across the harbour. The five remaining P-40Es began to scramble but two were flamed at once, while a third was damaged and finally crashed. The remaining pair also got into the sky but only lasted a briefly before they were also destroyed while one A6M flown by Hajime Toyoshima was the only Japanese fighter loss,[14] although seven were damaged slightly by ground fire. Six A6Ms strafed the auxiliary field at Bathurst Island and also shot up three American PBYs.

The carrier-based bombers sank the American destroyer *Peary*, seven transports and many smaller ships and badly damaged two further warships, the American seaplane tender *William B Preston* and Australian sloop *Swan*, and six further transports from the forty-seven ships moored in the harbour that day. On the way to the carriers they also sank the freight *Don Isidro* as well. When the land-based bombers arrived shortly afterwards they completed the job, flattening hangars, buildings, the hospital and workshops and finishing off the two damaged P-40s, destroying also six Hudsons and several light aircraft and causing wholesale panic and desertion among the service personnel.[15] Other than the single A6M the Japanese lost just two dive-bombers and one B5N. As a result of this devastating attack the official

British naval historian was to later record: 'Darwin was put out of action as a base for several months. The last reinforcement link to Java was thus broken.'[16]

On 19 February twenty-three A6Ms took off from Balikpapan to strike this assembly; preceded by weather planes they made the 430-mile hop without loss and they arrived over Soerabaya at 1130 at 16,000ft to find the Allies waiting for them. In a six-minute encounter the A6Ms claimed forty enemy aircraft destroyed for the loss of three of their own. Saburo Sakai alone claimed three P-36 scalps and a bombing raid on Madura caught most of the others on the ground later. The Japanese lost another three A6Ms from a force of eighteen dispatched the following day, 20 February, all downed by anti-aircraft fire while making low-level strafing attacks. This attack was repeated in the same force on the 25th and three B-17s and a floatplane were torched but no fighters were encountered. In total the campaign cost ten A6Ms. On 28 February a final attack was made flying escort to twelve G4Ms against the port of Tjilatjap. No opposition was met so the Zeros visited Malang and Bandjermasin to Bali while 3 *Kōkūtai* conducted similar swift advances via Davao, Manado to Kendrai in the Celebes, where it split, one section moving down to Amboina and then to Dili, Timor Island, while the other went via Makassar also to Bali.

As the long night of Japanese occupation settled over the former colonies of America, Britain and Holland a huge gap was opening up between the Royal Navy, now banished to the central Indian Ocean, and the remnants of the American fleet at Hawaii. Through this gap the Japanese, their appetite whetted by the very ease of the conquests, were threatening to flow, with either the occupation, or at the very least, the isolation of the whole vast Australia continent a very real threat. But, while preparing for the next moves south and east, the IJN was to administer one last blow to Britain's failing sea power, designed to secure their western flank from final threat or interference.

Chapter 8

Peak and Nadir

The attacks on Ceylon

The Nagumo Task Force spend a fortnight recuperating from its mighty endeavours and then, on 26 March, sailed west into the Indian Ocean (less the carrier *Kaga*, which was still refitting) with five carriers escorted by four battleships, two heavy and one light cruiser and eleven destroyers to carry out Operation *C*. Additionally Vice-Admiral Jisaburo Ozawa with the carrier *Ryūjō*, still with sixteen A5Ms under Lieutenant Takahide Aioi, as her fighter complement,[1] and escorted by five heavy and one light cruiser and four destroyers, sortied into the Indian Ocean, as related, and subsequently created havoc and mayhem there, being almost totally unopposed by any strong British naval or air forces. Nagumo, however, *was* challenged. Much speculation has been heard that this was the prelude to the invasion of Ceylon (now known as Sri Lanka) and even of India, but the Nagumo and Ozawa incursions were *never* more than just that, raids designed to either cripple or deter the Royal Navy and keep the Japanese western flank clear while they consolidated their vast conquests to the east and stretched out to deal with the remaining Americans unfettered. The Ozawa raid was designed to disrupt the flow of reinforcements to the crumbling Burma front and give the far-from-enthusiastic Indians something to think about.

The British Admiralty had cobbled together a ramshackle fleet in the hope of holding the Indian Ocean. At full stretch against the combined navies and air forces of Germany and Italy in the Atlantic and Mediterranean most of the ships and aircraft that could be spared were not the best. All five battleships dated back to World War I and only one, *Warspite*, had been modernized. There were three aircraft carriers, one the small and ancient *Hermes* of little fighting value, Admiral Somerville recording, '*Hermes* cannot fly off T/B[2] unless good breeze' due to her slow speed, but two others, *Formidable* and *Indomitable* were brand-new carriers with armour decks. Unfortunately aircraft carriers are only as good as the aircraft they carry and with regard to fighters *Formidable* and *Indomitable* only had thirty-five between them at the outset of the operation, fourteen F4Fs Martlets, nine Hawker Sea Hurricanes and twelve Fairey Fulmar two-seaters. Whereas the *Kidō Butai*'s five big carriers, *Akagi, Sōryū, Hiryū, Shōkaku* and *Zuikaku* carried about 350 modern aircraft, the complement of the two British carriers was pathetically small and individually outclassed, while the strength of the RAF and Fleet Air Arm ashore on Ceylon was equally dire. Again Somerville bluntly noted in his diary, 'Decided land-based striking force practically useless as Blenheims no experience and Swordfish have not got the range. So it all depends on the carriers.' But the carriers were in as poor a state. Indeed by 8 April, with the battle in full swing, Somerville signalled to the Admiralty, 'State of fighter aircraft in Fleet is: Martlet [The Royal Navy name for the F4F Wildcat] 6, Fulmar 8, Hurricane I – 10 and Hurricane II -1.' This was a total for *both* British carriers of twenty-five fighter aircraft, of vastly inferior performance. No wonder the admiral was pleading with London for, 'More and first class fighters.' He requested '… immediate dispatch more Fulmars as replacements', asking that they be fitted with extra fuel tanks for them, and also long-range tanks for the Martlets and Hurricanes. He questioned, 'When will Barracuda replace Albacore and Firefly the Fulmar?'[3] Of the aircraft mentioned the Blenheims were light twin-engined bombers, already obsolete and with a top speed of 266mph (428km/h); Hurricanes were Hawker Sea Hurricanes; the Fulmar was the Fairey Fulmar, a two-seater scout fighter make-over (O.8/38) from the original P.4/34 light bomber design with a top speed of 272 mph (437.74 km/h) and the agility of Thames barge – a few later flew with No. 273 Squadron in Ceylon also; the Albacore was the Fairey Albacore TSR (Torpedo Spotter Reconnaissance), incredibly at this date yet another biplane supposed to be an improvement of the same company's Fairey Swordfish, itself a wire-and-strut contraption known to its aircrews as the 'Stringbag'.[4] The longed-for Barracuda and Firefly were both Fairey-built aircraft, one a combined dive- and torpedo-bomber, with a maximum speed of 228mph (367 km/h), and which, like all such compromises, was not brilliant at either; the latter was a monoplane fighter with a top speed of just 316mph (508km/h); neither of these aircraft became serviceable until September/October 1943 and then only in penny packets.

It is just as well that the Eastern Fleet's tiny fighter force was never brought to battle by the *Kidō Butai* with over 130 A6Ms embarked. However, the British fighters ashore were most certainly put to the test as was the A6M.

Although forewarned of the Japanese attacks by Intelligence, when they did not occur as predicted on 1 April, Somerville, who had sortied from his base at Addu Atoll (Port 'X') in the Maldive Islands sortied out to offer battle, while the main ports of Ceylon and India, Calcutta, Madras, Trincomalee and Colombo were largely cleared of shipping. He decided that, in his own boastful words, 'Still no news of the enemy, I fear they have taken fright which is a pity because if I could have given them a good crack now it would have been very timely. Unfortunately I can't hang about indefinitely waiting for them.'⁵ He duly returned to his secret base, but prematurely split up his already inferior force, sending the *Hermes* to Trincomalee and two heavy cruisers to Colombo. However, he was very soon forced to eat humble pie. The Japanese were unaware of Addu Atoll but struck hard at the two latter harbours.

Warning was given by a Canadian pilot of a PBY Catalina at 1600 on 4 April, 350 miles south-east of Ceylon. He reported all five carriers and accompanying warships before six A6Ms of the CAP from *Akagi* and *Zuikaku* sighted him, being reinforced by six more scrambled from *Hiryū*. The flying boat managed to get away two detailed sighting reports in the seven minutes remaining to her before she was shot into the sea in the midst of the third transmission. The pilot, Squadron-Leader L. J. Birchall, RCAF (whom the Canadian Press immediately dubbed 'the Saviour of Ceylon!) and five others were later rescued. Their message initiated a general alert ashore and many ships were again sent away to sea, including the two heavy cruisers who were instructed to rejoin the fleet. However, thirteen Royal Navy ships and twenty-one merchantmen still remained in Colombo harbour when the Japanese struck early next day. The fifty-three B5N attack bombers and thirty-eight D3A dive-bombers, had an escort of thirty-six A6Ms under Lieutenant-Commander Shigeru Itaya (*Akagi*), Lieutenant Iyozo Fujita (*Sōryū*), and Lieutenant Sumio Nono (*Hiryū)* and Lieutenant Masatoshi Makino (*Zuikaku*).

Almost as soon as the *Hiryū* fighters arrived over the port at 0732 they found a formation of six Fleet Air Arm Fairey Swordfish from No. 788

Squadron who lumbered slowly into their path *en route* from China Bay to Ratmalana, who identified these radial-engined aircraft as 'Hurricanes, with a large red dot painted on the wings and fuselage'. All six were dispatched within minutes with very few survivors. Rather less antiquated serious opposition came in the form of No. 30 Squadron with twenty-one Hurricane IIBs and 258 Squadron with fourteen Hurricane I and IIBs, joined by three Fairey Fulmar from Nos 803 and 806 Squadrons FAA who took off from Racecourse and Ratmalana airfields and clawed their way skyward. The A6Ms were dumping their long-range tanks as they attacked. In the brief swirling fight that followed no fewer than twenty-one Hurricanes were destroyed and others damaged to varying degrees, against a single A6M, piloted by Sachio Higashi from the *Sōryū*, lost. In addition three more, *Hiryū* fighters, were damaged but able to land back safely on their carrier. Six D3A dive-bombers were also lost, mainly to AA fire. British naval losses were the Armed Merchant Cruiser *Hector* and the destroyer *Tenedos*, while the Submarine Depot Ship *Lucia* was damaged while lesser vessels and merchant ships were damaged and port facilities wrecked. A Supermarine Walrus amphibian from the light cruiser *Glasgow*, which was sent to patrol offshore from China Bay, was also lost when it crashed at Clampalmin.

The nine-plane CAP over Nagumo's ships meanwhile was taking a steady toll of any searching British aircraft; a PBY Catalina was destroyed at 0842 and a Fleet Air Arm Albacore from No. 827 Squadron Fleet Air Arm (FAA)[6] was forced into the sea by Masato Hino, Noboru Todaka and Kenji Kotani from *Hiryū*, who drove off a second which, although heavily hit, managed to land back aboard *Indomitable*. The fleets were very close, Nagumo search planes were watched on the Eastern Fleets radar screens that day but the main fleets (fortunately for Somerville) never became engaged and withdrew to the Maldives once more.[7] What the Japanese *did* find were the isolated heavy cruisers *Cornwall* and *Dorsetshire* steaming hard to join Somerville's force. A strong force of fifty-three unescorted Aichi D3A dive-bombers was dispatched, caught the cruisers by surprise even though one had an operational radar set, and sank them both with a record number of hits and near misses within seven minutes.[8]

On 9 April the *Kidō Butai* was re-located at 0716 by a PBY from No. 413 Squadron. The Japanese had resumed the attack on Ceylon by steaming into a launching position one hundred miles from the port of Trincomalee and began flying off a strike force from 0600. The British floatplane was quickly intercepted and destroyed by two A6Ms from *Hiryū*, again piloted by Masato Hino and Kenji Kotani. The five carriers between them sent off ninety-one Nakajima B5N attack bombers, escorted by forty-one A6Ms, the *Hiryū* and *Akagi* each contributing six, under Lieutenant Yasuhiro Shigematsu and Lieutenant-Commander Shigeru Itaya, the *Zuikaku* and *Shōkaku* ten apiece led by Lieutenant Masatoshi Makino and Lieutenant Tadashi Kaneko respectively and nine more from *Sōryū* under Lieutenant Masaharu Sugunami. This mass was detected by radar during its approach enabling the British to scramble all available fighters, twelve more Hurricanes, to reinforce three patrolling Hurricanes from No. 261 Squadron.

Almost immediately two A6Ms, piloted by Lieutenant Masatoshi Makino and Naval Airman 1st Class Tatsu Matsumoto, were surprised and shot down. A third A6M, piloted by Fujito Hayashi also failed to return. Two B5Ns were also lost. In return eight Hurricanes were destroyed and three more damaged in the air and another destroyed on the ground as were three Wildebeest torpedo-bombers. The bombers blasted China Bay airfield while A6Ms strafed causing much damage to aircraft and installations. Two Fleet Air F4Fs did not even take off while one Fulmar of No. 814 Squadron was destroyed. There was also a Walrus and three Albacores lost aboard the freighter *Sagaing*, which was bombed and beached. The 15-inch gunned monitor *Erebus* was also heavily hit and badly damaged. British naval losses did not end there, however, for among the ships hurried out to sea were the carrier *Hermes* (with just one Swordfish aboard in her hangars), the Australian destroyer *Vampire*, corvette *Hollyhock*, and Royal Fleet Auxiliary *Athelstone*, and two merchantmen, *British Sergeant* and *Norviken*, all of which were destroyed by eight-five unescorted D3A dive-bombers, which deliberately spared the Hospital Ship *Vita* and indeed directed her to survivors in the water. Eight Fulmars from 803 and 806 FAA Squadrons arrived too late to save the ships, but tangled with retiring D3As, shooting down four but losing two Fulmars in the process.

Meanwhile a counter-strike by eleven Bristol Blenheim bombers of No. 11 Squadron had been mounted, the RAF machines departing Racecourse airstrip at 0820 under Squadron-Leader Kenneth Ault. Two of these medium bombers aborted the search early on and returned to base, the other nine succeeded in penetrating the *Kidō Butai*'s CAP at 1048. Despite the fact that the *Hiryū* apparently sighted these aircraft, but, inexplicably failed to pass on any warning, and that a CAP of twenty A6Ms were aloft, eight from *Hiryū*, six from *Sōryū*, three from *Akagi* and three from *Zuikaku*, the British aircraft achieved complete surprise (none of the Japanese warships had radar at this stage of the war). The medium bombers were able to carry out unopposed bombing runs on the aircraft carrier *Akagi* and the heavy cruiser *Tone*, both of which were near-missed but undamaged. Failure to detect the British forces was deemed '… a very serious matter …' by the High Command[9] as indeed it was, but little practical action could be done with reliable radar.

As usual, the standard RAF level bombing method proved totally useless in hitting speeding warships. The RAF had rejected dive-bombing in the 1930s and stubbornly clung to their false doctrine despite the numerous examples of the accuracy of the dive-bomber set time-and-time again by the Fleet Air Arm and Luftwaffe off Norway, the Low Countries and France and in the Mediterranean and just recently re-emphasized by the D3As. The Blenheims might have achieved a stunning blow otherwise, but it was not to be and the A6Ms, after their initial lapse, did not give them much chance of escape. Four of the nine bombers were shot down immediately, for the loss of one A6M piloted by Lieutenant Sumio Nono from *Hiryū*. Worse was to come, as the five remaining British bombers made their way back to Ceylon they met the returning *Hiryū* A6Ms and were quickly destroyed or were so damaged that they crash-landed and were written off. The A6Ms lost one aircraft, piloted by Toshio Makinoda, in the process.

Winston Churchill was to later to boast that the Japanese had suffered a severe setback, claiming that finally, '… they had met bone' … but this can be dismissed as a typical piece of risible, even fatuous, political spin on what really took place.[10] In private he was reduced to pleading with Roosevelt to take the heat off the British to which the American Premier, no lover or supporter of the British Empire, was less than enthusiastic. Politicians of course have little connection with facts and more disappointing, and with far less excuse, the post-war account of events from the Air Intelligence

Officer on the scene at the time, refused to accept that the Japanese losses had been grossly exaggerated.[11]

The really sobering lesson from this raid for the Japanese ought to have been the fragility of the CAP and the force as a whole in detecting incoming enemy aircraft. Never mind that the actual bombing methods employed by the British were flawed and ineffective, the fact that they could approach with impunity should have given the Japanese deep pause for thought.

For a total loss of just eleven (three A6M, six D3As and one B5N)[12] aircraft the Nagumo force had sunk one aircraft carrier, two heavy cruisers, two destroyers, one armed merchant cruiser, one corvette and several merchant vessels, damaging many more. They had also destroyed forty-eight British aircraft in the air and many others on the ground. Satisfied with this result their foray ended and the five carriers and their escorts departed, never to return. Many had claimed this was a defeat but there was never ever any Japanese intention of invading and occupying Ceylon at this time;, there was no troop convoy, or, indeed, available troops at this period of the war.[13]

If it was a crushing British victory as Churchill and others have claimed, the men on the spot did not view it in the same way at the time. Admiral Somerville wrote to Admiral Sir Dudley North on 10 April, that the Japanese aircraft, '... certainly are the devil and we've got to revise all our ideas. You see we've never been up against carrier borne aircraft before ... It's a damned unpleasant lesson we have to learn. My poor Albacores, Swordfish and Fulmars are useless against the Japs unless can catch them at night.' Still that same old illusion. Later, on 2 May, he wrote to the First Sea Lord, Admiral Sir Dudley Pound, stating, 'It is no use disguising the fact that for day striking we are outclassed by the Japanese ...'. He summed up accurately enough, however, '... our FAA, suffering as it does from arrested development for so many years, would not be able to compete on all round terms with an FAA [i. e. the Japanese] which has devoted itself to producing aircraft fit for sailors to fly in.'

Admiral Geoffrey Layton was even more blunt, writing, 'The FAA aircraft are proving more of an embarrassment than a help ... as they cannot operate by day in the presence of Japanese fighters and only tend to congest airfields.'[14]

Not for two long years did the Royal Navy even begin to menace, to even the slightest extent, events in the Pacific. Some victory!

A6M3 Model 22

Even at the height of its achievements development work was continuing with the A6M fighter. Planning to increase the fuel capacity had already preceded the Model 32, and this need was reinforced early in 1942. With the obvious failure of the Model 32 in that regard it was decided to revert once more to the folding wing-tips, giving a 39ft 4 in (12m) wingspan. These folding tips were latched down and upon landing were each raised by hand. It retained the more powerful *Sakai*-21 engine, which gave the heavier aircraft a speed of 335.5mph (540km/h), only slightly less than the earlier model. To compensate for the higher fuel use and restore the essential outstanding reach of this little fighter, two 12-gallon (45.42-litre) fuel tanks were added, one in each wing, commencing with serial number 3344, which was the first Type 22, adding one hundred miles' range over the Model 21. This ensured that the Model 22 turned out to have the best range of any A6M model at 887.5 miles (1,428km) plus eighty minutes of full power potential. With the ghastly attrition of the Guadalcanal campaign under way, this was the best news of all to their hard-pressed Japanese Navy fighter pilots. Of course, it would have been better, and certainly would have placed much less strain on them, had the Japanese been able to quickly construct a chain of usable airstrips down the Solomons Island chain, thus obviating the need for such wearing journeys to and from the battlefield, but although some such airstrips were hewn out of the virgin jungle on remote islands, the Japanese were never able to match the construction expertise, extent and machinery that the American SEEBEE organization[15] could devote to such tasks. So range was still vital and reliance on the durability and dogged courage of their dwindling numbers of air aces took the place of sheer physical muscle on the ground. The Model 32 had an overall length of 29ft 9in (9.067m), just an inch longer the original Model 11 and powered by the Nakajima 'Prosperity' 21 (Ha 35) radial. This aircraft began to be produced in November 1942 and was officially accepted on 29 January 1943.

Also, before too many of this Model had come off the production lines, the trim tab that hitherto had protruded from abaft the lower rudder, was considerably enlarged in size and recessed into the rudder itself. Experiments were also made with this Model to increase the offensive punch of the aircraft. The A6M3 Model 22*Koh* (22a or 1st sub-type) designation was employed for those Model 22s that had the long-barrel Type 99 Model 2–3 20mm cannon fitted that protruded from the wing. Based on the Swiss Oerlikon FFL, this gun had the higher muzzle velocity of 2,490ft/sec (759m/sec), weighed 80lb (36kg) and had a firing rate of 490rpm. A few later production models A6M3-22*Kai* were experimentally equipped with the 30mm (1.2in) cannon, which had 90 rounds and weighed 102lb (51kg), had a muzzle velocity of 2,330 ft/sec (710m/sec) and were tested operationally from Rabaul. In total 560 A6M3 Model 22s were built at the Mitsubishi plant in the period 1942/43.

Battle of the Coral Sea

Between 4 and 8 May 1942 a confused action between rival carrier formations took place in the southern Pacific. It was the first-air-to-air naval battle during which the surface ships of both sides never sighted each other. It was a battle noted for the errors that took place and the missed opportunities that frustrated both commanders. Even although the Japanese Navy was planning and assembling forces for a great final show-down with the US Navy in the central Pacific, one-third of the *Kidō Butai*, the fleet carriers *Shōkaku* and *Zuikaku*, was allowed to participate in this side-show, which under the terminology Operation *MO*, saw the dispatch of a Japanese invasion convoy to take Port Moresby, New Guinea. At the same time the plan to severe communications between Australia and the United States by extending their air bases down the Solomon Islands chain and then ultimately on to Fiji and beyond, further embroiled limited Japanese forces and clashed with American holding actions in the same area. A light carrier, *Shōhō*, was also involved with a mixed range of tasks that ultimately proved beyond her capacity to fulfil. Overall command was vested in Vice-Admiral Shigeyoshi Inoue. The same Allied Intelligence sources that had revealed the Indian Ocean sortie and shared it under the COPEK system[16] gave advance warning to the Americans of what was afoot and they sent two of their own carriers, in separate groups, to contest the issue. In overall command of the American forces was Vice-Admiral Frank J Fletcher, who, as H. P. Wilmott pointed out, had the outstanding advantage of knowing his opponents' '… assumed order of battle, timetable and objectives'.[17] Under his command Fletcher, like Nagumo a cruiser man in charge of a carrier battle, had the carriers *Lexington* and *Yorktown*, with a total of thirty-eight F4F fighters, seventy SBD dive-bombers and twenty-five TBD torpedo-bombers embarked, with Rear-Admiral Aubrey Fitch exercising Tactical Command. There was also an Australian/American cruiser squadron under Rear-Admiral John Crace, RAN, and a separate fuelling group of two oilers and two destroyers.

The A6M strength aboard the three Japanese carriers comprised twenty-one in *Shōkaku* and twenty-five aboard *Zuikaku*, plus nine A6Ms destined to reinforce Rabaul. The little *Shōhō*, commanded by Captain Izawa Ishinosuke, had only been in commission since January, and after aircraft ferry duties she had sailed from Truk on 30 April along with four heavy cruisers and a destroyer.[18] She was carrying eight A6Ms under Lieutenant Kenjirō Nōtomi. She also had some unassembled A6Ms and four A5Ms. Suggestions that *Shōhō* should join up with the fleet carriers to form an integrated force made some sense in that her flight deck would serve as a floating reserve but such considerations did not rate highly and were rejected. Her lack of speed would have restricted the fleet carriers and as surprise (and success) was assumed priority was given to her role of covering the invasion convoy, which the Army Command was demanding air cover for.

When the Japanese occupation waded ashore at Tulagi to establish a base in the Solomons on 2 May the *Shōhō* provided three A6Ms as air cover, but when there was no enemy attack that day she withdrew. The American bombers arrived the next day and *Shōhō* reversed course, too late to take part in any air combat, although she lost one fighter piloted by Petty Officer 2nd Class Toshikazu Tamura to an accident over Tulagi that day, before the battle proper commenced. She put back into Rabaul leaving the next day to shield the troop convoy and began air operations on 5 May. From dawn on 7 May a two-plane CAP was maintained over the force with four A6Ms and two Type 96s. At 0800 a warning was received from

Japanese scouts shadowing the US Task Forces that they were launching heavy formations of aircraft and preparations were made to fly off every available aircraft from Shōhō. Four A6Ms and one B5N were preparing to land to refuel and join this force, having been relieved by three Type 96s, but before this could be implemented at 1100 the US striking force, ninety-three aircraft, which included ten F4F-3s from *Lexington* under Lieutenant-Commander Paul H. Ramsey and eight F4F-3s from *Yorktown* commanded by Lieutenant-Commander James H. Flatley, Jr, made a mass assault on the carrier, mistaking her for the main Japanese carrier force. Despite the best efforts of her slender air cover, during which at least three American aircraft were confirmed destroyed, the Shōhō was totally overwhelmed, being hit by seven torpedoes and thirteen bombs and she sank with heavy loss of life in twenty minutes, the American force commander jubilantly radioing 'Scratch one flat-top!' As the ancient little *Hermes* had vanished a few weeks earlier, overwhelmed by aircraft, so departed the brand-new Shōhō, equally swamped from the air. The vulnerability of aircraft carriers was becoming increasingly obvious. Without any, or sufficient, aircraft, they became mere unarmoured targets.

One A6M was lost in the brief aerial skirmish that of Warrant Officer Shigemune Imamura, a China veteran. Also lost were three more pilots, Petty Officers 2nd Class Takeo Inoue, Yukio Hayakawa and Hachirō Kuwabara, all killed aboard when the carrier was hit. The three surviving A6Ms under Nōtomi made for the nearest friendly haven, making forced landings at the temporary Deboyne Atoll seaplane base in the Louisiade Archipelago off New Guinea. Another A6M piloted by Petty Officer 2nd Class Okura Shigeru from the *Zuikaku* was also forced to ditch in the lagoon during the battle. The fighters had destroyed three Douglas SBD dive-bombers in return.

While the American misdirected strike had hit the little carrier instead of Inoue's pair of fleet carriers from the 5th *Kōkū-sentai*, the Japanese had made a similar mistake and devoted their main effort against the oiler *Neosho* and destroyer *Sims*, both of which were sunk. It had been a difficult learning curve for both sides.

The final Japanese sorties that day were mounted by land-based aircraft, 4 *Kōkūtai* dispatching twelve G4M land attack planes from Rabaul, escorted by eleven A6Ms of the Tainan *Kōkūtai*, which failed to find any enemy ships. A second strike was sent that consisted of twenty Mitsubishi G3Ms land attack bombers of the Genzan *Kōkūtai* escorted by further A6Ms. They bombed Crace's cruiser force without scoring any hits, and lost four bombers to the ships AA fire. All this groping around by both sides had achieved very little, but the battle proper was resumed the following day.

On 8 May the carrier forces of both combatants located each other and launched their respective strikes. The Japanese escorting A6Ms, from *Shōkaku* under their *buntaichō*, Lieutenant Takumi Hoashi, included Petty Officers Jirō Matsuda, Korenobu Nishide, Masao Sasakibra, Shunji Horiguchi and Ichirō Yamamoto, Warrant Officer Yukuo Hanzawa and Seaman 1st Class Shigeru Kawano. Nine A6Ms from *Zuikaku*'s 2 *Chūtai* were led by the *buntaichō* Lieutenant Yūzō Tsukamoto, with Petty Officers Tomio Kamei, Satoshi Kanō, Ginji Kiyomatsu, Shigeru Makino, Shigenobu Nakata and Shigeru Okura along with Seamen 1st Class Nobutaka Kurata and Toshitsugu Nisugi. The fighters were escorting thirty-three D3A dive-bombers and eighteen B5N torpedo-bombers. The American strike forces totalled fifteen F4Fs, thirty-nine SBDs and twenty-one TBDs. Incredibly the two air striking forces passed each other *en route* to their respective targets! The two American carriers, as usual, made separate attacks, the *Yorktown* planes arriving first.

The Japanese CAP was provided by ten A6Ms under Lieutenant Kiyokuma Okajima from *Zuikaku* and nine from *Shōkaku* under Ensign Abe Yasujirō, later relieved by Petty Officer 2nd Class Miyazawa Takeo. Operating in the murky weather conditions they had no radar to pierce the overcast and direct them against the enemy, and, forced to rely totally on eye-contact, they had problems with interceptions. By the time the leading American bombers arrived overhead three of *Zuikaku* 1st *Chūtai* A6Ms were aloft, piloted by Petty Officers 1st Class Junjirō Itō and Tetsuzō Iwamoto and Seaman 1st Class Mae Shichijirō, along with seven from *Shōkaku*'s 2 *Chūtai*, Petty Officers Hisdashi Ichinose, Sadamu Komachi, Yoshimi Minami, Takeo Miyazawa, Kenji Okabe and Yoshizō Tanaka and Seaman 1st Class Kōchi Imamura. Six more A6Ms were hastily scrambled once the attack developed, a further four from *Zuikaku*'s 1 *Chūtai* under Lieutenant Kiyokuma Okajima, the *buntaichō*, with Petty Officers Kenta Komiyama,

Saneatsu Kuroki and Gorō Sakkaida, and two from *Shōkaku*'s 2 *Chūtai*, Ensign Yasujirō Abe and Petty Officer Jinichirō Kawanishi.

The CAP of nineteen A6Ms suffered the loss of just two fighters: Petty Officer 1st Class Takeo Mayazawa from *Shōkaku* who, was, erroneously, credited with destroying one TBD Devastator, and deliberately ramming a second to prevent it making a launch at his home carrier, and Petty Officer 2nd Class Hisashi Ichinose from *Zuikaku*. Two bomb hits were registered on the *Shōkakū* but she continued to steam at full speed as her engines were untouched. Despite the bomb hits on *Shōkaku*, and loss of the arrestor gear, Warrant Officer Yukuo Hanzawa managed to land his A6M safely back aboard, while other *Shōkaku* survivors were diverted and landed aboard the *Zuikaku*.

Half-an-hour passed before the *Lexington* aircraft finally arrived and they were met by the thirteen A6Ms in the air at the time, seven from *Zuikaku*'s 1 *Chūtai*, led by the *buntaichō* Lieutenant Kiyokuma Okajima, with Petty Officers Junjirō Itō, Tetsuzō Iwamoto, Kenta Komiyama, Saneatsu Kuroki and Gorō Sakkaida with Seaman 1st Class Shichijirō; and six piloted by Ensign Yasujirō Abe, Petty Officers Jinichirō Kawanishi, Sadamu Komachi, Kenji Okabe, Yoshizō Tanaka and Seaman 1st Class Kōichi Imamura.

They destroyed three of the F4Fs but another hit was registered on the *Shōkaku* in this attack, and 109 of her crew were killed, but she was able to withdraw relatively intact. The *Lexington* airmen alone claimed to have hit her with two bombs and five torpedoes in this attack, but apart from one bomb strike the rest were total imagination!

The Japanese striking force contacted their target later that morning. Forewarned by radar the Americans had ample time to assemble a force of eight *Yorktown* and five *Lexington* F4Fs supplemented by no fewer than eighteen SBDs deployed in a defensive role. Nine more F4Fs were scrambled away from *Lexington* as the attack developed and yet four more from *Yorktown*. This massive defence force should have guaranteed immunity but it did not; the *Yorktown* was hit by one bomb and near-missed by five or six others; the *Lexington* fared worse, being struck by two torpedoes and two bombs. She later blew up and had to be abandoned and then finally sank, taking with her into the depths all her thirty-six surviving aircraft.

The two Japanese carriers returned home separately, at the end of the month, and their surviving fighter units resumed training exercises. The *Shōkakū* had to be docked at Kure for damage repairs,[19] while the *Zuikaku* replenished her vastly depleted air complement.[20] The latter vessel was back in commission again, too late to participate in the Midway operation other than to make a sortie from the Inland Sea on 15 June to support the fleet units withdrawing from that battle.

Battle of Midway

The launching of sixteen North American B-25 Mitchell bombers from the aircraft-carrier *Hornet* on 18 April 1942, to make surprise attacks on various Japanese targets was a humiliating experience for the Japanese Navy who found that, despite their overwhelming conquests and easy victories over one third of the globe, they had been powerless to prevent it. For twenty years the main Japanese naval plan had been to lure the American fleet westward, subject it to debilitating attrition with attacks by submarines and aircraft, whittle down its numbers and then engage and destroy it in one final cataclysmic surface battle. The plan was really little more than an enlarged and modernized version of how Admiral Heihachirō Tōgō's overwhelming victory of the Battle of Tsushima had been achieved over the Russian fleet in May 1905. Although the opinion of Navy High Command was divided on aspects of his concept, Admiral Yamamoto finally got his way, as he had done previously, by threatening to resign, and the operation was put into motion. Briefly, the idea was to attack and occupy Midway Atoll, a western extension of the Hawaii archipelago group, and thus provoke the Americans at Pearl Harbor to dispatch a relief force. The Japanese hoped the US Navy would commit their main remaining strength so that they could destroy it totally and finish the job started by the Pearl Harbor assault. Waiting in ambush for such an American response would be the full power of the IJN, ten battleships with accompanying light forces. The principal *agent provocateur* was, once more, to be the *Kidō Butai*, which would beat down the Midway air defences paving the way for the warship bombardments and landing of ground forces. Nagumo's carriers were subsequently to move into a covering position to eliminate any opposing carriers prior to the main and, it was hoped final, fleet surface action. Once such a happy outcome was achieved, the Japanese thinking went, Americans would see that to go on fighting was hopeless and Japan might be able to negotiate a ceasefire from a position of strength. In hindsight of course, this would never have happened, but there appeared to very few viable options. Although Yamamoto was renowned as a leading exponent of naval air power, it can be seen that, in the final analysis, his plan depended upon the 18- and 16-inch guns of his battleships to achieve the longed-final reckoning with the enemy, just as with his predecessors.

If bringing the US fleet to its destruction was the aim, which it was, the occupation of Midway being always a necessary, but secondary, aim, then the basis of the Yamamoto plan appeared sound enough. However, success always depended upon the enemy reacting exactly as hoped, never a very sound basis for any war operation. It also relied a great deal on secrecy, for the main Japanese fleet was not to be in place until *after* the atoll had been crushed. Only after that had been done was it expected that the US Navy would sortie looking for revenge, and by which time Yamamoto's big ships would be ready for them. That secrecy, however was fatefully to be denied them by the exceptional code-breaking of the Allied Intelligence teams in the field, notably that headed up by the brilliant, if unpredictable, Commander Joe Rocheford and the OIC Station *Hypo* group at Pearl Harbor who had cracked many the crucial Japanese naval code.

Unprecedented intelligence information gave the US Task Force commanders huge amounts of priceless data prior the battle, thus enabling the C-in-C Pacific, Admiral Chester W. Nimitz, to plan his own counter-ambush with both submarines and two carrier task groups. His commander at sea, Fletcher once more, knew even more details about the Midway operation than he had done about the Coral Sea scenario – the date of the attack, the direction it was coming from with the wind coming from the east to aid take-off, the intentions of the commanders, the fact that *Zuikaku* was *not* included, the fact that after launching their air strike the Nagumo force was to continue to hold their course straight down toward Midway for three-and-a-half hours to aid their subsequent recovery, even down to the names of each of the individual ships making up the composition of the *Kidō Butai*, all of which would be promulgated verbally to Nimitz's admirals in the field of course by COMPAC at the pre-battle meetings.[21]

Nimitz also refused to commit his remaining old battleships, keeping them on the West Coast out of harm's way; they had not been modernized like the Japanese veterans and nor had they the speed to evade adverse action. Instead, Nimitz decided to use his three remaining carriers to lurk on the edge of the Japanese approach and hit the Japanese ships while their aircraft were away attacking Midway. He also set up a large covering submarine ambush of his own (which, incidentally, proved largely ineffective). He warned his commanders, Fletcher and Rear-Admiral Raymond Spruance, to avoid losing their carriers and not take any undue risks. Fletcher certainly interpreted this order to the letter to the extent that the ambush was very nearly compromised because the US carriers found themselves out of place at the crucial opening phase. Nonetheless, the American plan was to prove to be a far more sound operation than the Japanese plan. Why was this?

The Japanese seemed to go out of their way to compromise their own battle preparations. Firstly they detached two of their six big carriers to cover the Port Moresby and Tulagi operations, both of which could have well been delayed for, had Yamamoto's Midway plan worked, both objectives could have been taken with almost no opposition anyway. This resulted in both *Shōkakū* and *Zuikaku* being unavailable for the really vital fight off Midway, as we have seen, with the most disastrous results. Four smaller carriers were allocated to the operation, but these, like most of the Japanese battleships and heavy cruisers, were scattered all over the central and northern Pacific in separate squadrons, far astern of the *Kidō Butai* and thus totally unable to assist them when the battle reached its climax. This was a total waste of fighting power, which nullified the overwhelming paper superiority that the IJN had on paper. Further dispersing of available power occurred when Yamamoto also agreed to the invasion and occupation of certain bases in the Aleutian Islands, far to the north. Again, this could have easily been achieved once the main battle had been won, as it was it merely drew off Japanese strength for a secondary, and totally, irrelevant purpose. And so, in essence, the Battle of Midway came down to a duel between four Japanese fleet carriers and three American fleet carriers plus Midway itself, which was, in effect, a fourth, and truly 'unsinkable', aircraft carrier.[22]

For the purposes of this study the battle can be split in three phases, the Japanese attack on Midway itself; the American attacks on the *Kidō Butai*; and *Hiryū*'s gallant attempts to fight back against the odds.

The strike on Midway

The A6M strength of twenty-seven fighters for the attack on Midway comprised nine from *Akagi* under Lieutenant Aya-o Shirane, with Petty Officers Seiji Ishii, Shinaji Iwama, Yōzō Kawada, Tetsuo Kikuchi, Koreo Kimura, Sakae Mori, Shigetaka Ōmori and Seaman 1st Class Masahi Ishida; nine from *Kaga* led by Lieutenant Masao Iisuka with Petty Officers Hiromi Itō, Tsugo Ogiwara, Kiyonobu Suzuki, Matsutaro Takaoka, Yoshikazu Nagahama and Seamen 1st Class Ei-ichi Takahashi, Matsutaro Takaoka and Yoshio Egawa; nine from *Hiryū* commanded by Yasuhiro Shigematsu, leading Petty Officers Yutaka Chiyōshima, Toshiaki Harada, Kazuo Muranaka, Haruo Nitta, Takaaki Satō, Michisuke Tokuda, Warrant Officer Yoshijirō Minegishi and Seaman 1st Class Shigeru Hayashi; and nine from *Sōryū* led by Lieutenant Masaji Suganami, with Ensign Hira Tanaka, Petty Officers Nobutoshi Furukawa, Iwao Mira, Mitsuomi Noda, Kyoichirō Ogino, Takeo Sugiyama, Kaname Yoshimatsu and Seaman 1st Class Yoshio Iwabuchi. They were escorting thirty-six Aichi D3A dive-bombers, half each from *Akagi* and *Kaga*, and thirty-six Nakajima B5N bombers in their Attack mode armed with bombs from *Shōkaku* and *Zuikaku*. The entire air striking force was under overall command of Lieutenant Jōichi Tomonaga, the *hikōtaichō* of the *Hiryū*. This mass commenced lifting off from each of the four carriers at 0426 and by 0445, so efficient was the Japanese launch procedure, they were *en route* to the south-east and Midway Atoll. Behind them they left the first elements of an eleven A6M CAP preparing for their first stint in what was to prove a very busy and eventful day.

The American defenders meanwhile had also been astir early. Captain Cyril Thomas Simard ordered his heavy aircraft into the air to conduct searches. Twenty-two PBYs and fifteen B-17s were got away; there was certainly to be no repeat of the Philippines fiasco at Midway if he could avoid it. When the PBYs began reporting the incoming Japanese strike from 0530 onward, the remaining Midway aircraft were not ordered into the air twenty minutes later. At 0600 they hustled into the air from the crowded runways and by 0610 all had likewise departed clawing to gain altitude. The intercepting fighters comprising four F4F Wildcats and twenty Brewster F2A Buffaloes of Marine Fighter Squadron VMF-221 were thus in the air waiting when the leading Japanese aircraft sighted Midway at a distance of forty miles around 0615 at 310–320 degrees. The squadron was operating in small units, a five-plane division of F2A-3s under Major Floyd B. Parks, a six-plane division of F2A-3s under Captain Daniel J. Hennessy, a seven-plane division of six F2A-3s and a F4F-3 under Captain Kirk Armistead, a two-planed division of F4F-3s under Captain John F. Carey and a two-plane division of F4F-3s under Captain James P. McCarthy. He estimated the enemy strength at eighty bombers, of which fifty were claimed destroyed.[23]

However, the original defence plan had already disintegrated. Instead of dividing into two groups, one to tackle the fighter escorts and the other to deal with the bombers, some aircraft were vectored thirty miles out and an altitude of 12,000ft (4,267.2m), rising to 14,000ft (3,657.6m), directly into the path of the oncoming enemy, while others, which included the patrolling F4Fs, were sent out further westward in case the radar plot proved faulty. One fighter, piloted by Lieutenant C. S. Hughes, was forced to turn back after suffering engine problems and force-landed on Eastern Island, but the rest soon became embroiled with the Japanese.

The air battle here commenced at 0621 when a surprise diving attack destroyed three B5Ns right at the outset. Thereafter the A6Ms intervened and summarily dealt with the audacious Americans who did not have long to enjoy their victories. The Commanding Officer of the Marine fighters stated in his report that the A6Ms:

… were flying at approximately the same level, or at lower altitude than the bombers. Fighters worked in sections or division of from three to nine planes. Our initial contact was made at approximately 14,000ft (3,657.6m). All of the divisions of this squadron were broken up after their first attack, and were to operate as single planes.

He concluded: 'The F2A-3 is sadly out-classed in all respects by the Japanese OO fighters.'

Very few of the Buffalos survived their first and last encounter with the A6M, and twenty-five American fighters were destroyed, just a single F2A and a single F4F were still flyable at the end of the one-sided battle. Ten staggered back to Eastern Island shot to pieces, of which very few ever took to air again. Captain Armistead gave a graphic account of what it was like to be on the receiving end of an A6M attack:

I looked back over my shoulder and about 2,000 feet (609.60m) below and behind me I saw three fighters in column, climbing up towards me, which I assumed to be planes of my division. However, they climbed at a very high rate, and a very steep path. When the nearest plane was about 500 feet (152.40m) below and behind me I realized that it was a Japanese Zero Fighter. I kicked over in a violent 'split S' and received three 20mm shells, one in the right wing gun, one in the right wing root tank, and one in the top left side of the engine cowling. I also received about twenty 7.7 rounds in the left aileron, which mangled the tab on the aileron, and sawed off a portion of the aileron. I continued in a vertical dive at full throttle, corkscrewing to the left, due to the effect of the damaged aileron. At about 3,000 feet, I started to pull out, and managed to hold the plane level at an altitude of 500 feet. As the speed decreased, the stick pressure became more manageable, and by giving it full left tab, at a low speed, the pressure was negligible.

He finally got down at 0899. Armistad continued:

The Zero Fighter is exceptionally maneuverable, with an astounding rate of climb. It is capable of closing the range on an F2A-3 in a climb to such an extent that it seems useless to even try to make more than one such pass at any target. It is my belief that they can climb at least 5,000 feet a minute, as these fighters climbing up at me were pointed an angle of 500 in their climb. I do not believe that they were zooming after a dive, because I am morally certain that at the time I attacked the bombers there were no enemy fighters above 14,000 feet. In fact, I believe that they were below the bombers at that time.

He concluded:

> The Zero Fighter is faster in level flight than the F2A-3. It is much
> more maneuverable than the F2A-3. It can out-climb the F2A-3. It has
> more fire power than the F2A-3.

Were there any weaknesses that he detected? Yes, one at least:

> In general, the Japanese airplanes appear to be very vulnerable to 50
> cal. gun fire. They burst into flame in nearly all cases upon my receiving
> any bullets. It is my belief that the use of incendiary bullets greatly
> increases the effectiveness of attack against Japanese aircraft.

Similar sentiments were expressed by Captain William C. Humberd, who
after attacking a D3A dive-bomber and about to attack another, received the
surprise of his life.

> I came up on other side and started another approach when, about half
> way through run, I heard a loud noise and turning around I saw a large
> hole in hood of my plane and also two Type 00 Navy fighters on me
> about 200 yards astern, then I immediately pushed over in steep dive in
> which one followed me.

There was naturally much bitterness that men had been sent to their deaths
in such inadequate machines. Captain Philip R. White wrote in his report:

> The F2A-3 is not a combat aeroplane. It is inferior to the planes we
> were fighting in every respect. The Japanese Zero Fighter can run
> circles around the F2A-3. It is my belief that any commander that
> orders pilots out for combat in a F2A-3 should consider the pilot as lost
> before leaving the ground.

Second Lieutenant Charles M. Kunz recorded:

In my opinion the 00 fighter has been by far underestimated. I think it is probably one of the finest fighters in the present war. As for as the F2A-3, it should be in Miami as a training plane, rather than be used as a first line fighter.

Lieutenant Hyde Phillips stated unequivocally, 'Zero Fighters outnumbered our fighters, had greater speed, and vastly great[er] maneuverability. The Japanese planes were flown with skill and daring. Brewsters and Grummans were no match for the Zero Fighters.'[24]

By contrast, Japanese fighter losses were minimal, two aircraft and three pilots. The *Akagi* lost one fighter, Petty Officer 1st Class Shinaji Iwama being shot down over Eastern Island by anti-aircraft fire. The *Kaga*'s losses were Petty Officer 1st Class Hiromi Itō shot down by fighters, while although Petty Officer 1st Class Yoshizō Tanaka gallantly nursed his A6M back aboard the carrier, he expired due to his wounds in his cockpit after touching down. Bomber losses were far from the fifty claimed by the Marine Corps flyers; just four B5Ns and a single D3A were shot down, while four further B5Ns returned damaged and had to ditch near the fleet, all but one of the crews being rescued safely.[25]

Surveying their handiwork, Lieutenant Jōichi Tomonaga made a considered judgement. Although Midway's fighter defences had just about been wiped out and much damage done to installations, he therefore radioed that he considered that a second strike was necessary in order to complete the job. It was to prove a fateful decision, and one that was, ultimately, to doom the *Kidō Butai*. In truth, Midway's aerial sting had by this time been drawn and the atoll's air power could offer little more in the way of resistance. Moreover, much more damage had been done to the land defences than was realized by Tomonaga's aerial survey. However, a second strike had always been on the cards as a possibility, and Nagumo, no doubt with memories of the criticisms to which he had been subjected for not making a third attack on Pearl Harbor's oil tanks and dock installation, was not going to open himself up to the same criticism again. He ordered the strike force (which he had been pre-warned by Yamamoto to keep ready in case of any nasty surprises), to be re-armed from ship strike weapons, torpedoes, to bombs for use against land targets. Work commenced in this complex change-over as soon as possible, but meantime other events had occurred.

The British being the only other naval power to operate carriers were naturally very interested in the tactics employed and the various lessons to be learnt from the Midway combats. A very detailed report was circulated by the Admiralty in London to the heads of all the concerned departments for comments and action.[26]

The British liaison officer's report was scathing on American fighter tactics at Midway Atoll itself.

The superiority of the Japanese Zero fighter over the American fighters in climb and manoeuvrability is very evident, but this superiority was aided by the faulty tactics of the American fighters. The latter apparently made no attempt to hold off the Japanese fighters with a portion of their fighter force while the remainder dealt with the bombers … They appear to have gone 'bald-headed' for the Japanese bombers in small un-coordinated detachments, with the result that the escorting Zero fighters, in spite of their inferior (*sic*) armament and lack of armour, shot them to ribbons. In fact, the Zero fighters were presented with the one form of combat in which their lack of armour did not matter.[27]

However, on the other side, the same report also noted:

Zero fighters again out-performed and out-manoeuvred F4F-4s but were much more vulnerable and again there are reports of Zeros being reluctant to attack aircraft in formation. Even so few as two would cause them to open fire ineffectually at long range. It is obvious in every report that comes in that the superior courage and skill of US aircraft crews more than made up for deficiency of their equipment.

The defence of the *Kidō Butai*

The Midway strike aircraft, four Army Martin B-26 Marauder torpedo-bombers, four Navy Grumman TBF Avenger torpedo-bombers, sixteen Marine Corps Douglas SBD Dauntless dive-bombers and eleven Marine Corps Vought SB2U-3 Vindicator dive-bombers, all got away as well, but fragmented and each group made their own individual attacks. As the morning wore on they were followed by successive waves of American carrier planes, each attacking semi-independently as they arrived on the scene, with little co-ordination. The American attacks somewhat resembled waves breaking on a beach in succession and allowed the hard-pressed Japanese CAP time to land, re-arm (the 20mm cannon's small ammunition capacity being a particular bugbear in this respect, so many were the targets being offered up) and even refuel between each attack. This approach meant that each ripple could be dealt with in turn, and they were, ruthlessly and efficiently; but it also had a cumulative wearing effect on the A6M pilots themselves who no sooner dealt with one group than another appeared. Eventually this was to prove a subtle, but fatal, erosion of their capacity to defend the fleet.

The Japanese CAP consisted of thirty-six A6Ms over the Nagumo Force and another seven were flown off to reinforce them during the combat. The first aircraft to arrive were the four torpedo-equipped B-26s but their commander made the fatal mistake of circling briefly while he selected his targets and in that interval two of the Marauders were shot down and the other so riddled with bullets that they were written off on their return. They announced four torpedo hits, but achieved nothing whatsoever other than the destruction of one A6M piloted by Petty Officer 3rd Class Toichirō Hanyu from *Akagi*. The four TBF Avengers torpedo-bombers of VT-8's detachment attacked at about the same time, marking this aircraft's debut in combat. They went for the *Hiryū* but her six-plane A6M detachment met them before they could launch and sent three into the sea immediately. The others dropped but scored no hits at all, although the ball gunner of one Avenger accounted for the A6M of Petty Officer 2nd Class Ichirō Sakai from the *Hiryū*. Nonetheless only one TBM staggered back to Eastern Island shot to pieces with all her crew dead or wounded.

Next up were the Marine Corps dive-bombers, sixteen SBDs in two divisions. The first group made glide attacks, which were ineffectual, but this approach enabled the A6Ms to get in among them and no fewer than eight dive-bombers were destroyed. In reply Warrant Officer Yoshimi Kodama of *Hiryū* was shot down and killed by the Marine flyers. The surviving Marine SBDs were all damaged to varying degrees, one aircraft had more than 200 holes in it on landing, and although they claimed three hits on one carrier, they achieved absolutely no hits at all.

There was an interval during which fourteen B-17s pattern bombed the Nagumo force from a high altitude, 25,000ft. They reported that there was '… no great difficulty' in hitting ships at this height. They duly made enormous claims[28] to back this up, claiming three direct hits and many near misses and that they left three carriers on fire and blazing. These absurd claims were taken at face value by the American press back at Hawaii, which resulted in headlines from Honolulu to New York that the big bombers had smashed the Japanese fleet and won the battle just about single-handed. The truth was that, as usual, altitude bombing had failed to score a single hit on any Japanese ship. No B-17s were lost, although they, again quite falsely, claimed to have also destroyed two A6Ms.

After this charade, the next group of Marine aircraft finally reached the *Kidō Butai*. These were the eleven Vought SB2U-3 long-range Vindicator dive-bombers (christened wearily by their despairing aircrews as 'Wind Indicators' as their worn fabric tended to peel up and flutter when airborne) led by Major Benjamin W. Norris. The *Akagi* A6Ms intercepted these as they began to form up for a shallow dive-bombing attack. One Marine pilot, Major Allan H. Ringblom reported later on, 'The amazing nonchalance of Zero pilots who did vertical rolls right through our formation …' He considered this an enormously impressive demonstration of superiority.[29] Hiding in the clouds for a brief period to escape these attentions the Marines re-emerged and attacked the battleship *Haruna*, claiming two hits and also that they had destroyed two A6Ms. Again, this was not the case, the battleship was not hit at all and three of the Vindicators were destroyed, the rest being harried for a long while on their return flight and most were badly shot up.

From glide-bombing and altitude bombing the Nagumo Force now faced the ultimate threat, mass torpedo-bombers. For by now the first of the US Navy carrier aircraft belatedly began to arrive on the scene. Also at this time the Japanese had landed back aboard the bulk of the Midway strike, but they had also been made aware that American carriers were in the area and were preparing to attack them in turn. This had to be delayed as further attacks continually washed over the *Kidō Butai* and required avoiding action. The first to arrive were the *Hornet*'s fifteen TBD-1s of VT-8 led by Lieutenant-Commander John Waldron, which had broken away from the rest of her attack force some time earlier and now attacked alone and without support. The ten F4F-4 Wildcat fighters of VF-6 under Lieutenant James S. Gray were overhead but at an altitude of 22,000ft could offer no relief. The American fighters stayed up above for an hour and then, with falling fuel gauges, they went home while down below another lesson in butchery was taking place, unaware that three A6Ms had been scrambled from *Sōryū* to attack them and were hurtling upward intent on battle, but these were soon diverted to easier prey, however. Twenty A6Ms led by Lieutenant-Commander Shigeru Itaya hit the lumbering Devastators while they were still some eight miles distant and began hacking them apart with their usual expertise, well before they could position themselves to launch torpedoes against the *Sōryū*, the closest carrier of the force. With a quarter of an hour every single torpedo-bomber had been shot into the sea, leaving just one survivor watching events from the sea.

Almost at once yet another force of Devastators appeared on the southern horizon, this being VT-6 from the *Enterprise*, led by Lieutenant-Commander Eugene Lindsey. Again ignored by the now departing F4Fs way above, they also went stoically to the meet their fate. By this time twenty-seven A6Ms were prowling the skies and, having knocked down the last of Waldron's aircraft, turned quickly toward the new prey for a repeat performance. The Japanese fighter pilots have often been criticized for concentrating so much on the low-flying torpedo-bombers and ignoring the high altitudes where dive-bombers were to make their approaches. It has to be remembered, once more, that they had no radar to warn them of what was on the way. They had been attacked previously by Navy-type dive-bombers and had no idea that yet more were on the way. It is also a hard fact, that a torpedo hit below the waterline was more likely to sink a ship, any ship, than a bomb hit above it, so the threat from the torpedo squadrons was acknowledged to be the greater and naturally required action when it appeared.

Appealing for assistance according to a pre-arranged plan, from the totally oblivious F4Fs from his home carrier, Lindsey's VT-6 now followed Waldron's route to annihilation. As the A6Ms, reinforced by a further nine scrambled away from their flight decks as reinforcements, closed in for the cull the rear gunners did what they could and were rewarded when Seaman 1st Class Shinpei Sano from *Akagi* was shot down and killed. This was the

Americans' sole consolation, however, for within seconds the slaughter was resumed and one-by-one six TBDs flamed into the water before they could drop their torpedoes, while of those eight that did none scored any hits at all and three more were destroyed. Having dropped their torpedoes, their only exit route was through the flak-ridden sky above the Japanese ships and, in the process, most of the torpedo-bombers met their end, one ditching on the way back to base. Just four TBDs survived the ordeal.

The *Yorktown* strike force had been delayed by Fletcher's superfluous 100-mile air search to the north earlier, which required further time for their subsequent recovery. Some distance behind Spruance's two carriers *Yorktown* finally launched her force late, and even then, at the very last minute and without informing the strike leader, a portion of the SBDs and some F4Fs were retained with the carrier, which was in variance to the already agreed plan and ran counter to US Navy doctrine to hit the enemy with everything you had as soon as possible. Nonetheless the reduced *Yorktown* group held together in the air better than the other two carriers' attackers, until almost the last moments. Then with a co-ordinated attack almost within their grasp, the fighters, the dive-bombers and the torpedo-bombers all went about their business separately. Two of the six VF-3 Wildcats, led by Machinist Tom F. Cheek, dropped down to protect the twelve TBDs at 2,600ft (9,792.48m) altitude, while the remaining four F4Fs under Jimmy Thach, eager to trial his long-practised beam defence fighter tactic against a live enemy at last, stayed up at 5,500ft (1,676.4m).

The Japanese 'Great CAP' was at a strength of thirty-five A6Ms at this point, with six more, three from *Kaga* led by Petty Officer 1st Class Kiyonobu Suzuki and the three from *Sōryū* that had abandoned the chase after Gray, rapidly joining them. Several A6Ms concentrated on Thach's formation, and almost immediately shot down the F4F of Ensign Edgar R. Bassett, and damaged that of his wingman, Lieutenant (j.g.) Brainard Macomber, but the latter was able to close and stick with the Thach and Ensign Robert A. Dibb section, which between them destroyed four A6Ms with the new tactic. This brisk self-preservation duelling did not help protect the *Yorktown* TBDs however, other than by drawing Zeros away from them. Ten miles out from the Nagumo ships the two remaining F4Fs piloted by Cheek and Ensign Daniel C. Sheedy, managed to shoot down the A6M of *Sōryū*'s Petty Officer

3rd Class Teruo Kawamata, who was later rescued, and the TBDs shot down another. One TBD had already gone as the torpedo-bombers, led by Lieutenant-Commander Lance E. Massey, descended for their final run-in at 150ft (45.72m) above the waves, with A6Ms swarming around them. Nine of the twelve TBDs were destroyed, Lieutenant Iōyzō Fujita alone claiming four, and only four managed to make their torpedo drops, which were, yet again, fruitless. Just seven torpedo-bombers, four of them damaged so badly that they were write-offs, remained from the fifty-one sent out a few hours before and from seventeen dive-bombers, eleven had been destroyed and eight heavily damaged.

At this point in the battle the Japanese were winning hands-down! Then came the crushing turning-point. With most of the A6Ms down at sea-level or duelling with Thach, there were none in reserve when two formations of SBDs, those from the *Enterprise* led by Lieutenant-Commander Clarence Wade McClusky and those from the *Yorktown* under Lieutenant-Commander Maxwell Franklin Leslie, suddenly and dramatically appeared above the *Kidō Butai* and commenced their vertical dives. Due to the delayed launch and the long searches, McClusky's bombers were at the extreme limits of their fuel, indeed engines were spluttering as they commenced their attacks, but, once committed nothing could have averted them other than direct hits from the heaviest of anti-aircraft guns. (Incredibly, after six months' war experience with the A6M in the Pacific some US Navy aircrew still filed reports that they had been attacked by German Messerschmitt Me.109 fighters!) Within seconds the carriers *Akagi*, *Kaga* and *Sōryū* had been hit and were covered in flames, fire and smoke. Normally bomb hits might have devastated flight decks and caused havoc with the aircraft and crew, but would not have sunk such ships outright. What turned this attack from a seriously damaging assault to outright carnage was, of course, the fateful change-over of ordnance that left weaponry strewn around the hangar decks and these fuelled the enormous furnace that the carriers immediately became. All three lingered for a long time, but all three were finally lost. Of the thirty A6Ms that remained airborne ten of *Kaga*'s fighters, seven of *Akagi*'s fighters and six each from the *Hiryū* and *Sōryū*, all save one managed to land safely aboard the *Hiryū*, while one *Akagi* Zero ran out of fuel and had to ditch.

In summary, of the total of forty-three A6Ms of the so-termed 'Great CAP', thirteen were destroyed – six by F4Fs, three to the SBDs defensive fire, one to the TBM defensive fire, one Lieutenant Iyozō Fujita from *Hiryū* was hit by the force's own flak, and forced to bale out but was rescued by the destroyer *Nowaki*, and two more were forced to ditch due to lack of deck space after the carriers were hit. Two casualties from the *Hiryū* were Petty Officers Masato Hino, Genzō Nagasawa, Huruo Nitta and Michisuke Tokuda, while *Kaga* lost Ensign Hiroyuki Yamaguchi, and Petty Officers Iwao Hirayama, Shigeto Sawano and Kazuyoshi Toyoda along with Seaman 1st Class Ei-ichi Takahashi.

Hiryū versus *Yorktown*, *Enterprise* and *Yorktown*

Although suddenly left alone after the disablement of her three companions, *Hiryū*'s redoubtable Rear-Admiral Tamon Yamaguchi, who had earlier repeatedly urged his senior officer to allow him to launch his fully prepared dive-bombers while there was still time, refused to crumble, or to run.[30] Vengeance was what the Japanese wanted at that moment, not just Yamaguchi but *all* the Japanese, including Nagumo, who proposed a night surface attack, and Yamamoto, who sought the same. After landing aboard as many of the orphans from the CAP as he could manage, he began organizing a counter-attack against what he thought to be just two enemy carriers.

Because of congestion aboard *Hiryū* the small Japanese striking force was eventually flown off in two under-strength segments. The first force was eighteen Aichi D3A dive-bombers under Lieutenant Michio Kobayashi (*buntaichō*) and these were escorted by just six A6Ms from 1 and 2 *chūtai*, led by Lieutenant Yasuhiro Shigematsu.

The fighters became embroiled with a brief battle with the outgoing American strike, and two A6Ms, flown by Warrant Officer Yoshijirō Minegishi and Petty Officer 1st Class Hitoshi Sasaki, were damaged and had to return to *Hiryū*, the latter being forced to ditch. The remaining quartet had to hasten after the dive-bombers but were too late to offer much protection, although the American fighter pilots were overawed enough to report these four as *eighteen* Zeros! In the ensuing fight against the fifteen F4Fs of the American CAP, three A6Ms were lost, those piloted by Petty

Officer 2nd Class Todaka Noburu, Petty Officer 3rd Class Chiyoshima Yutaka and Seaman 1st Class Yoshimoto Suekichi, with only Lieutenant Yasuhiro Shigematsu surviving to return to his fleet. One F4F, piloted by Ensign Stephen W. Groves, was destroyed in return while the dive-bombers scored three bomb hits on the *Yorktown*, setting her on fire.

The second *Hiryū* strike force comprised ten B5Ns under Lieutenant Jōichi Tomonaga, *hikōtaichō*, escorted by six A6Ms under the command of Lieutenant Shigeru Mori, with Petty Officers Makoto Bandō (*Kaga*), Kenji Kotani, Akira Yamamoto (*Kaga*), Tōru Yamamoto and Warrant Officer Yoshijirō Minegishi, a mixed force of *Hiryū*'s 1 and 2 *shotai* plus *Kaga* survivors. *Yorktown* had six F4Fs overhead and eight more were quickly launched once radar warnings were received but four of these totally missed the incoming Japanese and two more F4Fs, piloted by Lieutenant (j.g.) William S. Woollen and Ensign Harry B. Gibbs, were quickly shot down by the A6Ms, both by Minegishi and Kotani. This pair also nailed a third Wildcat, piloted by Ensign George A. Hopper, Jr, just after it had taken off from the flight deck, and they damaged two more, but two A6Ms were lost. Meanwhile the B5Ns had slammed two 18-inch 1,764lb aerial torpedoes deep into the *Yorktown*'s belly and she took on a heavy list. The Japanese were jubilant, thinking she was the second, previously undamaged, carrier.

Before a third strike could be organized from *Hiryū*, the Americans got in the final blow, twenty-five SBDs from *Enterprise*, one of which turned back, and sixteen SBDs from *Hornet*, but no fighter escort could be spared. There were fourteen A6Ms overhead when the Americans arrived, three *Hiryū* aircraft, six survivors from *Sōryū*, four from *Kaga* and one from *Akagi*. The A6Ms managed to destroy three of the dive-bombers but could not prevent such a mass of aircraft from scoring four direct hits. She sank later and the fifteen A6Ms were forced to ditch, although most of the pilots were quickly rescued. These included, from *Akagi*, Lieutenant Masanobu Ibusuki and Lieutenant Ayao Shirane and Petty Officer 1st Class Shigetaka Ōmori rescued by the light cruiser *Nagara* and Petty Officer 2nd Class Seiji Iishi also saved by an escort along with Petty Officer 1st Class Masao Taniguchi who was rescued by a destroyer; from *Kaga*, Petty Officer 1st Class Kiyonobu Suzuki and Seaman 1st Class Takahashi Nakaue, both being saved by the destroyer *Hagikaze*, as well as Lieutenant Masao Iisuka and Petty

Officer Yoshikazu Nagahama who were both rescued by the light cruiser *Nagara* and Seaman 1st Class Yoshio Egawa also plucked from the sea safely by an escort; from *Hiryū*, Petty Officer 1st Class Kazuo Muranaka who was rescued by the destroyer *Nowaki;* from *Sōryū*, Petty Officer 1st Class Kaname Harada, Petty Officer 2nd Class Yoshimatsu Kaname, Petty Officer 1st Class Munesaburō and Petty Officer 1st Class Takeo Sugiyama, again all being safely rescued by destroyers.

In summary, although the Battle of Midway turned out to be a stunning defeat for the Japanese and a severe setback to their expansion plans, it did not halt them. Tulagi in the Solomons was occupied and work commenced on constructing an airfield on neighbouring Guadalcanal across the strait. The occupation of Port Moresby, which had been abandoned as a sea-borne attack, nonetheless was pressed forward as a land campaign, not abandoned. Rabaul continued to be expanded and reinforced as did Buna; the drive to isolate Australia was slowed but the intention remained. Furthermore, as some kind of consolation prize for the Japanese public to conceal the magnitude of their Navy's first-ever major defeat, their limited Aleutian targets were occupied and held, however futile this fact was other than as a gesture.

One thing that must be stressed is that, despite the loss of their four best carriers, and the death of many of their finest airmen, the Imperial Navy's air power was *not* completely destroyed at Midway. The percentage of aircrew casualties was under 25 per cent of their front-line total, high enough when replacements were at such a premium, but totally destroyed they were certainly not as subsequent carrier battles were soon to demonstrate. The persistence of the myth that Midway finished the IJN as an air power continues even to modern times seems unstoppable. For example, a 2012 quotation has it that, '... the cream of her seasoned pilots, air crews, ground crews (*sic*) maintenance, armorers and flight decks crews', all just, '... vanished beneath the waves ...'[31]

Chapter 9

Grim Attrition

With the end of the Midway encounter the A6M entered a new phase. Elation at easy victories now became tempered with steely determination. The opening phase had been a walk-over, now the air war in the Pacific entered a new, more testing period. It started with a disaster of a different kind, one that was to come home to roost in the years ahead.

The Aleutians and capture of an intact Zero

In contrast to the epic and cataclysmic battle at Midway Atoll, the Japanese occupation of the Aleutians was little more than an irrelevant footnote, except for one factor, the capture, almost intact, of another A6M. Although, as we have seen, previous examples had been indeed obtained they had not been thoroughly examined or if they had been what data had been obtained had not been passed down to the Allied combat pilots in the field who had to learn its attributes (and weaknesses) the hard way.[1] By contrast another RAF pilot who flew with No. 258 Hurricane Squadron in Burma wrote how, even when the facts were presented to them, some pilots refused to credit them. 'We were warned of a speed which matched our own and, difficult to believe, in fact hardly believed, a superior maneuverability.'[2] Even so many points on the design of the A6M remained obscure but what became known as 'The Aleutian Zero' resolved them.

The two small Japanese aircraft carriers of 4 *Kōkū-sentai* had been allotted to the Task Group of Rear Admiral Kakuji Kakuta that was cover a landing force to seize the Aleutian bases of Adak, Attu and Kiska, in order to protect their northern flank.[3] The air strength comprised the newly built *Junyō* (which had only been commissioned on 3 May), with thirteen Model 21 A6Ms commanded by Lieutenant Yoshio Shiga, with Fighter Division

Jiro Horikoshi (1903–1982). This young graduate of the *Kōkū Kenkyūjo* at the University of Tokyo became the chief designer at Mitsubishi Heavy Industries at an early age. He fashioned a ground-breaking fighter aircraft for the Imperial Japanese Navy that was both beautiful and deadly, the A6M *Rei-sen*, or Zero.

The classic lines of the A6M *Rei-sen* fighter. The drop-tank gave this little fighter aircraft an unprecedented reach. Despite extensively reported combat victories in China this factor, her powerful armament and her agility, all came as an apparent surprise to the Western powers when the Pacific War opened in December 1941.

Lieutenant (j.g.) Stephen Jurika, Jr. (1910-1993). The last pre-war US Naval Air Attaché, he submitted two reports pre-war. That dated 9 November 1940, concerned what he termed the 'Mitsubishi Type Zero 1940 Fighter', an identification which he based on Chinese reports of a 'Type 100' airframe. His superiors told him to '… be more careful before sending in reports in future!'

An A6M salvaged after being shot down over Chengdu, China, after being re-assembled in 1942 at Liuchow by a team of Chinese engineers and examined by US General Nathan F. Twining. A detailed report, with sketches, was given to the Assistant US Naval Attaché James McHugh among other Americans, who duly forwarded it on to Washington eighteen months *before* Pearl Harbor.

A deck-load of A6Ms with their ground crew in attendance, powering up in readiness for take-off. A still from the Japanese information film of the Pearl Harbor attack. The IJN had by this time developed naval air operations to a high degree, combining the aircraft from six carriers into an efficient, powerful and fully-integrated striking group far in advance of Western thinking at the time.

A6Ms warming up aboard a Japanese carrier with the deck parties carrying out the final checks.

The signal is given, wheel chocks have been removed and the first A6M powers down the flight deck to the cheers and exultations of the ships company.

Lift-off - an A6M of 1 *Kōkū-sentai* leaves the flight deck of the carrier *Akagi* - a still from a Japanese information film.

The 940hp Nakajima *Sakae* radial engine recovered from one of the A6Ms that crashed during the Pearl Harbor attack was examined by the Americans in detail. The restrictions imposed by the IJN on the design team meant that the *Rei-sen* was always underpowered compared with its foreign opposite numbers, but nonetheless she swept the Pacific clear of them in a few short months.

The Ni'ihau Zero. The mount of Shigenori Nishikaighi, this aircraft was damaged over Pearl Harbor and made a forced landing on the most northerly island of the Hawaii chain. The pilots survived the landing but not the subsequent tussle with some of the locals.

The cockpit of one of the A6Ms that crashed during the Pearl Harbor attack. Note the radio equipment along the starboard bulkhead.

Designed as a carrier fighter, the A6M was destined to serve the first months of her combat career as a long-range, shore-based bomber escort in China and, later, in the same role during the long-drawn out South Pacific campaigns from 1942-45. Here chocked A6Ms start their engines prior to a mission.

These Model 21 *Rei-sens* are from 1 *Kōkū*-sentai, which were landed ashore at a Rabaul airfield from the carrier *Zuikaku* to participate in Operation *Ro-Go* in November 1943. The single white chevrons on the fuselage denote the unit and the double white chevrons the aircraft of the *Hikōtaichō*.

The early fighting formation adopted by the A6M *Kōkūtai* was the loose three-plane formation, the *shōtai*. Only later in the Pacific War did the Japanese aviators adopt the four-plane formations favoured by the Allies.

Warming up on a jungle airstrip with the attentive ground staff standing by, these A6Ms still retain their radio masts and thus landed ashore from active carriers.

A6M on the prowl! An air-to-air shot that shows off the distinctive elongated tail cone of the A6M. The large ailerons made this little fighter extremely manoeuvrable at lower altitudes and speeds, but, conversely her lightness and large wing-area told against her in dives.

Chui (Lieutenant) Yukio Seki (1921-1944). After serving in the surface fleet, including duty at Midway, Seki volunteered for flight training and, on qualification, was himself retained as an instructor. During the battle for Leyte his unit was selected to operate the first Kamikaze missions and on 25 October 1944, he led the five-A6M mission that carried out the attacks that sank the escort carrier *St Lo* and damaged four of her sister ships.

The famed Tainan *Kōkūtai*, which was established on 1 October 1941 and which after a year of outstanding service, was re-organized on 1 November 1942 as the 251 *Kōkūtai*, served ashore but probably contained the most A6M aces of any IJN fighter unit. Included in its ranks were such outstanding pilots as Tadashi Nakajima, Hiroyoshi Nishizawa, Toshio Ōta, Saburō Sakai, Jun-ichi Sasai, Masuzō Setō and many more.

Sleek, fast and agile, the A6M proved more than a match for the Allied fighter types early in the Pacific War, and continued to soldier on right through to the very end due to the lack of sufficient newer types. Here a *buntai* of 1 *Kōkū* Sentai Zero's heads out on a mission.

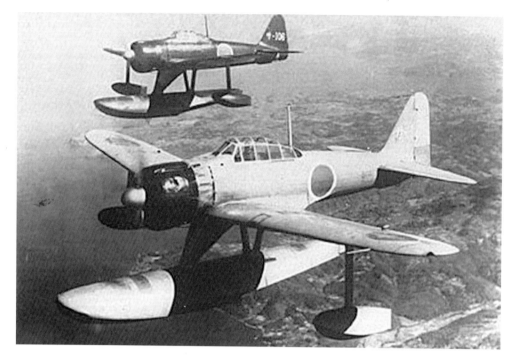

The A6M2-N *Suisen* seaplane fighter was an adaption of the *Rei-sen* that first flew on 8 December 1941 and which subsequently saw widespread use in the wastes of the Pacific, from Penang to the Aleutians and from isolated atolls all over the Pacific. Code-named 'Rufe' by the Allies some 327 were built.

The aircrew of the seven A6M2-N *Suisen* from 802 *Kōkūtai*, which were transferred to 902 *Kōkūtai*, at Truk, Caroline Islands, on 21 October 1943. They transferred to Greenwich Atoll, some 400 miles south-south-east of Truk, between November 1943 and early 1944 before returning to Truk, where they were all wiped out, mainly at their anchorages, on 17 February 1944 by American carrier aircraft during Operation 'Hailstone'.

The biggest identification differences between the A6M5 Model 52 and the earlier Model 32 can clearly be seen here, with the large individual exhaust pipes clearly visible, which replaced the more visually acceptable exhaust collector ring that vented them out of the single ventral egress of the earlier models on the *Sakae* engine. The idea was to increase speed, in which it was not very successful.

The A6M3 Model 22*Ko* introduced the 20mm wing cannon along with other refinements.

As the elderly Model 21 *Rei-sens* were gradually replaced by more updated versions, they were given an honorable 'retirement' role as an *enchu* (advanced training) aircraft. These are from the Ōita *Kōkūtai*, at Ōita Air Base and Naval Air Depot on Kyūshū. They have a white horizontal line painted along the rear fuselage to assist the trainees align themselves in formation flying.

An abandoned A6M3 of the 2 *Kōkūtai* standing forlornly on the much-bombed airfield of Lakunai, Buna, in Papua, New Guinea. One of two almost intact *Rei-sen* found by the Australian occupation forces on 27 December 1942. This and a sister were transshipped back to the Eagle Farm test facility in Australia for evaluation. Thirteen other A6M3 wrecks found on the abandoned strip were too badly damaged and were junked on the spot.

When the Allies invaded the Marshall Islands among the many wrecks they discovered was this A6M3 of 2 *Kōkūtai* with her 02 tail code. The Model 32's squared-off wing tips can be clearly seen in this view and this was brought about by simply deleting the folding-wing tips of the earlier models.

The Royal New Zealand Air Force obtained an A6M when a fairly intact one was discovered hidden at Kara airstrip, on Bougainville Island, eighteen months after it had been damaged. She was inspected and finally flown over to Piva by Wing Commander Bill Kofoed. Eventually, after much bickering, she arrived at Auckland on 20 October 1945 aboard the freighter *Wahine*. After various vicissitudes, and some weird paint schemes, she was finally preserved and put on display.

Another view of the Royal New Zealand Air Force's captured Zero fighter.

Among the first 'acquired' *Rei-sens* was the Nai'ihau A6M2. Once she was recovered from the island she was shipped to San Diego where she was repainted in American colours to reassure the Californian public and flown by test pilots for in-depth analysis. After the flight testing had finished she was flown over to Virginia and arrived at US Navy's Langley Research Center (LaRC), Hampton, Virginia, on 8 March 1943. The aircraft was fitted with flight data recorders by the National Advisory Committee for Aeronautics (NACA) team and given secret weekend wind tunnel tests, which not even Joe Chambers, who ran the tunnel facility, knew about and the data was sent by special messenger to Washington DC to be assimilated.

With her back to the wall the Japanese High Command finally gave in to persistent requests and sanctioned the use of a select number of suicide aircraft against the Allied fleet invading the Philippines at Leyte Gulf. The first missions were conducted by four special volunteer units and, after some early negative searches, they finally got in their attacks on 25 October 1944, when they sank one escort carrier and damaged four more. Here can be seen the final seconds of an attack dive by one specially-adapted A6M of the Seiki force, just before she impacts on the carrier *St Lo*.

Heavily hit the *St Lo* was set ablaze. Initially it was expected she would survive as did her sisters, but the fires spread and torpedoes and bombs cooked off in a series of enormous explosions that blew the little carrier apart and she quickly sank, chilling proof to the stunned American sailors that a new and dreadful form of warfare had arrived.

On the 25th also another escort carrier group was attacked by A6Ms in their Kamikaze role and the *Suwanee* was hit. The carrier was badly damaged with many casualties but managed to continue operations after a short pause. Here is a still from a dramatic piece of film shot from the carrier showing the *Rei-sen* hurtling into her.

Another dramatic photo showing an A6M Kamikaze hurtling down the side of the battleship *Missouri* off Okinawa on 11 April 1945, moments before she impacted. The photographer was a ship's baker, Len Schmidt. The heavily armoured 'Mighty Mo' suffered merely the indignity of a slight dent. The body of the Kamikaze pilot, Setsuo Ishino, was recovered and given a burial at sea with full military honours.

The bulk of the many thousands of combat-ready military aircraft that remained to the Japanese were held back in readiness of the expected invasion of the home islands. Thousands of Kamikazes awaited their final mission, which, in the event, never came. Immediately the Emperor ordered his military to cease fighting, most of these aircraft were made inoperational and littered the airfields. When the Allied occupation forces arrived these warplanes were gathered together and junked, as was the fate of these A6Ms and other aircraft at Atsugi *Kaigun-Hikōjō* (Naval Air Base.)

Preserved A6Ms. There are a large number of A6Ms on exhibition in museums around the world. I have been privileged to view and photograph a small selection of them myself, including those at the Imperial War Museum, Duxford, The USAF Museum at Dayton, Ohio and the San Diego Aerospace Museum. This one is at Yamamoto Museum.

Preserved A6Ms. National Air and Space Museum, Washington DC. This was a former 261 *Kōkūtai* aircraft, with the probable tail code of 61-108, which was abandoned at Aslito airfield, Saipan, and captured by US Marines. Along with a dozen other A6Ms she was shipped back to the States aboard the escort carrier *Copahee* for evaluation. Eventually acquired by the NASM in 1970 she has been a roof-hung display for many years.

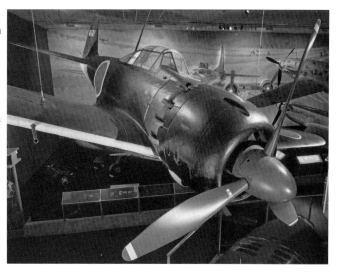

Preserved A6Ms. Yasukuni Shrine, Tokyo. At the invitation of the Head Priest, I was shown round by the Museum Curator, accompanied by Commander Sadac Seno, JMDF (Rtd), Commander Sadamu Takahashi, historian and Commander Zenji Abe, IJN (Rtd). The aircraft is a composite, but predominantly based on a Model 52, serial number 4241, abandoned at Rabaul. It was restored with part of other A6Ms to represent a Mode 52 machine, serial 4168, of the 281 *Kōkūtai*; it is tail coded 81-161 and is on display in the entrance hall where it appropriately enough faces the rising sun.

Preserved A6Ms. Nagoya Airport. This is a Model 22 aircraft, serial number 3621, tail code Y2-128 which belonged to the 252 *Kōkūtai* at Taroa Island airfield. It has had a very chequered history since she was 're-discovered' by Steve Aiken in 1970. I viewed her at the airport before she was moved and re-situated in the Tachiarai Peace Memorial Museum, in Fukubka Prefecture.

Officer Lieutenant Yasuhiro Shigematsu, and six A6Ms of 6 *Kōkūtai* under Lieutenant Zenjirō Miyano, which were earmarked for Midway once the island had been occupied, embarked; and the 1933-built *Ryūjō*, which had twenty Model 21 A6Ms embarked under the command of Lieutenant Kenjirō Nōtomi with Lieutenant Minoru Kobayahi as Fighter Divisional Officer. They sailed from Ōminato, Mutsu Bay, in northern Honshu with an escort of two heavy cruisers, *Maya* and *Takao*, three destroyers and an oiler.

Further south was Vice-Admiral Hosogaya Boshirō with the light cruisers *Kiso* and *Tama*, three destroyers, three escorts and four minesweepers escorting a troop convoy of our transports with 2,500 occupation forces under Rear Admiral Ōmori Sentarō. American air strength was vastly superior and consisted of ten B-17s, thirty-four B-18s bombers and ninety-five P-40 Warhawks and two squadrons of PBYs, but, in practice, they contributed little.

The Aleutians were notorious for their foul weather and on arrival the Japanese found low cloud base (300m) and murky visibility and each carrier was forced to operate more-or-less independently. Lieutenant Shiga led the first wave with thirteen A6Ms and twelve D3A dive-bombers from *Junyō*, and a further three A6Ms and six B5Ns from *Ryūjō* against the American base at Dutch Harbor, Amaknak Island, Fox Islands, on 3 June and the escorts destroyed a PBY Catalina. A second attack was again led by Lieutenant Shiga, with six A6Ms and fifteen D3As, but bad weather aborted this raid, although two further PBYs were destroyed by the fighters. The weather continued to be atrocious on 4 June but, at 1140, six *Junyō* A6Ms got airborne with eleven D3As, along with six A6Ms led by Lieutenant Masayuki and nine B5Ns from *Ryūjō*. While the attack was made the bombers hit the radio station, hit again the *Northwestern*, a barracks ship in the harbour, the PBY repair hangar, a warehouse, destroyed an anti-aircraft gun site and set ablaze six oil storage tanks.

During the strafing attacks on the harbour area one *shotai*, Petty Officer 1st Class Masu-aki Endo, with Petty Officers Tadayoshi Koga and Tsuguo Shikada, chopped down yet another PBY over Beaver Inlet, Egg Island, then turned a made a second run from 600ft in single line-ahead, during which machine-gun fire from the ground registered hits in both Shikada and Koga's plywood drop tanks, one bullet severing the return oil line between the oil cooler and the engine, according to a subsequent US report. Koga's machine began spewing out oil and his speed fell away as the engine began to stutter. The *shotai* headed toward Akutan Island, already pre-designated as an emergency landing site with the submarine *I-15* lying offshore to rescue any downed pilots. Koga lowered his undercarriage before it was noticed that the 'grass' was in fact bog. On touch-down the wheels dug into the mire and flipped Koga's A6M over onto her back breaking his neck. Reluctant to destroy the wreck in case Koga was still alive his two companions left it and returned to their carrier. The A6M and its nineteen-year old pilot were therefore left undisturbed and undetected for more than a month.[4]

Meanwhile a force of eight P-40s from Otter Point, Umnak, was encountered by *Jūnyō's* aircraft on their return flight over Otter Point, Umnak Island, which shot down two of the Japanese D3As before the A6Ms intervened and destroyed two P-40s before the rest fled. The two carriers and their escorts withdrew and rendezvoused with the carrier *Zuihō*, which had twelve Type 96 Claude fighters embarked. On 6 June the Japanese occupied Kiska, which became a seaplane base for *Rufes*, and Attu fell the following day. These bases remained in Japanese hands for the next eighteen months but were never of practical value. The recovery and detailed examination of Koga's A6M, by contrast, proved an unexpected treasure-trove for the US Navy.

Only by chance did the Americans locate the Zero; a PBY on patrol had, due to bad weather, strayed 240 miles off course and while making its way back to Dutch Harbor detected an aircraft on Akutan. Later a special search party found the aircraft considerably damaged from the landing, with Koga's body still hanging in his straps inside, and took steps to recover it. This took several attempts but eventually the aircraft was dragged out from the bog on a skid and taken by barge to Dutch Harbor for cleaning up and further examination where the total lack of armour protection, self-sealing fuel tanks, and IFF (Identification, Friend or Foe) devices gave vital knowledge of the A6M's areas of vulnerability immediately. The aircraft was then crated up and loaded aboard the Navy transport *St Mihiel* and taken to Seattle where it was trans-shipped for passage to US Naval Air Station North Island at San Diego, where it arrived on 12 August and was subsequently re-built to a full flying state under considerable secrecy in record time. Considerable work was involved requiring the complete re-building of the fin, both elevators, rudder and rear fuselage; the replacement of top fuselage skin and stringers and sliding cockpit; the repair of the pilots seat, fuselage around the cockpit area, entire engine cowling and cowl flaps; the rebuilding of a wing-tip, port landing flap, bullet holes and complete internal re-wiring and testing of all instruments and hydraulics, while the engine need considerable attention, although the propeller, strangely enough, was relatively intact. So much work was required and so many parts had to be fabricated on the spot with American materials, that some critics maintain that the subsequent flight-testing did not reflect the true full potential of the A6M. This may very well be true, but this aircraft was the best they had and Koga's machine, a true A6M or not, was vigorously flight-tested in the years ahead and did give valuable insights in what had up to then been the bane and great terror of the Pacific air war. It has been asserted that this aircraft was, '... critical in helping the Americans devise defensive and offensive tactics that in part resulted in the neutralization of the Zeke as an effective fighter'.[5] However, as we have seen Thach and others had already devised some defensive tactics to minimize the A6M's obvious superiority over the F4F, and, in addition *both* the Navy's massive new fighters, the Grumman F6F Hellcat and the Chance-Vought F4U Corsair, were already flying by the time this A6M arrived on the West Coast, so any claim that they had been designed as result of its examination will just not wash.

The first such aerial examination of the A6M was conducted from North Island by Navy test pilot Lieutenant-Commander Eddie R. Sanders, who carried out two dozen flights in the period 20 September to 15 October 1942, and Commander Fred Trapnell, both transferred from Anacostia NAS. Among their observations, which were duly promulgated out to the fleet pilots and training units from November 1942 onward, were the confirmation of the already very apparent fact that at low speeds the A6M could easily out-turn any American fighter and this was to remain the case to the very end of the war, but that at 200 knots (370.4 km/h) or above the excellent aileron control rapidly faded away and slowed the roll, which, it was revealed, was slower to starboard than to port. The float-type carburettor frequently cut-out under negative-gravity acceleration. It was also interesting that in Sander's official report of 29 September, he commented that the A6M was:

... equipped with complete instruments, *some of which appear to be superior to ours*;[6] two-way radio (frequency 4596 KC); radio compass (Fairchild); oxygen with regulator to control flow with changes in altitude; droppable belly tank; provision for two bomb racks on wings; flotation bags in wings and fuselage, which are constantly inflated and secured in several places to the structure with a vent to the atmosphere which can be closed at will; and instead of fuel boost pump or tank pressure, there are controllable air scoops below the gas tanks, for cooling the gas apparently.

Subsequently, this A6M was flight-tested by conducting aerial competitive duels against current fighter aircraft – both Navy (Vought F4U Corsair and Grumman F4F-4 Wildcat) and Army (Bell P-39D-1 Airacobra, Curtiss P-40-F Warhawk, Lockheed P-38F Lightning and North American P-51 Mustang). Testing continued throughout the war first at the Tactical Air Intelligence Center at Anacostia and then back at San Diego where it flew with a captured Type 52 from Guam. In February 1945, however, the Aleutian Zero met its final demise at the hands of the enemy, in the chunky form of a Curtiss SB2C Helldiver whose pilot failed to see Commander Richard G. Crommelin taxiing her out. The 'Beast' simply ran over the little Japanese fighter and the SB2C's propeller chewed her rear fuselage up in chunks. The remains were junked, but she had played a significant part in the defeat of her sisters far away across the broad Pacific.

Guadalcanal and the Solomons

To the unfortunate Japanese soldiers condemned to serve on Guadalcanal during the abortive attempts to wrestle back control of Lunga Point airstrip, it was '*Ga Tò*' (Starvation island). But the island also proved a starvation diet for the IJN over the period August 1942 to February 1943, for, despite some hard-fought surface and air victories over the American fleet, the end result was failure. Troops and ships were fed piecemeal, always too little and too late, and although the island was almost re-taken in October and the American carriers reduced to just one active vessel the following month, final victory eluded Yamamoto.

Battle of Eastern Solomons

Fought soon after the Midway epic, this third air-sea battle took place on 24/25 August and came about with the Japanese response to the US Marines landings at Tulagi, Florida and Guadalcanal islands from 7 August onward and the capture of the partly completed airstrip at Lunga Point, which was named Henderson Field.

Overall command was exercised by Admiral Isoroku Yamamoto with Rear-Admiral Chūichi Nagumo still commanding at sea with two fleet carriers, one light carrier, two battleships, sixteen cruisers and twenty-five destroyers deployed operating in support of the *Ka* offensive to re-take the island. Land forces assigned to this task left Truk Lagoon, the 2 Battalion of 28 Infantry Regiment under Colonel Kiyonao Ichiki and 5 Yokosuka Special Naval Landing Force aboard three troop transports on 16 August escorted by four heavy cruisers, a light cruiser and eight destroyers. Rear-Admiral Hiroaki Abe with the Advance Force had two battleships, three heavy cruisers one light cruiser and three destroyers; Vice-Admiral Nobutake Kondō had the Advance Force with the seaplane carrier *Chitose*, five heavy cruisers, one light cruiser and six destroyers. Nagumo had the Main Body, carriers *Shōkaku* (with twenty-seven A6Ms under Lieutenant Hisayoshi Miyajima, and twenty-seven D3As and eighteen B5Ns embarked), *Zuikaku* (also having twenty-seven A6Ms, led by Lieutenant Aya-o Shirane, with twenty-seven D3As and eighteen B5Ns embarked); and *Ryūjō* (with twenty-four A6Ms under Lieutenant Kenjirō Nōtomi, and nine B5Ns aboard), the latter ship being seconded to the 1 *Kōkūtai* from the 2 *Kōkūtai* with one heavy cruisers and eight destroyers.

Their American equivalents were under overall command of Admiral Robert Ghormley with Rear-Admiral Frank Jack Fletcher once again commanding three fleet carriers, *Enterprise*, *Saratoga* and *Wasp*, with a battleship, six heavy cruisers, one light cruiser, two AA cruisers and eighteen destroyers. Twenty-two more aircraft were based at Lunga Point and there were long-range PBY floatplanes and Boeing B-17s at Santa Cruz Island and Espiritu Santo respectively. Fletcher had pulled out the American carriers after just one day; leaving the Marines ashore unsupported and the resulting night surface action off Savo Island destroyed the American cruiser covering force. On 23 August Fletcher detached the *Wasp*, heavy cruisers *Australia*,

San Francisco and *Salt Lake City*, light cruiser *Hobart*, AA cruiser *San Juan* and destroyers of Task Forces 18 and 44, to Efate island for refuelling, even though just reaching there involved two days' steaming, thus reducing the size of his force by one-third.

There were three separate Japanese attacks, but only two hit home. The *Ryūjō* was detached with a heavy cruiser and destroyer escort, to carry out an attack on Lunga Point airstrip. At 1120 she duly launched six A6Ms led by Lieutenant Kenjirō Nōtomi, escorting five B5N2s. These were followed at 1248 by a further nine A6Ms, each of which carried a pair of 60kg bombs. A combined assault had been planned with twenty-four G4M and fourteen further A6Ms dispatched from Rabaul, but bad weather had already aborted that attack and *Ryūjō*'s aircraft were forced to act alone. Ten F4Fs and two P-400s intercepted and two Marine Corps F4Fs were destroyed for the loss of four B5Ns. As the carrier had been badly damaged and later sank, the survivors had to try and land back at Rabaul and three A6Ms were lost *en route* there.

The Japanese fleet carriers launched two waves against the US carriers, the first at 1450, comprising four A6Ms escorting eighteen D3As led by Lieutenant-Commander Mamoru Seki, from *Shōkaku*, and six A6Ms commanded by Lieutenant (j.g.) Saneyasu Hidaka, and nine D3As from *Zuikaku*. They destroyed four US aircraft and scored bomb hits on *Enterprise*. Three A6Ms were lost there, including Petty Officer 1st Class Shigeru Makino.

The second wave, which got away at 1600, comprised three A6Ms escorting nine D3As from *Shōkaku* and six A6Ms with eighteen further D3As from *Zuikaku*, all under Lieutenant Sadamu Takahashi, but these were forced to abort their mission without locating the American force. Arriving back after nightfall Nagumo ordered the carriers searchlights switched on to guide them in, all save five D3As made it back aboard, with some aircrews being rescued by destroyers after ditching.

The Americans had a huge CAP of fifty-three F4F-3s overhead with good radar warning, but these were poorly handled and most of these were misdirected and failed to intercept, while of those that did, four were destroyed by their own flak defences while the A6Ms kept the rest away from their charges most efficiently and destroyed two Wildcats. The main thrust of the dive-bombing was against *Enterprise* and the D3As scored three direct hits, which put her out of action for two months. Although the Americans claimed to have destroyed seventy Japanese aircraft when only forty-two in total made the attack, twenty-five aircraft failed to return. Likewise their air striking forces achieved nothing other than two near-misses on the *Chitose* and many had to land at Lunga Point.

Meanwhile, after considerable hesitation, at 1340 Fletcher had *Saratoga* send a thirty-eight plane striking force against *Ryūjō*, which had been pinpointed by a PBY four hours earlier. The *Ryūjō*, in the absence of the majority of her aircraft away attacking Guadalcanal, had just seven A6Ms, which destroyed one TBF. The little Japanese carrier was hit by an estimated four bombs and also hit by a torpedo that hit right aft and flooded the starboard engine-room and which caused a 21-degree list and brought her to a halt. Later the damaged carrier was subjected to another ineffectual high-level bombing by B-17s, which were attacked by A6Ms and later lost one of their number which crash-landed, but the badly damaged and abandoned *Ryūjō* sank that night taking with her the four remaining of her aircraft. All her CAP had to ditch but the pilots were rescued by escorting destroyers. The Japanese heavy ships also failed to make contact for a surface action and by nightfall each fleet had withdrawn leaving an unsatisfactory outcome from both viewpoints. Total Japanese A6M losses were put at thirty-three.[7]

Subsequently the *Shōkaku* flew off fifteen A6Ms led by Lieutenant Hideki Shingō to the airfield at Buka airfield, Bougainville, closer to the action, from where they conducted attacks on Guadalcanal between 28 August and 4 September, destroying fifteen US aircraft in actions on 29 and 30 August and 2 September, but lost six, including Lieutenant Shingō himself and Lieutenant Masanobu Ibusuki, both of whom had to make force-landings.

Battle of Santa Cruz

This was the fourth carrier-versus-carrier battle of the Pacific War and was fought on 26 October 1942. The Japanese had planned a major ground counter-attack at Guadalcanal between 20 and 25 October, by further elements of Lieutenant-General Hyakutake's 17 Army, which had earlier been ferried in from Rabaul with the aim, once again, of re-taking Henderson

Field (known to the Japanese as Lunga Point or Runga Point – which they code-named RXI). In case the US Fleet might once more attempt to influence the battle on the island, Yamamoto moved strong forces into the area of the southern Solomons in the hope of inflicting a decisive defeat upon them. When the *Oka* regiment prematurely signalled on 25 October that they had taken the airfield, the Japanese warships moved south, and the two fleets finally made air contact with the north of Santa Cruz Island about 250 miles (400m) south-west of San Cristobal.

The Japanese forces, under overall command from the *Yamato* back at Truk Lagoon, consisted of the *Kidō Butai* with *Shōkaku* (now finally equipped with radar), *Zuikaku* and *Zuihō* of 1 *Kōkūtai*, escorted by nine destroyers under Vice-Admiral Chuichi Nagumo; the 2 *Kōkūtai* (re-named from 4 *Kōkūtai*) with the carrier *Junyō* and two destroyers, under Rear-Admiral Sentaro Omori;[8] the Main Body, with heavy cruisers *Atago*, *Maya*, *Myōkō* and *Takao*, and seven destroyers, and Vice-Admiral Takeo Kurita's Support Group, battleships *Haruna* and *Kongō* with two destroyers; the Vanguard group of Rear-Admiral Hiroake Abe, with battleships *Hiei* and *Kirishima*, heavy cruisers *Chikuma*, *Suzuya* and *Tone* with eight destroyers, plus a supply group of four tankers and one destroyer. As can be seen Yamamoto's penchant for the complex splitting of separated forces in groups still persisted, despite the dire example of the Midway debacle. The air complements of the four Japanese carriers comprised: *Shōkaku* – twenty A6M2s, under Lieutenant Masanobu Ibusuki, along with twenty-one D3A1 dive-bombers, one Yokosuka D4Y1 dive-bomber, and twenty-four B5N2 torpedo-bombers; *Zuikaku* – twenty A6M2s, led by Lieutenant Aya-o Shirane, along with twenty-three D3A1s and twenty B5N2s; *Zuihō* – twenty A6Ms, commanded by Lieutenant Saneyasu Hikdaka, plus nine B5N2s. Finally the *Junyō* had twenty-one A6Ms embarked, many of them piloted by survivors from Midway, as well as eighteen B5Ns and nine D3As. After intensive training practice at Saeki the carrier arrived at Truk and, when *Hiyō* dropped out of the operation, Lieutenant Yoshio Shiga and part of her *Kōkūtai* transferred to *Junyō* to replace heavy losses received in attacks on Guadalcanal earlier.[9]

Just about the time the Japanese moved again, changes to the US Fleet were afoot. After his performance at Eastern Solomons, came the torpedoing of the *Saratoga* on 31 August, which put her out of action for three months, followed soon after by the loss of the *Wasp* on 15 September, Rear-Admiral Fletcher had been sent back to the States. Admiral Robert Ghormley also went and was replaced in command by his old friend Admiral William F. 'Bull' Halsey, now recovered from his long hospitalization at Pearl Harbor. Halsey had just arrived at Noumea on 18 October when the storm broke, but, true to form, and in contrast to the previous hesitant decisions of some of the previous base and sea commanders in the area, on learning the Japanese fleet was out 'Bull' sent one simple signal – 'Attack – Repeat – Attack.'[10]

The American forces comprised the carrier *Enterprise* with thirty-six F4F-4 fighters embarked, along with forty-four SBD-3 dive-bombers and fourteen TBF-1 torpedo-bombers, escorted by the battleship *South Dakota*, heavy cruiser *Portland* and anti-aircraft cruiser *San Juan* and eight destroyers (Task Force 16, under Rear-Admiral Thomas C. Kinkaid) and the carrier *Hornet*, with thirty-seven F4F-4s, and thirty SBDs and sixteen TBF-1s on board, escorted by the heavy cruisers *Northampton* and *Pensacola* and the anti-aircraft cruisers *Juneau* and *San Diego*, with six destroyers (Task Force 17 under Rear-Admiral George D. Murray). There were also at this time sixteen F4F-4s at Henderson Field, Guadalcanal, with twenty SBD-3s, two TBF-1s and twelve Army fighters, P-39/P-400s Airacobras. There were also numerous PBYs (some fitted with torpedoes) and land-based Army B-17s under Rear-Admiral Fitch in support and these had sighted the Japanese forces as early as the 23rd. These long-range units made attacks on 25 October but, as usual, failed to score any hits. Neither of the two opponents' carrier aircraft managed to locate the other but *Junyō*'s bombers attacked US Marines near the disputed airfield.

At 0250 on 26 October a PBY made contact and reported back to Kinkaid but the account was delayed for three hours and in that long period one of *Tone*'s scouts located the Americans. As usual then the Japanese struck first sending away a sixty-four plane strike. At 0510 the *Shōkaku* contributed four A6Ms, under Lieutenant Hisayoshi Miyajima, plus eight *Zuikaku* fighters under Lieutenant Aya-o Shirane while the *Zuihō* contributed nine A6Ms, under Lieutenant Saneyasu Hidaka with Lieutenant (j.g.) Shū-ichi Utsumi,

Warrant Officer Masa-aki Kawahara, and Petty Officers Masao Kawasaki, Masaichi Kondō, Zenpei Matsumoto, Jirō Mitsumoto, Yasuhiro Nakamura and Shizuta Takagi. The *Zuihō shotai* engaged incoming American strikes heading for the fleet and destroyed three F4Fs and two TBF Avengers, so damaging a further F4F and two more TBFs that they had to turn back to their carrier. This was all well done, but during the melee the A6M group had become disorientated and four of them, Utsumi, Kawasaki, Matsumoto and Takagi, failed to find their way back to their carrier and were lost.

Meanwhile at 0540 the *Zuihō* was surprised by two SBDs lurking in the clouds and struck by one bomb and damaged. She could still launch aircraft but could no longer land them back aboard.

For her first attack at 0705 the *Junyō* put up twelve A6Ms under Lieutenant Yasuhiro Shiga escorting seventeen B5Ns. Nagumo then ordered her to close her force for close co-operation. The D3As attacked *Enterprise* but scored no direct hits, although they did hit the battleship *South Dakota* and the AA cruiser *San Juan* losing eight dive-bombers in the process. At 1106 *Junyō* got away a second strike, with eight A6Ms escorting seven B5Ns.

The Japanese strike force was detected at a distance of forty miles (65km) and no fewer than thirty-seven F4Fs joined the CAP to block them. Despite this the majority of the American fighter aircraft failed to engage and only four D3As were destroyed, in return for which the A6Ms destroyed six Americans. The remaining sixteen Japanese dive-bombers thus had only to face the AA fire the *Hornet* Task Force.[11] The dive-bombers scored three direct hits on *Hornet* and, additionally, a fourth D3A was hit by anti-aircraft fire and set on fire, the pilot deliberately choosing to make a suicide crash into the carrier, which caused more damage. B5Ns then added two torpedo hits to the tally and disabled her engines, while another D3A made a deliberate suicide run into her and she wallowed to a halt. Meanwhile the destroyer *Porter* took a torpedo hit and had to be put down by gunfire.

For the second Japanese attack *Shōkaku* sent five A6Ms under Fighter Division Officer Lieutenant Hideki Shingō (who was lost) with nineteen D3As; they were joined by four A6Ms from *Zuikaku* led by Warrant Officer Shigemi Katsuma with sixteen B5Ns. These attacked the *Enterprise* Task Force and again eluded most of the defending F4Fs, losing just two dive-bombers. For the loss of eight further D3As they scored two direct hits and one very near miss on *Enterprise* badly damaging her. The following torpedo-bombers lost three of their number to F4Fs but failed to score any hits on the carrier, although the destroyer *Smith* was badly damaged, and lost five more B5Ns in the process. The A6Ms fared better and between them they destroyed five American fighters. The *Junyō* put up twelve A6Ms under Lieutenant Yasuhiro Shiga escorting eighteen B5Ns.

Meanwhile hastening up into the battle the *Junyō* launched twelve A6Ms escorting seventeen D3As and these scored one near miss on the *Enterprise* and hit the battleship *South Dakota* and the AA cruiser *San Juan* but lost eleven aircraft in the process.

Despite her depleted air complement the *Zuikaku* mustered yet a third strike, with five A6Ms under Lieutenant Aya-o Shirane, with two D3As and seven B5Ns and, likewise the *Junyō* got away eight A6Ms escorting seven B5Ns. The little *Junyō* had still not shot her bolt, and conducted yet a third wave at extreme range with six A6Ms, with four B5Ns and managed to hit *Hornet* a second time. The indefatigable Shirane and one companion were lost in combat while the remaining three Zeros ran out of fuel and were lost. Meanwhile the *Hornet* had listed over and was abandoned by her crew, aided on their way by another two bomb hits from the *Zuikaku* team. Two US destroyers were ordered to sink her to prevent her being captured by the Japanese but she stubbornly refused to do down and they had to flee when powerful Japanese surface forces arrived. In the end two Japanese destroyers completed the task for them as the carrier was too damaged to salvage.

Against the opposing American strikes the Japanese fighter defenders had performed far better than their opposite numbers. The *Shōkakū*'s radar set had detected the incoming American strike at seventy-eight miles' range at 0640. A total of just twenty-four A6Ms were available to form the CAP during the day and they destroyed nine enemy bombers, including one which Petty Officer 1st Class Shigetaka Omori took out by ramming, when the enemy was about to bomb the carrier. The *Zuihō*'s three A6M contribution engaged the escorting *Hornet* F4Fs, which left the SBDs unprotected and four of them were quickly shot down. One of *Hornet*'s SBD pilots recorded this thus: 'The Zero fighters engaged our four fighters and quickly shot down two of them. The other two fighters, trying to survive, disappeared into some clouds. That was the end of our fighter support. We were on our own.'

After he had made his dive attack and was try to escape, Fisher also graphically described what it was like to be on the receiving end of an A6M attack:

When I finally leveled off at 300 feet, my gunner yelled, 'We've got a Zero on our tail!' Putting it mildly, it was a horrifying feeling. I couldn't out maneuver the Zero. With a Zero on its tail, a SBD dive-bomber has a slight advantage over a single fighter because of the gunner's rapid-firing, twin 30-calibre guns. So I dove closer to the water where the fighter couldn't get in a position below us – a dangerous spot because the gunner couldn't position his guns to bear down on the Zero. My gunner, ARM 3/c Ferguson, practically shot off our rudder trying to hit the Zero. Both [our] wings were riddled with small jagged holes after being hit with 7.7mm bullets. One bullet passed between my legs, shattering my engine's cylinder temperature gauge. Finally, the Zero fired his 20mm cannons, and a shell exploded in the radio transmitter located behind my armored seat. A radio-frequency manual was blown to bits with confetti flying all over the cockpit. The concussion from the exploding shell inside the confines of the cockpit canopy felt like I had been hit a hard blow on top of my head. Simultaneously, I felt a red-hot burning sensation in my right arm just below my shoulder. Shrapnel fragments flying around in the cockpit had hit my upper right arm just above the elbow. Momentarily stunned, I had lost my vision, but my mind was visualizing the shimmering, wavering faces of my mother and Annie. I didn't want to die, but felt completely helpless. After recovering from the shock of the concussion and as my vision cleared, the Zero fighter, with its big red 'meatball' insignia, was flying off my right wing, just like a wingman. The pilot was staring at me! When our eyes met, he drifted back behind us. Ferguson had been shot in both thighs with 7.7mm bullets and a piece of shrapnel had gouged some flesh out of the calf of his right leg. Ferguson managed to reload his jammed guns, in spite of his wounds, and waited for the Zero to get into firing range. The Zero pilot evidently felt we were cold turkey and moved slowly into position for the kill. Ferguson fired first and hit the engine of the Zero. The Zero, with its engine smoking, pulled up sharply away from us and then disappeared. We had miraculously survived: Ferguson had not panicked. He had saved both our lives.[12]

The defence could not prevent the *Shōkaku* suffering three bomb hits, which severely damaged the vessel, but did not sink her. Both these Japanese carriers survived but had to withdraw from the battle. The *Hornet*'s TBFs failed to attack the carriers at all and instead concentrated unsuccessfully on the cruiser *Tone*, and nor did the *Enterprise* torpedo-bombers fare any better when they assailed the heavy cruiser *Suzuya*. Only three *Shōkakū* A6Ms were lost in combat. However, aircraft from *Hornet* did later manage to hit the heavy cruiser *Chikuma* with one bomb and one torpedo, but she survived. Losses among the Japanese strike force were very heavy, the *Shōkakū* had only four A6Ms and one B5N when she was detached with the damaged *Zuihō* at the end of the engagement; the *Zuikaku* was better off, having thirty-eight A6Ms, ten D3As and nineteen B5Ns when the battle ended. With the loss of one fleet carrier and severe damage to a second, plus the other damage, the American force withdrew but due to the heavy aviation losses the Japanese, although they could claim a victory, were unable to force the issue and Guadalcanal remained in American hands.

The *Rufe* in the Solomons

While land-based and carrier-based A6Ms slugged it out over and around the Solomon Islands, the A6M2-N *Suisen* was also moved into the area as an alternative fighter in that sea-girt theatre of war. Thus began the saga of the *Kamikawa Maru* and her brood. As early as 10 August 1942 the *Kamikawa Maru* had been allocated to join the *Chitose* in 11 *Koku Sentai* (Seaplane Tender Division), 2 Fleet and on the 23rd she left Yokosuka for the Shortland Islands, Bougainville Island south-east of Rabaul at the head of the Solomon chain, where she arrived five days later. From 4 September she became part of *Homen Koku Butai* under Rear-Admiral Takatsugu Jōjima. The main operating base for the unit was Shortland Harbour with an advance base at Rekata Bay, Santa Isabel Island, strategically closer to the disputed airfield at Lunga Point, Guadalcanal. The main aircraft complement at this time comprised eleven Nakajima A6M2-N fighters, under the command of

Lieutenant Jiro Ono, aided by a pair of Mitsubishi F1M2s and Aichi E13A1s for reconnaissance duties

The float fighters were soon in demand and, on 13 September, scored their first victory when two A6M2-Ns destroyed an SBD that was landing at Lunga Point. During the fierce battles ashore the next day *Kamikawa Maru* and *Chitose*, along with the auxiliary tenders *Sanyo Maru* and *Sanuki Maru*, mounted an attack with nineteen F1Ms carrying 60kg bombs, and four A6M2-Ns provided the escort. They were intercepted by four F4Fs and in the fight Lieutenant (j.g.) Masashi Kawashima and Warrant Officer Kawamura were lost.

Between 4 September and 7 November, the *Rufes* had carried out 360 sorties in 211 separate missions and claimed fourteen Allied aircraft destroyed, while losing nine of its own. Following this the *Kamikawa Maru* returned to Yokosuka in October and was fitted with radar, before embarking new aircraft and returning to the Solomons once more and commencing flying A6M2-Ns as fighter protection for troop convoys and destroyers running men into Guadalcanal. By 8 October losses and accidents had reduced her complement to just five *Suisen* and she once more had to replenish. On return *Kamikawa Maru* was based at Buin in October, where she was attacked by B-17s five times but received only minor damage. By 3 November she was back at Shortland once more and again participated in the famed 'Tokyo Express' troop runs into Guadalcanal. One important convoy comprised eleven destroyers under Captain Torajiro Sato with six of 802 (the former 14 *Kōkūtai*) *Kōkūtai's* A6M2-Ns providing air support assisted by four F1M2 from *Kamikawa Maru*. This convoy was assailed by seven Marine Corps SBDs from VMSB-132, three of *Hornet's* TBMs and eight Army Bell P-39s from 67 Fighter Squadron escorted by twenty-one Marine F4Fs from VMF-11. One F4F was destroyed against one float fighter, even though the Americans claimed ten and the convoy landed its troops successfully without loss.

Between 11 November Rear Admiral Raizo Tanaka's destroyers escorted a fast convoy with 14,500 soldiers from 38 Infantry Division, plus guns and supplies to Guadalcanal and *Kamikawa Maru's* A5M-Ns again provide air cover. This was followed by another replenishment visit to Yokosuka and further operations from Shortland between 5 and 12 December with the

802 *Kōkūtai* whose ace pilot became Hisaō Jitō with three kills while Keizo Yamazaki nailed a P-38.

In March 1943 the A6M2-Ns had proved such a thorn in the flesh of the Americans on Guadalcanal that a special mission was mounted to destroy them. Eight P-38s of 70 Fighter Squadron and eight of the big new Marine Corps Chance-Vought F-4U-1s, were sent against the Faisi-Poporang area, on 29 March, but due to the weather only five P-38s and a single Corsair eventually reached the target area near Shortland, Alu Island, at 0620, badly damaging seven of the floatplanes at their moorings.

To continue the story of 802 *Kōkūtai*, they later moved to Jaluit Atoll in the Marshall Islands where they were re-designated as 902 *Kōkūtai* on 21 October 1943 with seven A6M2-Ns. They were stationed for a period at the advance base of Greenwich Atoll, some 400 miles SSE of Truk, but were back at Truk by the beginning of February 1944 with an establishment of eight *Suisen*. When the great American carrier raid hit Truk on 17 February, two A6M2-Ns were airborne and attempted to intercept but were swept aside by the hordes of F6Fs who also totally destroyed the rest of the unit while they were still at their moorings.

Disaster in the Bismarck Sea

On 28 February 1943, a Japanese troop convoy of eight transports, carrying 6,900 men, escorted by eight destroyers, sortied from Simpson Harbour, Rabaul, on their way to land the HQ unit of 18 Army plus strong reinforcements, including elements of 51 Division, at Lae, New Guinea. It was known that powerful Allied air forces had assembled in the area and continuous air cover was planned over the ships by both Navy and Army fighter patrols. However, the Allies mounted strong attacks on the Japanese airfields. While the convoy was still within short range, north of New Britain, fighter cover was relatively easy to maintain, and both 204 *Kōkūtai* and 253 *Kōkūtai* shared the mission with the Army aircraft. Things remained placid on the 2nd but the following day the Allied attacks began. There were eighteen A6Ms of 253 *Kōkūtai* and fourteen of 204 *Kōkūtai* over the convoy this morning. One transport was sunk by B-17s and two were damaged.

On 3 March while off Finschhafen, Huon Peninsula, Papua, New Guinea, the Allied attacks reached a crescendo, with altitude bombing by B-17s and B-24s, and low-level attacks from A-20s, B-26s, and Australian Bristol Beaufighters and Bristol Beauforts. With the Japanese fighters up high the deadly 'skip-bombing' strikes by B-25s proved very effective. Fourteen A6Ms from 253 *Kōkūtai* working out of Surumi (now Gasmata), on the south coast of New Britain, and twelve from 204 *Kōkūtai* were aided by eighteen fighters from the *Zuihō* operating from Kavieng, but all to no avail. One B-17 was shot down by Leading Seaman Masanao Maki from *Zuihō*, and the A6Ms shot down three P-38s, and a B-25 but lost eight of their own number. The Japanese convoy was almost wiped out, losing all eight transports and four escorting destroyers. With hundreds of troops struggling in the water Allied planes roared in strafing at wave-top level and the result was carnage. In the end about 1,500 soldiers reached Lae, another 2,700 were rescued by destroyers and landed back at Rabaul but 2,890 were killed. It was a major disaster for the Japanese.

As a late postscript to this defeat, in August 1944 a section of A6Ms from 201 *Kōkūtai* based at Legaspi, Mactan Island, adjacent to Cebu on the Camotes Sea, asking for volunteers to practise their own form of *chōhi bakugeki* (skip-bombing). The whole group volunteered and selected pilots commenced training under the eye of instructors from the Yokosuka *kōkūtai*. A practice range was established in the nearby Bohol Strait and the method was refined. The accepted method became a high-speed approach at 280mph (450km/h), at wave-top height, 3ft (10m), carrying a 551lb (250kg) bomb. The release was delayed to with 1,000ft (304m) of the target vessel before bomb release. Such an approach profile gave each ship's gunner a perfect target for any weapon that would bear and it was expected that the chances of surviving such an attack were minimal. In the event, the American fleet made two overwhelming attacks on Cebu and Legaspi on 12 and 13 September, inflicting heavy losses on both those A6Ms that managed to get airborne and those destroyed still on the ground. Further fighting followed on 21 and 22 September, which used up even more priceless aircraft from the Group. The fighting that followed meant that the skip-bombers were never ever used in action and the chance of avenging Bismarck Sea never came.

The last Gamble – Operation *I-Go sakusen*

Admiral Yamamoto now launched one final attempt at a mass aerial assault in an attempt to blunt the Allied advances in the South Pacific. Working from both carriers and shore bases at Rabaul, where Yamamoto and his air staff flew to from Truk to oversee the attacks, Bougainville and the Shortlands the offensive included aircraft from the carrier *Hiyō* at Truk, her *Kōkūtai* moving to Ballale in the Shortlands on 7 April 1943 and later operating out of Rabaul. *Junyō* also added her *Kōkūtai* giving a total landed from the fleet of ninety-five A6Ms and sixty-five D3As, plus B5Ns. 11 *Kōkū-kantai* had eighty-six A6Ms, seventy-two G4Ms and sixty-seven single-engined bombers on hand.

A mass attack was launched against Tulagi and Guadalcanal on 1 April 1943. No fewer than fifty-eight A6M3s from the 204, 251 and 582 *Kōkūtai* left their bases and headed south down the Solomons. They were intercepted by Allied fighters in the vicinity of Russell Islands and eighteen A6Ms were claimed destroyed for the loss of six Allied aircraft.

On 7 April an even larger force, 110 A6Ms escorting sixty-seven D3A2 dive-bombers, set out down the Slot to hit Lunga Point and Tulagi. They were met by sixty-seven Allied fighters who claimed to have destroyed twenty-one of them for the loss of seven of their own. The dive-bombers sank the destroyer *Aaron Ward*, the New Zealand corvette *Moa* and the US oiler *Kanawha* and damaged another oiler and a transport.

On 11 April Allied shipping in Oro Bay, Buna, New Guinea, was attacked by twenty-two D3A3s escorted by seventy-two A6Ms, and were met by fifty Allied fighters who claimed six Japanese aircraft destroyed for no loss. However, the fifteen *Zuihō* fighters alone claimed two enemy destroyed, by Warrant Officers Tsutomu Iwai and Akira Yamamoto respectively, without loss to themselves; the twenty-seven *Zuikaku* A6Ms claimed one destroyed by Petty Officer 1st Class Yoshio Ch-Ishi, for the loss of two of their own; and the twenty-one A6Ms of the *Hiyō* Group claimed one enemy destroyed by Warrant Officer Misugu Mori. The *Junyō*'s nine-fighter contribution made no claims.

The following day an even larger force, a total of 131 A6M3s, was sent out, comprising twenty-three from *Zuikaku*, fifteen from *Junyō*, seventeen from

Hiyō, fourteen from *Zuihō*, twenty-four from *204 Kōkūtai*, eighteen from 253 *Kōkūtai*, and twenty from 582 *Kōkūtai*, along with forty-three G4M2 land bombers of 705 and 751 *Kōkūtai*, under Commander Masaichi Suzuki, which attacked Port Moresby from Rabaul, Buin and Kavieng. Some forty-four Allied fighters, P-38s of 39 Fighter Squadron and P-39s from 80 Fighter Squadron, rose to meet them. In the ensuing melee two P-38s and four P-39 Airacobras were shot down, while five Japanese bombers were destroyed in the air, and two more crashed on landing. Two A6Ms of 253 *Kōkūtai* failed to return. Only a few small craft were damaged and some Allied aircraft were destroyed on the ground, including two RAAF Beaufighters, and three American B-25s, while many more were badly damaged and facilities destroyed including a petrol dump that was set ablaze at Kila Kila airfield, Joyce Bay.

Finally, on 14 April, 188 aircraft raided Milne Bay. The carriers contributed seventy-five A6Ms, with twenty-one from 204 *Kōkūtai*, seventeen from 253 *Kōkūtai* and eighteen more from 582 *Kōkūtai*. Twenty-four Curtiss Kittyhawk Mk 1As intercepted and shot down seven Japanese aircraft for the loss of three of their own, including one *Junyō* fighter, with both Ensigns Yukiharu Ozeki and Shō-ichi claiming kills. Two transports in the bay, the British *Gorgon*, which was hit several times and the Dutchman *van Outhoorn*, were damaged, while the RAN minesweepers *Kapunda* and *Wagga* were also badly hit.

Yamamoto, believing the highly exaggerated claims of his airmen, called off the offensive on 16 April, but, in reality, the results on both sides had been trifling, Japanese losses being estimated at fifty-five aircraft in exchange for the destruction of a destroyer, a corvette, a tanker, two cargo ships and twenty-five aircraft.[13] The *I-Go* offensive did not even dent the Allied advance. At a post-offensive conference held on 17 April Yamamoto's staff concluded from these results that the A6M's performance remained 'excellent' and was still superior to any American fighter yet encountered. One change that did affect the A6M was the recommendation that in future a degree of armour protection was a requirement.

Yamamoto ambushed

Meanwhile American Intelligence had intercepted and de-coded the flight plan of Admirals Isoroku Yamamoto and Chief of Staff Vice-Admiral Matome Ugaki who were *en route* to Ballale airfield in two G4M bombers of 205 *Kōkūtai* with an escort of six 204 *Kōkūtai* A6Ms under Lieutenant Kenji Yanagiya. Despite attempts to dissuade this flight taking place for fear of ambush, Yamamoto insisted. A powerful force of sixteen P-38Gs of 339 Fighter Squadron intercepted this group under Operation *Vengeance*, destroying both transports for the loss of one P-38G to the escorting A6Ms without any loss to themselves.[14] Admiral Yamamoto and most of his team were killed, only Ugaki and two others surviving. Admiral Mineichi Koga took over command. In a revenge mission of their own 582 *Kōkūtai* made two raids and destroyed two P-38s, one apiece by Warrant Officer Kazuo Tsunoda and Petty Officer 2nd Class Kiyoshi Sekiya.

Chapter 10

On the Back Foot

The passing of Yamamoto marked a watershed in the Pacific War. His predictions had come only too true, but many felt that he had lost his grip on affairs earlier and his passing made little immediate difference to the way the war was being conducted. The Allies had most certainly learnt many lessons and applied them. The Japanese were forced to do likewise, but they did not have the industrial muscle or the necessary organization to back them up and change was only brought about piecemeal.

Change of fighter formations

As related earlier, the IJNAF had gradually, but very slowly, abandoned its long-established tactical fighter formations in the light of wartime experience and adopted one loosely akin to the Allies 'finger-four'. The Yokosuka *Kōkūtai* had begun to study such methods as early as the autumn of 1942. From 1943 this usage extended to units in the field, but still on a trial basis. In April 1943 the concept began to see more frequent field usage with the 204 *Kōkūtai* led by Lieutenant Miyano Zenjirō. Following improved results during the course of the Solomons campaign other front-line units also practised it informally. However, it was not until as late as February 1944 that 1 *Kōkū-kantai*, a land-based unit formed in July 1943, wholly adopted the new four-plane *shotai*. The basic set-up then became the *daitai* (*Hikōtai*) comprising sixteen fighters, the *chutai* (division) based on eight machines, the four-plane *shotai* (section) and the *buntai* (pair) with two aircraft.

Rabaul under siege

Since its unopposed occupation Rabaul had gradually been built up by the Japanese to became the main bastion of their drive down the south-west

Pacific. Because of its strategic position Rabaul also became the main focus of the Allied drive northward from New Guinea and the Solomons; as such it was given the dubious title 'The Gibraltar of the Pacific' by the American press. Whatever the merits of the base its location was undeniably key and while the Japanese built it up steadily as a hub, and the garrison at one point numbered 80,000, the Allies did all they could to neutralize it from the air. Eventually they would by-pass it totally, but for a nine-month period from in 1942–43 intense air battles were fought from, and over, Rabaul, and anchorages of Simpson and Matupi harbours, which had a crucially debilitating effect on Japanese naval aviation. Both Admiral Yoshimasa Nakahara's *Dai-Jūichi Kanta* (11 Air Fleet) and later, Lieutenant-General Giichi Itahana's *Dai 6 Hikō Shidan* (6 Air Division) were subjected to tasks that eventually proved beyond their power. Distance proved key at the start, before the Allies started a step-by-step advance and thus the fact that Guadalcanal was 650 miles from Rabaul proved a handicap for the Japanese at first. Reinforcements were either flown in from Truk 795 miles distant via Kavieng, New Ireland, 145 miles distant, which had been occupied at the same time as Rabaul, or flown in from carriers. Lakunai and Vunakanu airstrips were expanded and the latter eventually covered two square miles, while a new Army Air Force airfield was constructed at Rapopo adjacent to St George's Channel, in April 1943, and Tobera further inland. Finally a fifth field was begun at Keravat to the south but was never completed and nor was another on Duke of York Island. The need to extend the airfield south resulted in the construction of Buka field in October 1942, and by February similar forward strips were in use at Kahili (Buin), Ballale, Vila and Munda.[1]

The *Tainan kaigun Kōkūtai* under Captain Masahisa Saitō, with Yasuna Kozono as Air Officer, flew into Rabaul from Bali and began conducting operations against Allied fighters working out of the Port Moresby airstrips or from Rabi, Milne Bay in south-western Papua, New Guinea. After their previous exploits in the Philippines and the Netherlands East Indies they already enjoyed a formidable reputation and were to go on to produce more fighter aces than any other unit in the IJN. With very experienced pilots they quickly established air superiority in the area claiming three hundred aerial victories against just twenty A6M losses. This unit flew the very first sortie against the American landings at Tulagi, Florida Island, on 7 August, when seventeen A6Ms escorted a twenty-seven strong force of G4Ms against the invasion fleet in Lunga Roads an overall flight distance of 1,112 miles with eight hours in the air and an air battle in between. They were met by eighteen F4Fs and sixteen SBDs from three American carriers and in a brief fight the A4Ms destroyed nine Wildcats and one of the dive-bombers, while losing two of their own number, Petty Officer 1st Class Takio Yoshida and Petty Officer 2nd Class Kunimatsu Nishiura. On the return five A6Ms put down at Buka and ten returned to Rabaul. One of those who returned, miraculously as he had been wounded and blinded, was Petty Officer 1st Class Saburō Sakai, who destroyed two aircraft and somehow nursed his aircraft back to base. He was hospitalized for two years but later returned to full combat duty. He went on to become one of Japan's leading surviving air aces by the end of the war. The mission leader, Lieutenant-Commander Tadashi Nakajima, also survived and continued to cull enemy aircraft at an unprecedented rate during his time at Rabaul, being credited with six kills on this mission alone. He had notched up a further twenty-four personal victories before he returned to Toyohashi that November. Such was his success that Admiral Ryūnosuke Kusaka later presented him with a sword with the inscription *Bukō Batsugun* (For Conspicuous Valour) and they lost count of the number of American aircraft he destroyed, with anything from eighty-seven to 120 mentioned.

At the end of May 1942 the *Chitose*'s *Kōkūtai*'s fighter group was in the progress of exchanging its Type 96 fighters for the A6M at Roi and Wake Islands and they were used as replenishments for the *Tainan* and 24 *Kōkū Sentai*, both sent to Rabaul while the remainder became 201 *Kōkūtai* on 1 December.

Prominent A6Ms units in this long rearguard action were the 201, 204, 252, 253 and 582 *Kōkūtai*. 204 had been set up on 1 November when 6 *Kokutai* was re-numbered and had both Model 21 and Model 23 aircraft under Captain Chisato Morita and worked from Buin until it relocated at Rabaul in April 1943 for the *I-Go* missions. The use of the outstanding A6M in the *bakusō* (fighter-bomber) role became more prevalent due to the high losses of the attack bombers, but this move in itself was self-defeating. It removed high-class fighter units from their design combat role; it led to higher losses from anti-aircraft fire (an attack by twenty-four A6Ms on targets off the Russell Islands on 7 June saw one-third of the force as armed as fighter-bombers but AA fire claimed nine of them when, as fighters, they would have mainly operated out of range of these weapons); the small bombs that the A6M carried, 30kg, were practically useless against ship targets (even the 500kg bombs used by the D3As and, later, by the A6Ms, were too small – the standard US Navy dive-bombers had been using 1,000lb bombs for several years). Nonetheless this process continued after Lieutenant Mitsugu Kofukuda handed over to Lieutenant Zenhjirō Miyano in March 1943. On 16 June Miyano died in the same kind of attack off Lunga Point and 204 *Kōkūtai* was left without a single operational officer. The remnants of 204, working from Buin, merged with the 582 *Kōkūtai* after the latter was subjected to similar heavy losses but soon even this combined group was further decimated. In October the few survivors were pulled back, initially to Rabaul but, at the end of January, right back to Truk to rebuild their strength under the command of Lieutenant Torajirō Haruta. In the process of this a devastating American carrier raid on 17 February caught the Japanese by surprise. Some fifty A6Ms of various types from 201, 204 and 501 *Kōkūtai* engaged the enemy and destroyed thirty but only at considerable cost, all three units being practically wiped out, just a single A6M being left operational at the end of the day. The unit was disbanded shortly afterward.

582 *Kōkūtai*, under Lieutenant Yoshio Kurakane, had arrived at Rabaul aboard the ferry carrier *Yawata Maru* on 6 August 1942 with fifteen Model 32s but due to their comparatively short-range were mainly used over targets in the northern New Guinea area and later moved to Buna. They had a series of victories against USAAF units here to start with, destroying nine P-39s on the 24, but lost two of their number while taking off from their home base three days later. At the end of September they moved to Buka from where they attacked targets at Guadalcanal. During the highly successful withdrawal of Japanese forces from the island (Operation *Ke-go*) the unit provided air cover and during the action off Rennell Island when the Japanese G4M torpedo-bombers sank the heavy cruiser *Chicago*, hit the heavy cruisers *Lousiville* and *Wichita* and badly damaged the destroyer *La Valette*. On 1 February 252 *Kōkūtai*, under Lieutenant Saburo Shindō, provided twenty-one of the eighty-one strong A6M escort for fifteen D3As, which sank the destroyer *De Haven* off Savo Island and in the ensuing air

fight they destroyed eight American fighters for the loss of four A6Ms and five of the Japanese dive-bombers. Between November and February ten thousand Japanese troops were withdrawn safely from Guadalcanal and the A6Ms provided air cover during the daylight hours that minimized attempts by the Americans to interrupt the flow.[2]

A different kind of mission was mounted on 10 February when the Japanese submarine *I-1* ran aground on Fish Reef, off Kamimbo Bay (Tambea), Cape Esperance, on the north coast of Guadalcanal Island and some top secret documents were inadvertently left aboard her when she was abandoned. To destroy the wreck and the documents a force of forty-two A6Ms, including fourteen from 582, were sent as escorts for a force of nine D3As to bomb her and the latter scored one direct hit on the submarine's conning tower.[3] The final series of missions by 582 *Kōkūtai* were conducted from Buin and Munda between May and July, including victories on 13 May, 7 June and 12 June in the area of Russell Island, but on 16 June sixteen A6Ms under Lieutenant-Commander Shindō, lost four of their number in an air battle over Lunga in which four American fighters were also destroyed. The unit was disbanded on 1 August with surviving pilots dispersed to other units.

252 *Kōkūtai* formed at Tateyama, Chiba Prefecture, near Tokyo Bay, on 20 September 1942 with Lieutenant Masaji Suganami as the fighter leader and was transported to Rabaul aboard the carrier *Taiyō* early in November. They were soon involved in the fierce naval battles off Guadalcanal, the first mission being the contribution of eleven Model 21s led by Lieutenant Shigehisa Yamamoto to the battles on 11 November with 253 and 582 *Kōkūtai;* on 12 November, with twelve A6Ms under Lieutenant Suganami escorting the torpedo-bomber assault; and on 13 November, again led by Lieutenant Yamamoto, when they vainly endeavoured to protect the badly damaged battleship *Hiei* with a six-strong CAP. While returning to base all six had to make water landings due to severe weather conditions. Next day Lieutenant Suganami was lost while trying to protect Japanese troop convoys running reinforcements into the island. These early heavy losses were replaced and the unit continued to operate from Rabaul and Ballale, as well as Munda and Lae in New Guinea. After five months of intense operations, 252 *Kōkūtai* was pulled back to Roi (Ruot) at Kwajalein Atoll,

Wake Island, Taroa at Maloelap Atoll, and lonely Nauru Island (Yaren or Pleasant Island).

The *Kanoya Kokutai*, after service in the Indian Ocean area, was transferred to Rabaul and then Kavieng, New Ireland, in September 1942 with the fighter group of two dozen Model 21s led by Lieutenant Toshitaka Itō. On 21 September they opened their operations with sorties against Port Moresby and a week later were in air battles over Guadalcanal where they shot down four American aircraft. On 1 October the fighter unit became the 253 *Kōkūtai* with Commander Yoshito Kobayashi in charge with a paper strength of forty-eight A6Ms, but these were dispersed around several airfields in the region. Over the following eight months it partook in many of the major actions over Guadalcanal and claimed over one hundred Allied aircraft destroyed for a total loss of thirty of its own pilots. In May 1943 the depleted unit was pulled back to Saipan to rest and replenish with the Model 52 and in August Lieutenant-Commander Harutoshi Okamoto took over command.

As the war of attrition intensified the IJN rotated the A6M units through these Rabaul airfields as best they could to cope with an ever deteriorating situation. Both the *Dai-Jūichi Kōkū Kantai*'s (11 Air Fleet) 25 and 26 *Kōkū Sentai* (Air Flotillas) re-organized their fighting units. The 201 *Kōkūtai* had been based in the northern Kurile Islands, but was ordered to Rabaul in July 1943 with a strength of forty-five Model 22s, which embarked aboard the carrier *Unyō* at Yokosuka for sea passage, arriving at Truk on the 15th. Meanwhile, due to the urgency of the situation, the commander of 201, Commander Chujiro Nakano, led a flight of eighteen A6Ms on a 3,000-mile (5,000km) flight south staging via Iwo Jima, Saipan and Truk directly to Rabaul where they arrived on 12 July to join 21 *Kōkū Sentai*. They were immediately involved in the fierce fighting around Buin (Kahili), south Bougainville Island and Buka Island to the north, which culminated on 14 September when a total of 117 A6M sorties were made to intercept five waves of American air attacks. These latter were designed to soften-up the Japanese defences prior to the Allied landings, which followed in November, and were among the largest air battles in that part of the Pacific.

This day saw Petty Officer 1st Class Takao Okumura claim no fewer than ten Allied aircraft destroyed in a single day, for which he was to have been awarded an inscribed ceremonial sword by Admiral Kusaka. Okumura was another China veteran having made his debut at Kunming on 7 October 1940 when he had claimed four victories. After surviving the sinking of *Ryūjō* in July 1942 and service with the *Tainan* unit (which later became 251 *Kōkūtai*), Okumuru destroyed two or three F4Fs on 13 September 1942 alone. Okumura transferred from 251 to 201 in May 1943, and then joined 204 *Kōkūtai*, whose combined sixty or so A6Ms fought under Rear-Admiral Munetaka Sakamaki. On 14 September each raid was intercepted in turn. The first attack was mounted by ten B-24s and seventeen F-4Us and they were met by twenty 201 and twenty-three 204 fighters. Okumura claimed one F-4U and a B-24 destroyed, but the Americans admitted only that five F-4Us were write-offs from severe damage and one B-24 was also damaged. The second wave consisted of twelve B-24s with an escort of twenty-three F4Us, but although twenty A6Ms were scrambled they failed to intercept. In the third attack ten more B-24s were escorted by eight P-40F/Ms and sixteen New Zealand P-40 Kittyhawks and were met by the A6Ms already in the air from the second raid. The RNZAF fighters failed to become involved but the P-40s lost three of their number and another was badly damaged while four more turned back. Okumura was credited with three of the twenty Allied aircraft claimed destroyed. There were no Japanese losses but, due to fuel shortage some A6Ms landed at Ballale, Shortlands, and two at Buin where they were strafed by F4Us and bombed by nine PB4Ys of the fourth wave. The fifth attack was also directed against Ballale with twenty-four Marine Crops TBFs and thirty-four SBDs escorted by forty F4Fs and fifteen P39s the latter not being engaged. The American fighters claimed eight A6Ns destroyed and in return two F6Fs were lost and one damaged, along with four TBFs. Both Okumura and his companion had refuelled by this time and engaged the enemy claiming one TBF and four F6Fs destroyed.

Meanwhile, having lost Lae and Salamaua in Papua, New Guinea the Japanese defence line screening Rabaul was crumbling. Although the Army had taken over chief responsibility for this area of air defence, the Navy still contributed patrols and it was during one of these, against the Allied landings at Finschhafen on 22 September that Okumura was killed. The Rabaul airfields sent a force of eight B5N torpedo-bombers against the invasion fleet off Cape Cretin, escorted by thirty-five A6Ms from 253 *Kōkūtai*, including twelve from 201 *Kōkūtai* under Lieutenant Shiro Kawai, from Buin, Okumura being among them. The torpedo-bombers attacked through heavy flak and lost six of their number, without scoring any hits (the American ships and defending P-38, P-40 and P-47 fighters claiming no fewer than eighteen bombers destroyed from the eight-plane force!). Meanwhile, the A6Ms clashed with the fighters and destroyed three P-38s and the A6Ms lost six (the Americans claiming twenty-one destroyed). Among those who did not return from this mission was Okumura, who received a posthumous promotion of one rank, and Warrant Officer Shunzō Hongō.

Such air battles were naturally ruinous and production was hard-pressed even to replace casualties, let alone increase the numbers,[4] but combat losses were not the main drain of experienced A6M pilots in the Solomons as the extended periods of patrols protecting troop reinforcements down the slot resulted in increasing fatigue from repeated long-range missions. There were also many forced water-landings, coupled with the primitive conditions at the jungle airstrips at the end of extended lines of communication, which reduced serviceability and a steady erosion of morale as well as expertise. It was estimated that at this time the A6M units were losing eight aircraft to accidents to five lost in battle. The need to increase production and pilot training resulted in a lowering of material standards and a drop in personnel attainment. Time taken to re-build numbers of men and aircraft after each major failed offensive increased, while the Allies, by contrast, gained the time they should not have been allowed, and steadily widened the gap in both fields. A steady descent into ultimate defeat was commenced that proved irreversible. Vice-Admiral Matome Ugaki, was bitterly recording in his diary entry of 8 June 1944 as New Guinea crumbled:- '... our Third Air Force (*sic*) has only thirteen Zero fighters.' He added, 'With this small strength we must meet more than three hundred enemy planes deployed west of Hollandia. This is worse than sweeping back the sea with a broom.' He blamed the faceless bureaucrats back home, 'What do they think of the [our] present plight, those responsible men in Tokyo who promised that so many planes would be produced by May? Shame on them!'[5]

Commander Ryoji Nomura, a veteran fighter pilot, was on the Staff at Rabaul between November 1942 and July 1943 and witnessed this rapid decline. In his post-war interrogation he stated that:

> The Naval land-based losses in the Rabaul-Solomons-New Guinea areas were extremely high and finally resulted in the destruction of the cream of the Naval Air Forces. The high losses were attributed in the order named to: 1) Superiority of American fighter aircraft; 2) Breakdown of Japanese aircraft supply system; 3) Inability of the Japanese to replace experienced pilots and maintenance personnel.[6]

Of course, he may have been telling the victors exactly what they wanted to hear, but his testimony rings true and is repeated by other veterans.

There was little sign of any waning of Rabaul's air strength on 2 November 1943. On that day the Allies got a bloody nose. The previous day had seen 1 *Kōkū Sentai* fly in a large number of A6M *Kōsen* from the carriers *Shōkakū*, *Zuikaku* and *Zuihō* to reinforce Rabaul. These struck at targets in the Bougainville area, and, after refuelling and rearming, they were available to meet a strong attack mounted by the 5 Air Force from New Guinea who sent 150 aircraft, B-25s escorted by P-38s against Rabaul. Some fifty-eight A6M *Kōsen* plus fifty-seven land-based fighters from 201, 204 and 253 *Kōkōtai* scrambled away and took the attackers head-on. The Americans lost nine B-25s and ten P-38s in the ensuring ensuing melee but eighteen A6Ms were destroyed from various causes.

Despite such pyrrhic victories, gradually and inexorably the Allied moved forward both up the Solomon chain and in New Guinea, and the noose tightened around Rabaul. Buin advance base was finally overwhelmed by constant air attacks, 204 *Kōkūtai* had been pulled back to Rabaul on 8 October and 201 itself was destroyed on 22 October by an air attack that destroyed eight A6Ms on the ground, while of those that got aloft to combat the enemy, three were lost and three more had to force land. The surviving nine, under Lieutenant (j.g.) Yoshio Ōba were then moved to Buka, where they found no respite, then back to Rabaul itself. With the death of Ōba on 23 December what little remained of the unit, thirty pilots, was pulled back to Saipan to be re-equipped. Commander Chujirō Nakano assembled twenty-three new A6Ms at Yokosuka and an advanced echelon under Warrant Officer Masao Taniguchi with eight of these moved down to Truk on the way to Rabaul, where they were almost immediately destroyed by the American carrier raid of the 17th, as were the four remaining aircraft at Saipan on the 23rd. Lieutenant Shirō Kawai led the remaining fighters to Truk but none ever reached Rabaul.

At the end of 1943 the main mount was the A6M3, both Model 22s nearing obsolescence, and some short-range Model 32s. In November 1943 the *Zuikaku* flew in to Tobera fifteen of the new A6M5s to join 204 *Kōkūtai*, with a now rare surviving China veteran, Lieutenant Tetsuzō Iwamoto, among the pilots, fresh from a six-month hitch at Paramushir Island in the Kuriles. Also operating for a three-week stint in which they lost 50 per cent of their strength was 652 *Kōkūtai* under Captain Kōji Shiroshima. They operated almost daily until withdrawn to Truk at the end of February.

For the Japanese the whole campaign was a wearing meat-grinder.[7] By September 1943 11 *Kōkū-kantai* had dwindled to around three hundred aircraft on strength, with the A6Ms of 201, 204 and 253 *Kōkūtai* having nominal strengths of fifty aircraft. Replacement fighters were fed into Rabaul at the rate of about forty machines a month and combat-exhausted pilots were similarly rotated. The *Rengō Kantai* (Combined Fleet) at Truk, as we have seen, also contributed by landing its carrier-based A6Ms ashore for specific operations from time to time. However, the standard of aircraft, maintenance and aircrew had all sharply deteriorated from August 1942. The A6M was scheduled for maintenance after 150 hours of air-flight, but in forward areas with limited facilities, this often had to be stretched to 200. Commander Takashi Miyazaki, who had commanded 4 Air Squadron at Rabaul from September 1942 to March 1943, and then became a Staff Officer of the 25 *Kōkū Sentai* from March 1943 to November 1944, stated later that:

In the beginning of the war, during 1942, if 100% of the planes were available for an attack one day, the next day 80% would be available, on the third day 50%. In 1943, at any one time, only 50% of the planes were ever available, and on the next day following an all-out operation only 30% would be available. By the end of 1943, only 40% at any one time would be serviceable. In 1942, the low availability was due to lack of supply; from 1943 on, it was due to lack of skill on the part of maintenance personnel and faulty manufacturing methods. Inspection of the aircraft and spare parts, prior to their delivery to Rabaul, was inadequate, and there were many poorly constructed and weak parts discovered. The Japanese tried to increase production so fast that proper examination was impossible.[8]

The November 1943 *Ro-Go* operation directed against the American landings at Bougainville was but a repeat performance, in terms of achievement, of the *I-Go* operation of the year before. Strong air attacks were launched on the 1st, 5th, 8th, 11th, 13th and 17th of the month and two hundred enemy aircraft were claimed destroyed. However, this great effort totally affected the outcome and Ozawa's 1 *Kōkū-sentai* (1 Carrier Division) lost 70 per cent of the 173 carrier-based aircraft it had committed along with 44 per cent of their aircrews, thus negating the painstaking rebuilding that had taken place. Among the heavy losses incurred were forty-three A6Ms from the eighty-two committed to battle.

In the end the Allies felt no compulsion to invade and capture Rabaul, instead it was left to wither on the vine and was was gradually run down.[9]

More captured Zeros

In January 1943 the Australians in New Guinea captured the airstrip at Buna and among the abandoned Japanese aircraft found relatively intact was an A6M3-32 with the characteristic clipped-wings that had led it to be mistaken for an entirely new fighter, which was duly codenamed 'Hap' and then 'Hamp'. Taken back to Hangar 7, Eagle Farm, this machine was flight tested on 20 July 1943 by Captain William Farrior after a captured Japanese pilot had been interrogated thoroughly on the instruments and controls. Farrior conducted a thirty-minute evaluation and further comparative tests were conducted against British and American fighter types in mock fighter duels. On the following day two more flight tests were carried out, but the programme was brought to an abrupt halt when while performing a slow roll the engine cut out due to an apparent carburettor blockage and the pilot was forced to force-land, during which the brakes grabbed and the aircraft ground-looped causing considerable damage.

The ATIU subsequently put together a flyable Zero from the parts of five different machines, also recovered from Buna. This composite machine was combat-tested in the same manner against a Spitfire V. The evaluation was that at altitudes below 20,000ft even this cobbled up machine outclassed the British fighter. The aircraft was later loaded aboard the escort carrier *Copahee* (CVE-12) for transport to the States, with the ultimate destination of Wright Field and further testing. As it was not a 'proper' Zero it is not known what value such testing had.

Chapter 11

Last Shout for the Little Warrior

T he new generation of Allied fighter aircraft was bigger, faster, more rugged, better armed and, more importantly, produced in awesome quantities. Skill and expertise were steadily and inevitably being ground down by sheer mass and that was a particularly American phenomenon.[1] Even so, on occasions the A6M was able to remind the ascendant Allies that she was not yet to be despised.

Zero versus Spitfire

The British equivalent of the A6M was the Supermarine Spitfire, whose fame during the Battle of Britain gave her an equal aura of invincibility in the air, although of course she was more of a 'point defence' fighter with very limited range. That invincibility had been severely dented over Dieppe by the German Focke-Wulf Fw190, but the legend persisted for a long while. In terms of manoeuvrability, climb rate and roll, it should have been on a par with the A6M. It was not a thug and did not rely on pure power and bulk like the Chance Vought F4UF or the Grumman F6F Hellcat; it was as refined and pure as the A6M, equalled it in armament, plus it had pilot protection. Comparative loaded weights were 5,313lb (2,410kg) for the A6M2 against 6,622lb (3,003kg) for the Spitfire. There are frequent references to the A6M fighting the British Supermarine Spitfire, both in Burma and over Ceylon in 1942, but these are pure fiction. The real clash between these two thoroughbreds did not take place until 1943, when, frustrated at the lack of Allied success in stopping the A6M, No. 1 (Fighter) Wing of Spitfire Vs was sent out to Australia. The unit comprised three squadrons, No. 54 (RAF), No. 452 (RAAF) and No. 475 (RAAF) equipped with the 'tropicalized' Spitfire Vc , fitted with sand filters for desert operations.[2] Led by famous Australian ace Wing Commander Clive 'Killer' Caldwell, RAAF,[3] it contained fourteen fully combat experienced pilots who had good records against the Luftwaffe in the Mediterranean among them four or five aces, and it was hoped it would to stop the rot. On arrival American veterans tried in vain to warn them what they were up against. James Morehead, who had mixed it with the A6M while flying P-40s and survived the experience, remembered advising the Spitfire boys, 'Don't think that because you could turn inside a German fighter that you could do the same with a Zero.'[4]

As we have seen the 3 *Kōkutai*, now the 202 *Kentai*, based at Kendari under Lieutenant-Commander Minoru Suzuki, after previously being fully engaged in the Solomons Campaign, began preparations in intensive training for long-range trans-ocean navigation and bomber escort missions in readiness for offensive operations to pre-empt Allied efforts over northern Australia. After some brief skirmishes during which few losses were incurred, the eagerly sought clash came on 2 May.

That morning twenty-seven A6Ms lifted off from Kupang, escorting twenty-five Type 1 land attack planes of 753 *Kōkutai* (the former *Takao* group), which had staged in from Kendari to make the wearying 500-mile hop to Darwin. The weather over the area was fine, with light winds and the Japanese bomber force approached at an altitude of 27,000ft (8,229.6m). The Australians were late in getting airborne, due to the usual radar problems encountered in this area and due to the same atmospheric conditions that constantly plagued Merlin engines on the ground, and had to climb up hard to reach their foe. At such altitudes it was found that the Spitfire's Merlin engine fell off sharply in performance. The A6Ms had the advantages of height and, agility. Nonetheless, in the fighting that followed the thirty-three Spitfires made a claim that they had destroyed four 'Type O' carrier fighters, No. 457 Squadron, which had three European veterans with twelve combat operations to their name, alone recording one definite and two probable kills, losing two Spitfire in return. But this was largely hot air for, according to one reliable source, the Japanese suffered no losses whatsoever, 'All of our aircraft, including land attack planes and Zero fighters, returned safely.' This one-sided result the Japanese attributed to various reasons, including the fact that the A6Ms had a high number of combat veterans, that they were fully rested and trained, and that the Australian pilots '… tended to prefer dogfights, at a time when the very same tactic was most favoured by the more experienced Zero fighter pilots'.[5] The Americans tended to agree with this analysis. Claire Chennault concluded, 'It was simply a matter of tactics. The RAF pilots were trained in methods that were excellent against German and Italian equipment but suicide against the acrobatic Japs.'[6] Even before the battle American Marine flyers with experience over Guadalcanal had lectured the Spitfire pilots that, although they had great expertise in Europe, to engage in close-in turning duels with the A6M was the height of folly. While this advice was taken on board superficially, it does not appear to have been heeded in practice in the heat of combat where the old habits automatically re-asserted themselves.

What is *absolutely* certain is that the Australians were forced to admit the loss of fourteen Spitfires. Eight years of research by one historian in which he interviewed Japanese survivors and accessed records not consulted before, concluded that this was indeed a defeat for the Spitfire and the figures appear to bear that out, despite immediate post-war Australian and British books that claimed the opposite.[7]

In mitigation the following breakdown was given on how this disastrous rate of exchange was brought about and it was determined that five Spitfires were lost to enemy action, four more were lost due to engine failures and malfunction of the propeller constant speed unit (CSU failure) and the destruction of a further five was said to be fuel starvation; there were both internal and external glycol leakage. However, what, in effect was really happening at this period was that the Japanese, many thousands of miles from their home islands, were able to maintain their A6Ms at a comparatively unsophisticated distant air base to such a high degree that they could fly 500 miles, defeat the enemy in aerial combat and fly 500 miles back again; whereas the Australians, even on their own home soil, could not maintain the short-range Spitfires sufficiently for them to operate a relatively simply home defence role effectively. The resilience of Rabaul for example, was substantiated by a modern historian, who recorded:

Rabaul was cut off in early 1944 but not captured by the Australians until after Japan's surrender. The Australians were startled to find how well organized the base remained and how healthy the garrison seemed. Mechanics at Rabaul were even capable of resurrecting a few aircraft from the scrap heap and wage a small guerrilla air war against advanced Allied bases.[8]

The Japanese raids continued until September when events to the northward saw them concentrate more on that area and aerial combat petered out. Only three A6Ms were lost over the Darwin region in that entire period while up to thirty-two Spitfires were written off in the same time-span.

Battle of the Philippine Sea

Despite the steady attrition of their carrier and surface fleet between the Midway battle and through the debilitating Solomon Islands campaign, the Japanese Navy, at first under Yamamoto, then sequentially under Admirals Mineichi Koga and Soemu Toyoda, still based their hopes and plans for the climatic final all-out naval battle, *Kantai Kessen*, that same old obsession. They were determined to bring such a battle forward in 1944, but their dithering in 1943 when they still had the edge, had long gone by the spring of 1944, for the colossal American aircraft production and shipbuilding programmers had been given vital time to build a fleet without comparison in size and power, far outmatching anything the Japanese had left to offer. Nonetheless the die was cast because any further delay would only increase the already formidable gap between the two sides. The Red Line became the Caroline and Palau Island groups, but the Americans achieved surprise by actually attacking further north, in the Mariana Islands (principally Guam, Saipan and Tinian) for which the Japanese were unprepared and on 14 June they invaded Saipan itself.

For Operation *A-Go* the Mobile Fleet under Vice-Admiral Jisaburo Ōzawa *1 Dai ichi Kōkū Sentai* (1 *Kōkū-sentai*) comprised the *Taiho*, with twenty-six A6M5s embarked led by Lieutenant Toshitada Kawazoe, along with twenty-three Yokosuka D4Y *Suisei* dive-bombers, seventeen Nakajima B6N *Tenzan* attack planes and two D3As; *Shōkakū* and *Zuikaku*, each with twenty-seven A6Ms under Lieutenant Yasuo Masuyama, which had completed training at Batu Pahat and Seletar in the Singapore area with the new Type 52 fighters and then at Lingua and Tawi Tawi south-west of Mindanao; twenty-four D4Ys, seventeen B6Ns and two D3As as 601 *Kōkūtai* under the command of

Commander Toshiiye Irisa.[9] They were accompanied by two heavy and one light cruiser and seven destroyers. *Dai ni Kōkū Sentai* (2 *Kōkū-sentai*) under Rear-Admiral Takatsugo Jōjima consisted of the *Jūnyō*, with twenty-seven A6M5s aboard commanded by Lieutenant Hiroshi Yoshimura, along with six B6Ns and eighteen D3As; *Hiyō* who fielded twenty-six A6M5s under Lieutenant Hōhei Kobayashi, six B6Ns and eighteen D3As; and *Ryuho*, with twenty-seven A6M5s under Lieutenant Saneyasu Hidaka, six B6Ns, all of 652 *Kōkūtai* led by Commander Shōichi Suzuki. Previous deployment at Rabaul from January 1944 had already seen half its strength lost in just three weeks before the survivors pulled back to Truk. Replacement pilots received just two months' training back at Iwakuni, Oita and Saeki before joining the re-built unit and this force was thus the weakest of the three. Seven out of ten pilots had only graduated in 1943/44. The bankruptcy of Japanese policy was revealed by the fact that, in order to give these immature tyros some stiffening in combat, training schools were depleted of their invaluable instructors, who were sent to the carriers and committed to battle, thus further disrupting the build-up of any meaningful aviation reserve for the needs of the moment. It was a self-inflicted downward cycle with only one end possible.

Surface escorts were one battleship, one heavy cruiser and seven destroyers. The Mobile Force vanguard ('C' Force) with *dai San Koku Sentai* (3 *Kōkū-sentai*) under Rear-Admiral Sueo Ōbayashi, consisted of the *Chitose*, *Chiyoda* and *Zuiho* each of which shared the sixty-three A6M5bs, forty-five of which were equipped as *bakusō* (fighter-bombers), as well as twenty-seven B6N and B5Ns of 653 *Kōkūtai* under Commander Gunji Kimura, with the fighters under Lieutenant Kenji Nakagawa. They were in company with four battleships, eight heavy cruisers, a light cruiser and seven destroyers. There was also an Oiler Group of six tankers with six destroyers.

Ashore under the command of Vice-Admiral Kakuji Kakuta, Base Air Commander Marianas, with his HQ on Tinian Island, just south of Saipan in the Northern Mariana Islands were approximately three hundred additional aircraft. The Japanese, with nine carriers and 750 aircraft on hand, felt supremely confident of victory. However, the American fleet (Task Force 58) under the very experienced Admiral Raymond A. Spruance, with Admiral Marc A. Mitscher controlling the carrier operations, heavily outnumbered the Japanese in every category. The Americans had seven fleet and eight light fleet carriers on hand and these fifteen carriers outnumbered the Japanese by almost two-to-one. Moreover each American carrier embarked many more aircraft, and the US ships between them could field no fewer than 956 aircraft. The Americans also had seven battleships against the five Japanese battleships, twenty-one cruisers against a Japanese total of nineteen of that type, and fifty-eight destroyers against twenty-seven Japanese ships. The surface ships never came to blows but the Americans cleverly positioned their main battleship force, with its enormous anti-aircraft fire power[10] ahead of the carrier groups thus presenting a killing ground through which the Japanese had to fly to reach their main targets. Again, the Japanese plan had high hopes that Kakuta's shore-based aircraft would combine with their carriers in combined strikes, which would inflict telling losses on the American fleet, with the knowledge that Japanese warplane inevitably out-ranged their American counterparts to give a further edge.

However, Spruance pre-empted all such hopes with early and continuous air strikes on the island air bases, which decimated Kakuta's aircraft before the Japanese could fully engage with their fleet, leaving the actual battle ratio of forces even more askew. Finally, the standard of training for the air crews that made up the bulk of the Japanese carrier units was of a very low order. Although the bulk of the remaining veteran pilots and aircrew featured in this last classic carrier-to-carrier battle, their numbers were leavened out by hundreds of fresh-faced novices. Two years was the accepted time it took to train new pilots up for carrier operations, but the relentless need to replace the heavy losses of veteran flyers from mid-1942 onward, plus increasing fuel problems, meant that this level of expertise had long since been abandoned by the IJN.

Between 11 and 13 June 1944 Mitscher's airmen conducted a series of powerful strikes against Japanese airfields on Guam and Rota, and practically eliminated the carefully husbanded air strength that was intended to work closely with the fleet. Rather than sit and be totally wiped out on the ground the surviving aircraft were committed while they could still be used, but inflicted little or no damage on the Americans and expended their final strength.

First sighting of the American fleet was made by an A6M5, one of fifty Guam-based aircraft, at 0550 on the 20th and, after sending his sighting report, he made an attack run against a destroyer but was shot down. Follow-up attacks were being readied at Orote airfield, Guam when a force of thirty F6Fs arrived overhead and in the resulting one-sided battle thirty-plus Japanese aircraft were destroyed but only a single F6F fell. These fighters were recalled to protect the fleet when the first Japanese carrier strikes began to be detected by radar at 0957. The 653 *Kōkūtai* flew off forty-five A6M5bs, fourteen A6M5s and eight B6N *Tenzans* led by Lieutenant Nakagawa. Later Ozawa sent in the more experienced 601 *Kōkūkai* flyers, with forty-eight A6Ms, fifty-three D3A2 dive-bombers and twenty-seven B6Ns.

Unfortunately this powerful force had to pass over the Japanese 2 Fleet, which was positioned one hundred miles in advance, on its way to the target and it was mistakenly caught in an intense friendly-fire AA barrage that broke up its pattern. While attempting to regain its cohesion in readiness to attack it became split into groups. These aircraft were caught by fully alerted American fighter defences some seventy miles (110km) out while the still disorientated airmen were re-assembling. The American fighters got in among these disorganized groups and quickly dispatched forty of them, again for the loss of just one F6F. The surviving Japanese aircraft attacked the destroyers *Stockham* and *Yarnall* of Admiral Lee's battleship force without success and a few penetrated to score one hit on the *South Dakota*, but none got past the battleships, and Mitscher's carriers remained unmolested.

The second group comprised 107 aircraft and was picked up at 1107. Again interception was made by masses of F6Fs about 60 miles (97km) out and the bulk was destroyed in fierce air fighting. 653 *Kōkūtai* lost thirty-two A6M5bs, eight A6M5 fighters and two of the B6Ns. About six broke through to attack the carriers, scoring hits on two of them, but only ten Japanese aircraft survived. In total the Japanese suffered the loss of thirty-two A6Ms, forty-one D3As and twenty-three D6Ns, 96 planes in total. Among the casualties were several fighter leaders, Lieutenant Toshitada Kawazoe of 1 *Daitai*, Lieutenant Ikurō Sakami of 2 *Daitai* and Lieutenant Fumio Yamagata of 3 *Daitai*. 652 *Kōkūtai* had launched fifteen A6Ms, twenty-five A6M5bs and seven B6Ns but they had become split up due to the weather and inexperience during the 350-mile flight, and lost two of the fighters, four *bakusō* and one B6N to no avail. A second strike was sent out two-and-a-half hours later, with six A6Ms and nine *Suisei* dive-bombers, to attack US carriers, losing one fighter and five dive-bombers but failing to score any hits.

Another group came in at 1300, consisting of just forty-seven aircraft, which was met by an almost equal number of American fighters 50 miles (80km) out from the ships. With the loss of seven of their number they attacked but also failed to score any hits whatsoever. A fourth wave from 601 *Kōkūtai* consisting of four A6Ms, ten D3As and four B6Ns was scraped together by 601, but was misdirected by the shadowing aircraft and after hunting diligently without success ran low on fuel and steered for Guam and Rota where they hoped to replenish. While *en route* thither they tangled with US fighters who destroyed nine of eighteen and the surviving D3As made dive-bombing attacks on the carriers *Bunker Hill* and *Wasp (II)* without success losing all but one of their number in the process. Another group of Vals were caught circling and preparing to land at Orote by twenty-seven F6Fs and were wiped out, every D3A being either shot down or write-offs.[11] The 653 *Kōkūtai* carriers had prepared a second striking force of five A6Ms, nine A6M5bs and five B6Ns, but their take-off was delayed by returning aircraft and although some got away this strike was finally cancelled. It had truly been a massacre with the Japanese losing over 350 aircraft for the loss of just a tenth of that number. The battle duly received the famous epithet of 'The Great Marianas Turkey Shoot' and effectively marked the end of the Imperial Navy's carrier force as a viable unit.

The seal of this overwhelming day of defeat was set by American submarines, one of which put one torpedo into the *Taihō*, which burst two of her aviation fuel tanks. She continued operating but her inexperienced crew brought about her demise by attempting to flush the dangerously explosive fumes from the ship but only succeeding in spreading them until they were finally ignited by an electric generator. She was torn apart by a series of massive explosions and sank with the bulk of her crew. Meanwhile, another submarine had hit the *Shōkaku* with three torpedoes and she quickly suffered the same fate as the *Taihō* with the same heavy casualties, including 376 officers and men from 601 *Kōkūtai*.

Despite his appalling losses Ozawa determined to resume the battle the next day with the 150 or so aircraft remaining to him in the fatally mistaken belief that Kakuta's air strength in the islands was still largely intact. The 653 *Kōkūtai* launched four A6Ms, ten A6M5bs and two B6Ns late in the day but incoming air attacks aborted their mission to counter-attack and claimed twenty enemies destroyed. By the end of the day this unit was reduced to just two A6M5s, three A6M5bs and six *Tenzans*.

On the 21st the Japanese had not been sighted by the American search planes until late in the day, and at extreme range and a heavy strike of more than 230 American aircraft did not arrive overhead until dusk. Some thirty-five A6Ms, including eight from 601 *Kōkūtai* under Ensign Yoshio Fukui, were aloft to defend the remaining carriers and claimed fifteen enemy aircraft destroyed, but they proved insufficient to stop the US aviators scoring more successes. Even so the small force of A6Ms had performed well against the F6Fs despite the odds being all against them. One American SB2C dive-bomber group expended its fury on the oiler force instead of the Japanese carriers, damaging two of them, which had to be scuttled later, but the rest held on for the main target. 652 *Kōkūtai* sent aloft nineteen A6Ms and seven A6M5bs as part of the CAP, claiming two F6Fs and nine TBFs destroyed, but eleven of this force were lost and three more had to ditch. This left 652 with just eleven A6Ms, five A5M5bs and one *Tenzan*. The *Hiyō* took several heavy bomb hits and four torpedoes, and again blew up after aviation fuel fires and sank. The *Chiyoda*, *Junyō* and *Zuikaku* and battleship *Haruna* also received damaging hits but all survived and reached port while the American lost twenty aircraft in the battle.

Due to the long range at which the attack had been launched the returning US aircraft, guided in by searchlights, lost a further eighty aircraft, which were forced to ditch due to lack of fuel. Ozawa withdrew his battered fleet the same night and Spruance, who decided his priority all along was the defence of the invasion forces at Saipan, was by then too far away to bring him to further battle. Ozawa had lost 430+ carrier planes and 200 land-based aircraft as well as three carriers. The latter losses were irrelevant for the Japanese only had enough aircraft remaining to fill one small carrier anyway. The 601 *Kōkūtai*, for example, only had four A6Ms, two D3A2s and one B6N on strength at this time. The Americans lost around 125 aircraft, mostly to lack of fuel.[12]

Operation *Shō-gō* (Battle of Leyte Gulf)

Sunset of the carrier fleet – Cape Engāno. 25–26 October 1944

At the massive sea/air battle of Leyte Gulf the once proud Japanese carrier fleet was reduced to the status of 'live bait' due to the appalling aircraft losses it had taken during the Philippine Sea encounter. Admiral Jisaburo Ozawa's Northern Force sortied out with his one operational fleet carrier, *Zuikaku*, as his flagship, accompanied by the three light carriers *Zuihō*, *Chiyoda* and *Chitose*. Having been totally destroyed 601 *Kōkūtai* had to be re-built from scratch between July and October and 3 *Kōkū-sentai* no longer existed and they became 1 Division.[13] 601 was re-established from scratch under 3 Fleet, mainly with pilots straight from training units and even so had a strength of only two *Hikōtai*, 161 under Lieutenant Hōhei Kobayashi, and 162 led by Lieutenant Sanyuki Hida, each with forty-eight A6M5s. With a few dive- and attack-bombers Ozawa had embarked aboard the four Japanese carriers a total of just 108 aircraft.

Two old battleships, *Hyūga* and *Ise*, were added to his force as 4 *Kōkū-sentai*. They had both been partly converted as intended hybrids, keeping many of their main guns but able to carry a limited number of aircraft. However, after many attempts to organize an agreed ratio of suitable types, no aircraft actually proved available and they sailed into battle with none aboard.[14] They were escorted by three light cruisers and nine destroyers. Ozawa was not found until late on the afternoon of 24 October.

Halsey duly swallowed the bait and set off after the Northern Force with overwhelming fire power, having five fleet carriers, five light carriers, six battleships, two heavy and six light cruisers and destroyers. In the American carriers no fewer than 600–1,000 were embarked.

Early on the 25th Halsey sent Vice-Admiral Willis A. Lee's six modern battleships of Task Force 34 on ahead at high speed, with the aim of being positioned to finish off with their seventy-two 16-inch guns any of Ozawa's ships that survived the coming days air strikes. Ozawa made his air attack at dawn that day, launching fifty-six aircraft, which comprised thirty A6M5s, nineteen A6M5bs, two *Suisei* dive-bombers and five B6Ns *Tenzans*.

Nearly all were overwhelmed by the CAP and ships gunfire with just a few surviving to land at airfields on Luzon, including six of the A6Ms, five attack and one dive-bomber. They had inflicted no damage on Halsey's ships.

Mitscher's counter-strike was rather more effective, his 180-strong force crushing the Japanese thirteen-plane CAP under Lieutenant Kobayashi with ease, although the A6Ms claimed twelve kills. Some 527 American sorties were conducted that day and the carriers *Zuihō* and *Zuikaku*, along with a light cruiser were all sunk.[15]

While these air strikes were being exchanged the beleaguered Admiral Kinkaid's 7th Fleet was continually calling for assistance having being in danger of being overwhelmed by the powerful surface forces of Admiral Nishimura in the Surigao Strait. Halsey recalled Lee's battleships, which were just about to sink the crippled carriers, and after refuelling them, sent them south in two sections, but they were again, too late and Kurita escaped. This left Halsey's carriers with no heavy ships to protect them and when the Japanese sent their two battleships south another crisis seemed imminent but no contact was made here either and the battle petered out on the 26th by which time Ozawa's carrier force was all but destroyed by further air attacks but not before the carrier *Chitose* was sunk with all hands and the destroyer *Hatsuzuki*, which had earlier rescued Lieutenant Kobayashi and some of his other ditched fighter pilots, had also been sent to the bottom by shelling, both by Rear-Admiral Lawrence T. DuBose's cruiser squadron led by the *Santa Fe*. None of the rescued pilots survived.

Zero versus Hellcat

In examining the factors involved in aerial combat, on paper at least, the Grumman F6F was superior to the A6M in acceleration, climb, dive, roll rate, top speed, hit damage survivability, and engine power. The Japanese fighter, with her low wing loading × lift coefficient, retained her edge on slow speed turning (via her smaller turning circle and higher turning rate), and visibility and could outperform the Hellcat in climb rate and manoeuvrability, while the improved 20mm cannon of the later Zero models packed a more powerful punch and had greater range than the F6F .50 Browning machine-guns. Given the reputation of the A6M the general tactic adopted by the American pilots was to gain superior altitude, dive down – fire and then zoom away and climb again. However, that required the twin advantages of surprise and height to be successful. If the surprise part of the factor was lost, then the height factor rapidly went also for the A6M could climb at a rate of 3,050ft/min (929.63m/min), outperforming both the US Army Curtis P-40 and the Navy's F4F. In a close turning duel at low altitude it was still suicidal to tangle with the A6M, although, as the quality of the Japanese pilots began to be seriously diluted, the danger was less and the American fighters were able to sustain heavier hitting.

But that was on *paper*. Saburo Sakai used his six years of front-line combat savvy and skill to out-fight no fewer than fifteen F6F Hellcats in his A6M even though he was blinded in one eye and exhausted. The standard of the A6M pilots certainly and undisputedly fell sharply as the war continued, but the rookie American pilots coming out of much longer training schedules, during which they had been carefully trained to conduct aerial deflection shooting, were hardly supermen either and had the advantage of hugely numerical superiority as well. Despite that, on 24 June 1945, Sakai, having already shot down two F6Fs already, took on the whole fifteen and routed them totally, causing some to flee and totally out-flying the others before landing back on Iwo Jima without a mark on his aircraft. In the end, no matter how good the aircraft, it was often the man who counted.[16]

By 1943 the war in the Pacific was fast slipping away from Japan. The massive ship-building programme of the United States Navy dwarfed the Imperial Japanese Navy and its own new construction. The new classes of *Essex* Class carriers and *Independence* Class light carriers were now finally joining the fleet and were being joined by hordes of brand-new battleships, cruisers and destroyers and this new build fleet easily replaced any losses that the Japanese could hope to inflict. Matching the new ships was a similar enormous output of military aircraft from newly constructed plants all over the USA entirely free of any threat of bombing or retaliation. A huge pilot training programme matched the tens of thousands of aircraft and, with regard to fighter types, the overwhelming numbers churned out were also new types, many of which obviously much outclassed the hitherto dominant A6M. The Grumman F6F Hellcat and the Chance-Vought F4U Corsair were both large and powerful new Navy and Marine Corps heavy fighters of high-speeds. The A6M weighed 5,500lb, the F4F 7,500lb, the F6F an astonishing 12,000lb.[17]

In addition converted General Motors East Coast automobile plants, as Eastern Aircraft Division, were building updated and improved versions of the F4F Wildcat as the new General Motors FM-1 of which more than a thousand were produced in 1942–43. These were pretty much straight copies of the F4F-4s, with reduced gun armament of four .50 calibre machine-guns. These were clearly inferior but were mainly employed on second-line duties with small escort-carriers (CVE or 'jeep' carriers) used by the US and Royal Navies in both the Atlantic and Pacific. More challenging to the A6M was the new Grumman XF4F-8, of which Eastern Aircraft built no fewer than 4,000 of under the designation FM-2. This aircraft featured the 1,350hp Wright R-1820-56 Cyclone single-row radial engine, and this power upgrade was coupled with a re-designed and much lightened build overall, 8,271lb, and a re-working of the vertical tail to increase stability. The result was a faster (332mph at 28,800ft) and more agile Wildcat taking on some of the attributes of its main opponent including improved range, speedier climb rate, longer range and being far more agile than the old F4F. The armament was unchanged but the extra range was superfluous however, as again they were operated from CVEs as close-in fighter support for the island-hopping campaign's many landing operations but, as such, they often came up against the improved A6M.

A6M5 Model 52

By the summer of 1943 the Americans in the Pacific were introducing several new fighter types that would eventually simply overwhelm the Japanese, producing huge, rugged machines with 2,000hp+ engines and heavy gun armaments, such as the Grumman F4F Hellcat, Chance-Vought F4U Corsair and Lockheed P-38 Lightning, which were churned out by the tens of thousands from factories totally immune from attack. In a futile attempt to match these new American fighters and also to speed their own production, which was lagging far behind demand due to casualties, the A6M was subjected to a range of improvements and modifications and in the summer of 1943 appeared in a new guise on the combat zone. This was the A6M5 Model 52, which was destined to be the most prolific of all Zero marks. The wings were of the shorter 36ft 2in (11 metre) span, with the clipped wings abandoned and rounded tips re-adopted. The ailerons were lengthened out to the tips of the wings and the flaps were also elongated accordingly to obviate any space in between. In order to improve the known weakness of its poor dive qualities the wings were thickened up with heavier gauge material and this resulted in a 410mph (659.83km/h) diving speed, while overall maximum speed was increased to 351mph (564.88km/h) in level flight by introducing individual exhausts, which protruded aft from notched flaps in the engine cowling (five to port, six to starboard, each vent requiring its own individual fuselage heat shield patch), instead of a single centralized exhaust collector ring.[18] The range of the Type 22 having proved key, the two 12-gallon (45.42 litres) wing tanks were retained in this model giving a range of 1,194 miles (1,921.6km). The power unit remained the 1,130hp *Sakae*-21 and armament reverted to two 20mm cannon and two 7.7mm machine-guns. Production problems at home had seen the introduction of large, tail-finned 66-gallon (300-litre) wooden drop tanks replacing the original under-belly type and the introduction of 33-gallon (150-litre) under-wing drop tanks. The Type 3 Mark 1 radio was installed to replace the Type 98*Ku* Mark 1 set and the new installation could be detected by a much shorter antenna mast, but the reputation for unreliability apparently continued, the main problem being the unshielded ignition systems, exacerbated by the effect of humid tropical conditions as well as hindered by the difficulty of access for proper maintenance in the field on jungle airstrips. There was also a persistent shortage of copper for the wiring and it was not until 1945 that the Second Research Institute was established to improve electronics in the fleet's aircraft.[19] Some land-based units were reputed to have discarded their radios completely, although, of course, they were a vital necessity for carrier-based A6Ms who did *not* abandon them as some have claimed.[20]

A prototype was converted from a Model 22 machine and made its debut in August 1943 achieving a maximum speed of 351.07mph (565km/h). This seemed to satisfy the Navy but this aircraft proved to be less agile than the Model 21, while the endurance was far inferior, three hours against eight. If it were expected that this would render the concept null-and-void this proved not to be the case and production was immediately ordered as the urgent need from the front predominated over any reservations. Although problems were encountered with the new engine exhaust venting design, which meant early models had to go to war without them, Mitsubishi eventually produced a total of 747 in the numerical range #3904 to #4650. These were rushed into service due to the worsening situation.

A further adaptation of the A6M5 was the Model 52 *KO* (a). The 20mm 100-round drum-fed cannon were upgraded to the Model 2-4, which was belt-fed, each carrying 125 rounds. Further thickening of the wing construction pushed the dive speed up still further, to around 460mph (740.3km/h). Mitsubishi produced 391 of this sub-type but they did not begin to enter front-line service until March 1944. They still lacked armour protection however, but the need to get them into battle quickly dominated. To address this latter problem another variant, the Model 52 *OTSU* (b) appeared in April 1944. The pilot was given a measure of protection with the introduction of an armoured glass plate almost 2 inches (45mm) thick. To try and solve the notorious tendency of the A6M to burn easily the internal main fuel tank was fitted with a CO_2 fire-extinguishing system. These defensive measures were matched by an increase in offensive power and range. The 7.7mm machine-gun mounted in the starboard wing was deleted and a more powerful 13-mm Type 3 machine gun was substituted. This weapon was a licence-built version of the German *Rheinmetall-Borsig Maschinengewer* MG-131 weapon, and weighed 37lb (17kg). It had a rate of fire of 900 rpm, was belt-fed and was of the percussion-ignition variant, which the IJN apparently considered more suitable for Pacific climate conditions. This enabled a smoothing of the wing under-surface and required an addition fairing where the cannon protruded from the leading edge of the wing. Ammunition access points were also modified. A number of *OTSU* aircraft also had provision for a pair of 33-gallon (150-litre) under-wing drop tanks. Both Mitsubishi and Nakajima production runs involved the *OTSU*, 470 being built by the former but no figures seem to be available for the latter plants output.

Subsequently further changes along these lines were progressively introduced to the A6M5, which resulted in the Model 51 *HEI* (c). The pilot was finally given protection on the scale that Allied flyers had long been used to as standard by the insertion of a sheet of one-third of an inch (8mm) thick armoured plate to the rear of his seat, with over 2 inches (55mm) of armoured glass sheet emplaced to protect his head from above. This added considerable weight but there was more for to further increase internal fuel stowage a 37-gallon (140-litre) fuel tank was inserted directly astern of the pilot, and this tank was made self-sealing. The armament was subject to further drastic revision. The type 13mm machine-gun, with 240rpg, was now fitted to *both* wings, beyond the wing-mounted cannon; the 7.7mm machine-gun mounted in the nose was eliminated while the 13mm fuselage-mounted weapon remained. Some of this sub-type later had their under-wing hard-points for 30–60kg (66–132lb) air-to-air bombs replaced by an air-to-air rocket carrier. Wooden drop-tanks with stabilizer fins and four-point support became the norm. These aircraft began to enter front-line service in November 1944.

Night-fighters (*Heisen*)

Despite the continuing western article of faith that the Japanese avoided night-fighting (Savo Island and other examples to the contrary notwithstanding) night fighter (*Heisen*) adaptations were in use both in the south-west Pacific and later in the defence of the home islands. One early attempt to use the A6M in this capacity had been made by the 4 *Kōkūtai*, which was established on 10 February 1942 at Truk under the command of Captain Gashi Moritama with twenty-seven Type 96 fighters and moved into Vunakanau airfield at Rabaul shortly afterward. American bombers were subjecting this area to nuisance night bombings with some frequency at this time. Three A6Ms arrived on 28 January and attempts were made at interceptions in conjunction with the bases searchlights, but this embryo effort proved futile.

It was not until of the advent of A6M5s properly equipped for night work that real progress was made. The selected Zeros were converted to this mission type by adding a fixed, angled Type 99 Mark 2 Model 4 20mm cannon firing obliquely upward and forward from the rear of the cockpit over the pilots head. This required a modification of the panelling of the after greenhouse, which was plated over astern for strength from the recoil. An additional Type 3 Sight was emplaced on top of the forward windshield frame.

Another 'in-the-field' adaptation was the fitting of some A6M5, A6M5a and A6M5bs with a fixed Type 99-2 Model 4 20mm cannon mounted in the aircraft fuselage behind the pilot. This weapon was angled to fire 30° forward and 30° to port when first installed. Later variations had an oblique firing angle of 10° to port and in both cases the barrel of the gun barrel pierced the aircraft's fuselage. Another modification resulted in the same cannon being recessed into the cockpit canopy rather than the fuselage itself. All methods found some disfavour with the pilots due to the weight penalty this involved and the difficulty in lining up the target. Units that experimented with this type of fixture were not dedicated only to night interceptions of course and among such was the 302 *Kōkutai* at Atsugi, near Tokyo, whose experienced commander, Yasuna Kozono, was apparently somewhat fixated on the use of slanted cannon, having successfully deployed it with 251*Ku* earlier, even considering it useful in fighter duelling (an enthusiasm *not* generally shared by his pilots or his superiors). Originally organized for the defence of Tokyo on 1 March 1944, with twenty-four night fighters, the 302 *Kōkutai* moved to Atsugi to replace the 203-*Ku*, which had shifted up to the Kuriles. Containing many experienced aviators, including redundant seaplane pilots, reinforced by university student cadets, the unit was given intensive training in the use of oblique-firing cannon. The A6M5s thus equipped, under Lieutenant Kushichirō Yamada and later Lieutenant Hiroshi Morioka, the unit's strength between January and March 1945 was never more than twenty strong. The additional weight of the emplaced cannon also detracted from the A6M5's climb performance, which meant that actual interceptions were rare and success almost non-existent. After participating in the defence of Okinawa the force was reduced to ten A6M5s. Along with its other aircraft types the unit was dispersed to be husbanded in readiness for the Allied invasion and flew its last mission on 15 August, when eight A65Ms joined a fight with six F6Fs over their airfield, losing six of their own number to just one Hellcat. When the order came to lay down their arms, the fanatical Kozono refused to accept the inevitable and vowed to carry on the fight regardless. He began to gather aircraft to organize an attack, but was restrained and confined to a mental ward and the disbandment of his unit under a new commander was undertaken.

Other units that specialized in oblique armed fighters, were the 332 *Kōkūtai* at Iwakuni, in Yamaguchi Prefecture, southern Japan, and on 6 November eight A6M5s equipped with this weapon moved to Atsugi for one month undertaking air defence of the Kantō region. The 131 *Kōkūtai* was re-organized as a night fighter outfit in March 1945, and based at Kanoya, Kyūshū, under Lieutenant-Commander Tadashi Minobe, flying their first night interceptions on 4 April. After sixty such missions the unit moved to the secret Iwakawa airbase on 20 May with ten A6M5 night fighters, in order to avoid continuous enemy bombing.

Engine boost system

While the Zero herself had been steadily improved, lack of a really powerful engine continued to restrict just what improvements could be made to the existing airframe, which these additions had now increased by 700lb (317.5 kg) additional weight with the same power plant. Mitsubishi requested the Navy Air Arsenal allow them to fit the more powerful Mitsubishi *Kinsei-62* radial to this aircraft, but the request was rejected outright. The Navy's solution was to insist on fitting the existing *Sakae-21* with a water-methanol injection system to boost its output for short bursts during combat.[21] However, such was the slow pace of development of this system that the *HEI* had to go into combat without it. Eventually one trial aircraft appeared late in 1944 fitted with the *Sakae 31a* radial. It was a far from successful prototype; the injection system was still in its experimental stage and was plagued with continual problems, while the modified engine generated *less* power not more. The A6M5c sub-type was built at the Nakajima Koizuma Plant, and attained a maximum speed of 346mph (556.83km/h) but only ninety-three ever appeared before the whole project was cancelled in the increasingly frenetic situation the Navy found itself that final winter of the war. Production was complex and still mired by problems, maintenance of the temperamental power plant in the field difficult.

Work on the water-methanol injection system continued, however, utilizing the Nakajima *Sakae-31* engine, which was a fourteen-cylinder, air-cooled radial, which was rated at 1,130hp (831.11kW) for take-off, 1,100hp (809kW) at 9,350ft (2,850m) and 980hp (720.79kW) at 19,685ft (6,000m).

With this power plant the climb rate to 26,250ft (8,001m) was 9 minutes 53 seconds. It provided a service-ceiling of 33,300ft (10,150m), and a maximum range of 956 miles (1,538.5km) at a cruising speed of 230 mph (370.15km/h). These aircraft had a wingspan of just over 36ft (10m), an overall length of almost 30ft (9.118m), a height of 11ft 6in (3.505m) and a wing area of 229.27ft^2 (21.300m^2). Weights were 4,519lbs (2,049kg) empty, 6,614lb (3,000.59kg) loaded. The armament comprised a single 13mm Type 3 machine-gun in the upper fuselage decking, two wing-mounted 13mm Type-3 machine-guns and two wing-mounted 20mm Type 99 cannon. Provision was also made for eight 22lb (10kg) rockets or two 132lb (60kg) rockets carried beneath the wings. For the first time the A6M was fitted with a CO^2 fire-suppression system.

A direct comparison was done later in the war between the A6M5 Model 52 ('Zeke-52'),[22] the F4U-1D, F6F-5 and the FM-2, which makes for interesting reading. With regard to speed the A6M5 was overall speedier, with the top speeds recorded being 335mph (539.13km/h) at 18,000 feet (5,486m) for the A6M5, against 321mph (516.6km/h) at 13,000ft (3,962.4m) for the FM-2. At sea level the FM-2 was marginally faster than the Zeke-52 by 6mph (9.66km/h) but as the altitude increased the A6M5's superiority became more and more marked, being 4mph (6.44km/h) faster at 5,000ft (1,524m); 12 mph (19.31 km/h) faster at 10,000ft (3,048m); 8mph (12.87km/h) faster at 15,000ft (4,572m), 19mph (30.58km/h) faster at 20,000ft (6,096m), 22mph (35.41km/h) faster at 25,000ft (7,620m) and 26mph 41.84km/h) faster at 30,000ft (9,144m). To get to those altitudes the two machines were evenly matched, with, at sea-level, the FM-2 exceeding the A6M5's rate of climb by 400ft/min (2.03m/s). However, at an altitude of 4,000ft (1,219.2m) the two aircraft were level, the FM-2 being 500ft/min (2.54 km/h) superior at 8,000ft (2,438.4m), with the rate of climb equalling out again at 13,000ft (914.49m). The A6M5's best climb speed was 105 knots (120.832mph) compared with the FM-2's 120 knots (138.094 mph).

In the field of combat that the A6M had hitherto made her own, the roll rate was found to be equal to the FM-2 at less than 160 knots (184.125mph), but the margin was with the FM-2 at high speeds, which was put down to high control forces. The Japanese fighter could still out-turn the Wildcat gaining one turn in eight at an altitude of 10,000ft (3,048m). In the dive, unexpectedly, the heavier American machine showed no great excess over the A6M5, the latter in fact being better in the initial acceleration and on a par afterward, with zooms following dives also being similar. With regard to pilots' all-round vision, the A6M5 excelled, notably rear-vision. The manoeuvring of the A6M5 was recorded as 'remarkable' at speeds under 175 knots (201.386mph), but this edge lessened as the speed factor went up, again due to high control forces, and above 200 knots (230.156mph/ 370.4 km/h) the FM-2 was considered to have a marginal advantage

The final suggested tactics for FM-2 pilots tangling with the Zero fighter remained, as they had for the previous three years, quite simple: 'DO NOT DOG-FIGHT WITH THE ZEKE 52.' Other advice was to maintain altitude advantage but, should a Zero appear on your tail, to '… roll and dive away into a high speed turn'. The A6M5's maximum safe dive speed was around 350mph, but she lost her roll agility.

Return to China

Three years after the last A6M units had departed from the Chinese mainland they returned again in a combat rôle. As early as May 1943, following heavy Allied bombing raids, nine A6Ms were once more based at San Ya airfield on Hainan Island to provide limited defensive air protection over the Hainan and Canton airspace. In October this section was beefed up with the establishment of 245 Wing based on Haikou, Hainan Island, with twenty-four A6Ms plus four Kates. Some of the A6Ms were detached for similar duties to Yangzi. Finally, in February 1944, 256 (Air Defence) Unit was established at Longhua airfield, Shanghai, with a strength of twenty-four A6Ms and eight Kates.[23]

With the war drawing ever closer to the home islands and the (perceived) success of the suicide method of attack, a *bakusō* version of the once nimble A6M became the last combat variant and was termed by some the *Kamikaze* variant, the A6M7 Model 62/63. Designed for the job instead of being retro-fitted conversions of earlier models,[24] the power plant was the 1,130hp (831.11kW) *Sakae-31-KOH* water-methanol injected radial, designated as Model 62. Others using the same engine but without the injector boost equipment fitted to it, were termed the Model 63. The injection gear necessitated the enlargement of the engine cowling to accommodate it. Further increases in weight to aid diving capability were incorporated by using heavier-gauge material in the tail assembly. Armament was generally as the Model 52c, with the Type 4 gun-sight, but in many the 13mm cannons were removed. The centre wing section was beefed up also to enable a 550lb (250kg) bomb to be carried on a recessed ventral rack instead of the 37-gallon (168.2 litres) drop-tank, and to compensate a 33-gallon (150-litre) drop tank could be accommodated under each wing or alternately air-to-air rocket bombs. Introduced as a means of bringing down the hordes of American four-engined bombers laying waste to her cities, the Japanese Navy introduced two type of *Tekkō-dan* (armour-piercing) rocket bombs toward the end of the war. The Type 3 No. 25 Mk 4 (*I-Gou*) weighing 315kg appeared as early as 1943 and had a launch speed of 100m/sec with a 3.5kg bursting charge. This was found to be inefficient for the job and was replaced from February 1945 onward by the more practical and efficient Type 3 No. 6 (*6-Gou*) air-to-air rocket bomb. Weighing just 145lb and with a velocity of 270m/sec, it was in three sections and had a rocket motor with a 5.5lb incendiary shrapnel warhead, consisting of 140 metal pellets embedded with white phosphorus, affixed. The warhead became activated by a clockwork adjustable-delay time fuse, which ejected them in a 60-degree cone.[25] This weapon appeared shortly after the first A6M7 Model 63 appeared in the spring of 1945. In the chaos of the final days of the Pacific War, and also by the deliberate destruction of some records, it is difficult to ascertain exactly how many of this variant were built. However, an entire Model 63 (#82729) has been on exhibition at the Arashiyama Museum, Kyoto City, having been brought up from the cold waters of freshwater Lake Biwa, north of Kyoto in 1976, in relatively good condition.

Training conversions

The A6M was a 'hot ship' and, although her reputation had outlived her undisputed merits by 1943, she continued to soldier on to the very end of the war. Like all such fighters the need to train increasing numbers of fresh young pilots, who had already qualified in the primary and intermediate training course, in the face of ever-mounting casualties, finally saw the modification of early types for which little combat value remained. The Model 21 survivors in particular were deemed particularlyly apt to have their now surplus airframes converted to the training (*Tsukuba*) role but it was not until March 1944 that they first appeared on the scene becoming the A6M2-K. The Naval Aeronautics Arsenal quickly did the necessary design work, following which the Hitachi *Kokuki* was allocated the mission of carrying out the task and eventually 273 conversions were carried out. The elongated cockpit canopy was extended aft to accommodate the instructor and dual-controls were emplaced, while the front cockpit for the trainee had an open canopy, accessible from both sides. The radio mast was moved to a middle position between pupil and instructor or even removed altogether. For added stability, an elongated running strake extended from the new rear end of the greenhouse to just before the horizontal stabilizers of the tail fin and the fire wall was shifted aft. To compensate for the additional weight the aircraft were stripped down; the 20mm cannon were removed from the wings but the nose-mounted 7.7mm machine-guns were retained to provide rudimentary gunnery training; the main landing gear doors likewise and the rail wheel was made permanently fixed in the landing position further forward, doing away with the covers, and making for easier maintenance, and with the tail cone often being deleted as well. A thicker tyre was substituted.

Plans were also being considered for a similar derivative of the Model 52, known as the A6M5-K, Interim Type O Training Model 22. The concept basically followed that of the A6M2-K but with the entire nose armament deleted. The Ohmura-based 21 Aircraft Arsenal actually produced a prototype conversion in 1945 but the war terminated before production could get underway at Hitachi. All of these trainers were able to offer less and less air time. By 1 January 1945 the average pilot training hours flown had fallen to a mere 275 hours for the entire fleet. Fresh-faced Imperial Navy pilots were being sent from the training cadres with about forty hours flying time; in contrast the US Navy combat pilots usually had more than 500 hours to their credit. There was no longer much question of teaching the rookies complex dog-fighting techniques; lack of fuel, lack of facilities and, above all, lack of time meant that many were sent off to face the enemy with just the sheer basics. Inevitable also, in those final days, was the sacrifice of numbers of even these training aircraft in *Kamikaze* missions.

A6M8 *HEI*(c)

Belated realization that all the many 'improvements' had, in general, added weight but slowed down the original concept until it was no longer able to catch, let alone destroy, many opponents, meant a reversion was made to shed some of the excess and get back to basics. The basis was the adoption of the new Mitsubishi *Kinsei* 14-cylinder air-cooled radial, which developed 1,560hp (1,163.76kW), which was still far less than contemporary American fighter engines of course. This power plant had a bigger diameter (more than 4 inches larger, at 103mm) than its predecessor and therefore entailed a corresponding enlargement of the cowling and the nose guns were deleted, resulting in a bigger profiled but smoother, forward profile. As a consequence the pilot's windshield was slightly modified to suit. This aircraft was designated as the Model 64, but only two examples were ever completed. Testing of the prototype in April 1945 revealed a maximum top speed of 349.83mph (563km/h), with a climb rate of 19,685ft (6,000m) in just under seven minutes.

Chapter 12

Final Sacrifice

With the war now reaching home territory Japan's plight was desperate. Cut off from the very sources of oil and essential war materials she had gone to war to obtain, her fleet obliterated, the bulk of her army on guard in Manchuria against the Soviet offensive, more and more desperate measures had to be resorted to in order to stave off the impending finale. Thoughts turned to the past to turn around the present. The providential intervention of great typhoons in past ages had wrecked the invasion fleets of the Mogul Empire on two occasions. Might such divine aid be invoked in her current dire peril? For the A6M the final chapter in her story was one of self-sacrifice, but on a scale never before envisaged.

Iwo Jima

The power of the American 3rd/5th Fleet[1] in the Pacific was, by the summer of 1944, overwhelming. Wherever the sixteen fleet and light fleet carriers with their 1,200 embarked aircraft and supporting warship groups wished to go, they *did* go. Attempts by the Japanese to build up the air power of various island garrisons proved in vain, for at any chosen point of impact the US carrier aircraft could always totally overwhelm any opposition. Like boys frantically trying to poke their fingers in the dyke as a tsunami surged in, the Japanese were always behind the loop, with always too little, too late to influence the inevitable. One example of this was the situation on Iwo Jima in the Bonin Islands, a mere five hundred miles from the Japanese mainland, which had been Japanese territory since 1875. There were two airfields on the island, which were capable of supporting up to eighty fighters, and since June the garrison had been steadily built up under Lieutenant-General Tadamichi Kuribayashi and the Japanese were in the process of moving their best units and pilots in to defend their home turf among them 301 and 601 *Kōkutai*. They were equipping with the powerful new Mitsubishi J2M *Raiden* point fighter (code-named 'Jack') designed by Horikoshi and powered by the 1,530hp *Kasei* engine, but at the last moment continuing problems with this power plant saw their substitution with the A6M Model 52. A6M production, which was to have been run down, was now re-boosted and in 1943 Mitsubishi at Nagoya produced 1,029 A6Ms and Nakajima, 1,967.[2] At the battle-front the US Navy was determined not to allow the Japanese to build up their air strength and the airfields on both Iwo and Guam were 'softened up' with numerous pre-emptive strikes in preparation for landings at Saipan.

The first American air attacks on Iwo were mounted on 15 June, and sixty F6Fs were met by eighteen A6Ms, ten from 1 *Chūtai*, led by Lieutenant Shigeo Jūni, with Chief Petty Officers Isamu Hirano, Suminori Kawabata and Kazuo Ōshi, Petty Officers Sotojirō Demura, Akio Nagashima, Mitsugu Yamazaki, and Takeo Yoshitake and Leading Seaman Kaihaku Kumagaya and Shūzo Nakagawa; and eight from 2 *Chūtai* under Lieutenant (j.g.) Chōbei Morita, with Warrant Officer Fukuju Kawakami, Petty Officers Yukio Kubota, Kaname Shibata and Hiroshi Shigemitsu, and Leading Seamen Kazuwa Honda, Mitsuo Shiraishi and Kesaji Sugihara, which between them claimed four aircraft destroyed but suffered horrendous losses of sixteen of their own with only Kawakami, who crash-landed, and Yamazaki surviving the encounter. This massacre was put down to inadequate training as the majority of the pilots had only previously flown two-seater floatplanes.

On 24 June fifty-nine fighters rose to meet the enemy, claiming the destruction of thirty-seven Americans but lost half their own number, and on 4 July 110 sorties were flown, with thirty-nine enemy machines claimed for the loss of twenty-three Japanese. The battle on 4 July 1944 was against the carriers of Admiral Marc Mitscher's Task Force 58 whose F6F pilots later commented that the aerial opposition encountered was strong. Twelve VF-31 from the carrier *Cabot* had twelve Hellcats flying top cover at 15,000ft that day but some thirty-one A6Ms, led by Lieutenant Kikumasa Fujita, managed to lure them into pursuit then rapidly made a climbing turn to 20,000ft and attacked them from above and out of the sun, a classic A6M manoeuvre that caught the Americans flat-footed. Lieutenant (j.g.) Cornelius Nicholas Nooy reported, 'We ran into a real hot Jap outfit and had our hands full. Planes were being shot down all over the sky and I couldn't tell whether they were Japs or ours.' Lieutenant Adolph Mencin, the XO, recalled: 'It was our toughest fight; we were out-numbered, and the Jap pilots were the best we ever encountered.' Lieutenant (j.g.) Robert Clark Wilson stated: 'In that predawn attack, we ran into some of the best pilots the Japans ever put up against us. Until our Hellcats thinned them out, the Zeros outnumbered us and had the altitude advantage.' The twelve American airmen claimed to have destroyed ten A6Ms in that encounter, but lost four F6Fs, those of Lieutenants (j.g.), Haig G. Elezian, Jr, Frank Hancock, Malcolm L. Loomis and Bob Wilson, only the latter pilot surviving.[3]

The Japanese A6Ms actually flew forty-five sorties this day and claimed a total of twenty-six enemy machines destroyed for the loss of fourteen, including several destroyed by anti-aircraft fire from the US warships conducting bombardments offshore. One successful pilot that day was a former flying instructor, Lieutenant Kunio Iwashita of the Yokosuka *Kōkūtai*; parts of this unit had reached Iwo on 22 June with nine A6Ms and further reinforcement arrived over the next two days. Many were intercepted *en route* to the island with Lieutenant Katsumi Koda near the Uracus Island (Farallon de Pajaros), in the northern Marianas, and seven A6Ms were destroyed.

On 5 July the Americans returned and Iwashita, who had been grounded with appendicitis the day before, volunteered to fight. Commander Katsutoshi Yagi allowed him to go under command of Peal Harbor and Midway veteran Iyozō Fujita, who was the *Butaichō*. Fujita took Iwashita aside and counselled him, 'One's first fight is the most risky. I will teach you how. Don't stray from me. Follow me tight.' The air raid warning sounded almost immediately and F6Fs were flying low over the airstrip and strafing even as the A6Ms clawed their way rapidly up through 328ft (100m) altitude. As he looked back Iwashita could see the big American fighters set ablaze aircraft and fuel tanks back at his base. He closed on a group of four F6Fs, which at first he mistook for Japanese aircraft. They were engrossed on creating mayhem and failed to see the lone A6M close from astern. Iwashita got to less than 30ft (9.14m) from the rear Hellcat before opening fire with his 20mm cannon. He recalled: 'The wing of the F6F broke up. I saw the goggles and white muffler of the young pilot and his face as he looked back in surprise. The F6F was instantly engulfed in flames and crashed into the sea. Mount Suribachi was close to us.' His victim had been Ensign Alberto Nisi from the carrier *Wasp*'s VF-14 Squadron.

The remaining three F6Fs instantly turned on the lone A6M seeking revenge, and Iwashita's aircraft had his cockpit canopy shattered and his port wing perforated before Fujita and the rest of his section arrived and drove the Americans away. Iwashita managed to crash-land his aircraft safely just before US cruisers offshore began a fierce bombardment. At the end of the week the Yokosuka group had lost thirty-one pilots and claimed to have destroyed twenty American fighters. The few survivors were flown back to Japan in a transport aircraft and Iwashita went on to fly further successful combat sorties in the Philippines, at Okinawa and over Japan, and in the end ferrying A6Ms around, surviving the war.[4]

Just nine A6Ms remained and these were dispatched as escorts for eight B5Ns against the American fleet, where they were intercepted and destroyed, just four fighters and one bomber managing to struggle back to Iwo. But the island was spared invasion at that time.

More *Suisen* operations

Despite the obvious limitations of the A6M2-N concept this little floatplane saw widespread war service and was quite successful in its limited sphere, notwithstanding the Solomon Islands losses. The *Rufe* served with 802 *Kōkūtai* from the Shortlands Anchorage, south of Bougainville, being based at Faisi Island, and also from Jaluit Atoll in the Marshall Islands; with 902 *Kōkūtai* from Dublon Island (which the Japanese called *Natsu Shima* – Summer Island – now known as Tonowas) in Truk Atoll; with 934 *Kōkūtai* from Aru Island in the Arafura Sea, south-west of New Guinea; and with 5 *Kōkūtai* (later 452 *Kōkūtai*) out of Kiska in the Aleutians where they fought with US Army P-38s (the *Rufes* claiming seventeen scalps for the loss of eight, before being disbanded on 1 October 1943), and from the Kurile Islands. Six A6M2-Ns were utilized as impromptu bombers in lieu of anything else and attacked Amchitka, but lost two of their number in the process. They also served with 936 *Kōkūtai* (the former 40 *Kōkūtai*) at Singapore, having a dozen B5N2s from November 1942, working from the Sembawang Royal Navy Base, just west of Seletar, where the British had built a ramp for their seaplanes and commenced a jetty, just over 98ft (30m), which the Japanese later completed. Two American submarines are thought to have been destroyed by A6M2-Ns, the *Grenadier* (SS-210) on 22 April 1943 by 936 *Kōkūtai* and the *Scamp* (SS-277) on 11 November 1944, by 453 *Kōkūtai*. On 19 April 1944, two of these A6M-Ns intercepted the Allied air strikes on Sabang, from the carriers *Saratoga* and *Illustrious*, damaging two SBDs. The 934 *Kōkūtai* worked from Kai and Aru Islands, south-east Maluku in the Arafura Sea, known as the Barrier Rim. This unit was credited with destroying three B-24s and three Australian Bristol Beaufighter. The 13 *Kōkūtai* was based at Brunei, North Borneo, in 1942–1945 with both B5N2 and E13A1 on its strength for convoy escort and anti-submarine patrolling; and was also employed by the *Otsu Kōkūtai* in defence of the home islands against Boeing B-29 Superfortresses attacks working from Biwa Lake, Honshū, toward the end of the war. Home defence units flew from Kashima, Ibraki, and Konoike (Gonoike) also, from where at least two victories over F6Fs were claimed by the A6M2-Ns.[5] The *Sasebo Kōkūtai* had A6M2-Ns at Chichi Jima (Peel Island) in the Bonin Group, north of Iwo Jima but in strong air attacks from Rear-Admiral 'Jocko' Clark's Task Group 58.1 destroyed or badly damaged every one while they were still on the water. The pilots, now without mounts, were re-allocated to the *Sasebo Kōkūtai*. The A6M2-N also saw much hard sea-service aboard the seaplane carrier *Kamikawa Maru* in the Solomons campaign, as described later.[6] Production ceased in 1943.

Enter the *Kamikazes* (神風特別攻撃隊)

The *Kamikazes* represented just one facet of the extreme Japanese measures originated to present a last-ditch defence against the American onslaught, under the overall title of *Tokku* (Special Attack) and the latter term is the one used by them. As in all things, the western usage of the term *Kamikaze* to apply generally to *all* such facets of self-sacrifice, has become the accepted norm. The Japanese term *Shimpū* (Divine Wind) so named after two opportune typhoons that legend had it had providentially arisen and destroyed two huge invasion fleets sent by Kublai Khan against Japan in

1274 and in 1281 applied to the air-to-sea arms of the *Tokku*. There have been many theories as to when exactly the idea of the suicide attack, as a given policy rather than as a personal decision, were adopted, and just as many speculations as to the originator. In my study on this subject[7] I have tried to list the precedents down through the war. Before proceeding in detail with how the A6M came to be involved, it should also be firmly held in mind that the lone 'suicidal' attack was far from just a Japanese concept. All nations' armed forces had embraced the 'take one with you' philosophy down the ages, from forlorn hopes such as King Leonidas and his Spartans who sacrificed themselves to hold the pass at Thermopylae against the Persian hordes of Xerxes in 480 BC, throughout succeeding centuries, and World War II was no exception. In the particular field of aerial warfare the examples of Major Katsushige Takada off Biak in May 1944 and Rear-Admiral Masabumi Arima's sacrifice on 15 October of the same year had been preceded by many similar actions by all other air forces. Russian fighter pilots such as Lieutenant II Ivanov of 46 Fighter Regiment became 'Heroes of the Soviet Union' for ramming Luftwaffe bombers, and even women pilots got into the act when First-Lieutenant Yekaterina Zelenko rammed a Bf.109. Major Ernst-Siegfried Steen of the Luftwaffe crashed his Junkers Ju.87 dive-bomber into the Soviet heavy cruiser *Kirov* and was awarded a posthumous Knight's Cross. The Americans were no exception to this list, with Captain Colin P. Kelly, Jr, for example lauded coast-to-coast by the press back home for his heroism in diving his huge B-17 bomber into the battleship *Haruna* and sinking her off the Philippines on 10 December 1941 – when in fact he did no such thing, only a light cruiser was present and she was not scratched, while *Haruna* herself was hundreds of miles away at the time.[8] That same day Lieutenant Samuel H. Marret of 34 Pursuit Squadron was killed when his P-35 fighter was caught in the up-blast from a bomb hit on a Japanese transport ship and the two stories became intertwined. Neither man committed suicide of course but the American press, hungry for some grain of success, invented stories to *say* they had, and, in doing so, also treated them as heroes for so doing. At Midway Marine Captain Richard E. Fleming is credited with diving his Vought SB2U dive-bomber into another 'battleship' (actually his target was the heavy cruiser *Mikuma*) at Midway, but his citation clearly stated he scored a near miss and crashed into the sea, the press knew otherwise; but other American pilots most certainly did self-sacrifice in this way, and were rightly hailed as heroes. So self-immolation for the defence of one's country was not an exclusive trait of the Japanese.

However, the Japanese most certainly embraced the concept (although not without considerable reservations on the part of many and outright rejection by many more) more than any other nation had done up to that point. The suggestion of deliberately crashing aircraft into enemy ships as a matter of policy had been raised at various times, by various people, only to meet rejection. The American landings at Leyte Gulf on 20 October, at the start of their campaign to re-conquer the Philippines, brought all such speculations to a high pitch.

When Vice-Admiral Takijirō Ōnishi, commanding 1 *Kōkū-kantai*, visited 201 *Kōkūtai* at their Mabalacat base (Clark Field) that day events did not auger well. Bombarding battleships and cruisers lined the coast, tens of thousands of American troops were in transports just offshore protected by dozens of small escort carriers, while over the horizon the all-powerful US Task Forces with their massed aircraft prowled in overwhelming strength. What was left of the Japanese surface fleet was to be committed to an all-out assault to drive the enemy back, but to facilitate their task, those carriers just had to be eliminated. The Admiral had been charged by the High Command to do just that, destroy the American carriers, but, from previous experience and failures, he had come to the conclusion that there was only one way left to achieve his brief and save his nation. Originally when the question of suicide attacks had been raised, Ōnishi had been rigorously opposed it; he called it 'heresy'.[9] Now faced with the direness of the situation he had put all such scruples behind him. He postulated to assembled officers that Japan's position was a desperate and extreme one. If the Philippines went then Japan would be cut off from the oil sources she had gone to war to obtain and then it was just a matter of time to total defeat. He put to them the option of loading their sleek little A6M fighter planes with 551lb (250kg) bombs and deliberately crash-diving (*Tai-Atari* – literally body-crash) them into the wooden flight-decks of the American carriers operating offshore. Such a revolutionary concept, deliberate suicide, would, one would have expected, have caused considerable pause, but it would appear that, after the briefest of consultations between Executive Officer Commander Asaichi Tamai and Lieutenant Masanobu Ibusuki, senior squadron leader (the Group commander, Captain Ei Yamamoto, was hospitalized after an accident at this time) they accepted the Admiral's option without reserve. The generally accepted versions of events presented are that the pilots of 201 were immediately assembled and the news broken; volunteers were called for; every man raised his hand. Almost in a trice then the *Kamikaze*s were born. Other accounts recall a considerable reluctance on the part of the chosen leader, Lieutenant Yukio Seki, but, upon reflection, he finally consented. Whatever the truth, and there must surely have been some pause, the ultimate outcome was the same and planning commenced. Four units were set up, named after elements in the poet Norinaga Motoori's epic one-line homage to Japan – *Shikishima-Tai* (traditional name of the Japanese islands); *Yamato-Tai* (the original name of the Japanese nation), *Asahi-Tai* (the rising sun) and *Yamazakura-Tai* (the mountain cherry blossom).

Admiral Ugaki duly noted this revolutionary step in his diary entry for 21 October.

> In view of the present situation, the 1 *Kōkū-kantai* is going to organize a *Kamikaze* Special Attack Corps with twenty-six carrier fighters of the 201st *Kōkūtai*, all of its present strength, of which thirteen were suicidal ones. They are divided into four units. They intend to destroy enemy carriers without fail – at least put them out of order for a while – before the thrust of the [our] surface force, when they come to the sea east of the Philippines.

He added in an emotional outburst of spiritual pride, 'Oh, what a noble spirit this is! We are not afraid of a million enemies or a thousand carriers because our whole force shares the same spirit!'[10]

The selection of the A6M as the first *Kamikaze* operator may appear a bizarre choice. The agile little fighter plane was renowned for her deftness and lightness and the options of various bomber types would seem more apt as pile-drivers to sink carriers. Ōnishi was certainly influenced by the fact that the group's earlier experiments with the *chōhi bakugeki* method made them stand out in this regard. Considered practically suicidal anyway they were used to toting bombs around and making high-speed approaches. Instead of bouncing the bomb off the water into the side of the ships, they could adopt varying approaches, which included a low-level approach with a final climb and dive, according to the conditions and scale of defences. That the A6M had the necessary speed to penetrate US defences whereas the Philippine Sea battle had shown that the dive-bombers and attack planes stood very little chance of doing so, decided the choice. The same problem remained, the size of bomb that the suicider *bakusō* could carry into battle to be an effective carrier-killer. It still remained in essence a 551lb (250kg) weapon when at least 1,100lb (500kg) was required to smash up such large ships as fleet carriers and fulfil the basic premise of the *Kamikaze*, 'one ship for one plane'. Of course all other types of aircraft were soon pressed into service, even floatplanes and flimsy wire-and-strut trainers, in fact anything that could be flown piloted by anyone capable of flying them; but it was the A6M that led the way, and indeed remained the mainstay of the earlier *Kamikaze* attacks.

How did their designer feel about this apparent waste of his outstanding design concept, the A6M? Did he feel it was being thrown away in a totally unsuitable manner? Did he resent the misuse of his brainchild? At the time he contributed an article for the *Asahi* newspaper group's publication *Kamikaze Special Attack Forces*, which he titled 'Compliment to the *Kamikaze* Special Attack Forces'. Horikoshi was to write, 'As I have witnessed the birth of the Zero, I know there is nothing to fear, since we have created an aircraft worthy of its task and the *Kamikaze* Special Attack Forces does the job that must be done.' This seemed to be a very clear and unequivocal endorsement of the role to which his creation had been assigned. Later he recalled that he reflected that this was not really the case, asking himself, 'Why were the Zeros used in such a way?' He mused, 'Of course, I could not say such things publicly at that time …'[11]

However Hirikoshi thought about things there is no doubt that the A6M carried out the strange new role that was thrust upon it very well indeed. Indeed, initially, the whole *Kamikaze* concept took the Allies totally by surprise. Not only were they amazed at the alien mind-set that could conceive, and carry out continuously, such a sacrificial effort, but at its effectiveness. The debut was made during the closing stages of the

Leyte Gulf battle, a sprawling encounter as labyrinthine and complex as all of the previous Japanese grand assaults from Midway onward, which saw the remnant of the still powerful surface fleet crushed and scattered to the four winds and yet another instance of a Japanese commander turning back with victory almost within his grasp. At Savo Island in 1942 with the Allied warships beaten and bewildered and with the American transport fleet at their mercy, the Japanese had turned back, a decision which led to the long-drawn out defeat in the Solomons. At Leyte Gulf, in the *Shō-Gō* Operation – with the whole American landing fleet within their grasp and the chance to justify the sacrifice of their whole fleet, command irresolution again took place at the critical moment and lost the Japanese their one last chance. But if the Americans had survived the massed salvoes of the Japanese battleships and heavy cruisers, the arrival of the *Kamikaze* gave them much pause for thought.

There were initially several abortive missions, on 21 October the *Shikishima-tai* failed to find the enemy carriers, while the *Yamato-tai* ('Spirit of Japan') flew a sortie from Cebu, from which Lieutenant (j.g.) Kōfu Kunō vanished without a trace. However, the Australian heavy cruiser *Australia* was hit and badly damaged by a suicide aircraft, the first of many such crashes endured by this ship. Similar failures by the *Shikishima-tai* were recorded on each succeeding day up to the 24 October. It was not until 25 October that the *Kamikaze*s made their mark when the Commander Yukio Seki's group of five *bakusō*, including Ensigns Iwao Nakano and Nobuo Tani and Petty Officers 1st Class Hajime Nagamine and Shigeo Oguro, with a four A6M fighter escort, attacked the eighteen escort carriers of Task Group 77 under Rear-Admiral Clifton A. F. Sprague off Samar where they had just narrowly escaped total destruction by Kurita's premature withdrawal. The carrier *St Lo* was sunk, and the *Kalin Bay*, *Kitkun Bay* and *White Plains* were all damaged. These attacks were all observed and confirmed by Warrant Officer Hiroyoshi Nishizawa of the escort. That same day Lieutenant Hiroyoshi Nishizawa was refused permission to lead his own group and his aircraft was instead flown by Petty Officer 1st Class Tomisaku Kastsumata, who crashed the escort carrier *Suwanee* off Surigao. Others of his group hit and damaged her sister ships, the *Sangamon* and *Santee*, in the same mission.[12]

After these initial victories the High Command in Tokyo enthusiastically embraced the *Kamikaze* concept and it rapidly became the most efficient method of anti-ship operation, although it never totally replaced conventional dive- and torpedo-bomber sorties entirely, and was itself supplemented by the *Oka* ('*Baka*') human-guided-bomb missions, *Maru-dai*, on which 252 *Kōküati* also flew as escorts, and other innovations. The missions themselves rapidly developed and Allied defensive methods, which included stronger fighter patrols, heavier radar-controlled gun barrages at longer ranges, picket-destroyers and proximity AA fuses, were countered by intelligent use of the land mass, mountains and cloud cover to shield approaches, the alternation and constant variation of altitudes and early morning and dusk attacks to take advantage of poor light, to keep up the pressure. Another tactic that confused the defending gunners was to make a determined run against a specific ship in the fleet and then, at the last moment, turn hard to port or starboard and crash an adjacent ship. Once the A6Ms were inside the warship formation at low level the gunners were restricted in their fire because the chances of hitting a friendly ship in the heat of the action were high.[13] In public the Allies derided the *Kamikaze* as 'wasteful', in private the US Navy was seriously worried as warship losses sharply escalated.

The use of the suicide attacks rapidly gained favour and the Japanese Army Air Force was also a contributor, indeed, some sources say they originated it. From being a purely voluntary operation before long the commanding officers of entire units were 'volunteering' them for this mission. Love of one's country, the need to protect one's family, peer pressure, even mental blackmail, the motivation varied from individual to individual. There was not the blanket blind obedience that nowadays many Americans allege existed. Even among those that volunteered and died, rational doubts were uppermost in the final thoughts. One young pilot, Lieutenant-Commander Iwatani, wrote:

I cannot predict the outcome of the air battles, but you will be making a mistake if you should regard Special Attack operations as normal methods. The right way is to attack the enemy with skill and return to the base with good results. A plane should be utilized over and over again. That's the way to fight a war. The current thinking is skewed.

Otherwise, you cannot expect to improve air power. There will be no progress if flyers continue to die.[14]

The A6M remained one of the principal aircraft utilized as *Kamikaze* during the Philippine campaign. The principal *-tai* (units) in which the A6M were involved either as suicider or as escort, were the *Kamikaze Tokubetsu Kōgekitai Asahi-, Baika-, Byakko-, Chihaya-, Hazakura-, Jimmu-, Junchū-, Kasagi-, Kashima-, Kasuga-, Kazaki-, Kikusui-, Kongō-, Kōtoku-, Niitaka-, Ōka-, Reisen-, Sakon-, Sakurai-, Seikō-, Shikishima-, Shinpei-, Shisei-, Shōmu-, Taigi-, Tenpei-, Tokimune-, Tsukuba-, Ukon-, Wakazakura-, Yamato-* and *Yamazakura-tai*. As far as can be ascertained approximately 230 A6Ms were despatched on suicide sorties from the Philippines, with a further eighty assigned as escorts.

The shock of being on the receiving end of one of the first A6M suicide attacks was recorded in the Action Report of the *St Lo*, all the more graphic because of its detachment.

At about 1051 AA fire was seen and heard forward and general quarters was sounded. Almost immediately thereafter, numerous planes, believed to include both friendly and enemy, were seen at 1000 – 3000 feet ahead and on the starboard bow. These planes moved aft to starboard and one of them when about abeam to starboard went into a right turn toward the *St. Lo*. The after starboard guns opened [fire] on him, but with no apparent effect. This plane, a Zeke 52, with a bomb under each wing, continued his right turn into the groove, and approached over the ramp [aft] very high speed.

After crossing the ramp at not over fifty feet, he appeared to push over sufficiently to hit the deck at about number 5 wire, 15 feet to the port side of the centre line. There was a tremendous crash and flash of an explosion as one or both bombs exploded. This plane continued up the deck leaving fragments strewn about and its remnants went over the bow. There is no certain evidence as to whether or not the bombs were released before the plane struck the deck.

The Captain's impression was that no serious damage had been suffered. There was a hole in the flight deck with smouldering edges which sprang into flames. Hoses were immediately run out from both sides of the flight deck and water started on the fire. He then noticed that smoke was coming through the hole from below, and that smoke was appearing on both sides of the ship, evidently coming from the hangar. He tried to contact the hangar deck for a report, but was unable to do so. Within one to one and a half minutes an explosion occurred on the hangar deck, which puffed smoke and flame through the hole in the deck and, he believes, bulged the flight deck near and aft of the hole. This was followed in a matter of seconds by a much more violent explosion, which rolled back a part of the flight deck, bursting through aft of the original hole. The next heavy explosion tore out more of the flight deck and also below the forward elevator out of its shaft. At this time, which he estimated as still shortly before 1100, he decided that the ship could not be saved. With the smoke and flame, he was even uncertain as to whether the after part still was on the ship, though later he had glimpses of it. All communication was lost, except the sound-powered phones, which apparently were in for some time although no reports could be obtained from aft. The word was passed 'stand by to abandon ship' and the order given to stop all engines. The order to the engines appeared to get through, and the word to stand by to abandon ship reached all parts of the ship, partly by sound-powered phone and partly by word of mouth, and the personnel assembled largely on the flight deck forward, and on the forecastle. During this time, some personnel had been blown overboard, and some had been driven over by fire.

Iwo Jima falls

Even before the Americans turned their eye to the occupation of Iwo Jima, it had been fully recognized by the Japanese defenders that they would not be able to count on the Navy fighters to defend them for very long, but would have to be self-reliant. 'Even the suicidal attacks by small groups of our Army and Navy airplanes … could be regarded only as a strategical ruse on our part.'[15] This, despite the fact that on 10 August Rear-Admiral Toshinosuka Ichimaru had arrived on the island with 2,216 naval personnel, including aviators and ground crew and that by the time of the invasion this had increased to 7,347. The two airfields at Motoyama were not expected to survive the landings but were kept going through frequent American softening-up bombings for as long as possible so that the A6Ms based there could intercept US bombing forays against the home islands from Saipan.

In the event the only assistance the Navy was able to mount was a *Kamikaze* attack launched by the *Kamikaze Tokubetsu Kogekitai Di 2 Mitate-tai* (Imperial Shield) from Katori air base. The unit had only just been established on 19 February, from the 601 *Kōkūtai* and 254 *Kōkūtai* under Lieutenant Hiroshi Murakawa. The strength of this unit was twelve A6Ms led by Lieutenant (j.g.) Senzō Iwashita, ten Yokosuka D4Y *Suisei* dive-bombers (code-named 'Judy') and eight Nakajima D6N *Tenzan* carrier attack bombers (code named 'Jill'). They had taken off when news of the American invasion came in that same day, but bad weather caused this mission to be aborted. The weather had cleared by the 21st and early that morning the unit again set off early in the day for the long flight south. They were staged through Hachijo Jima air base in the Bonin Islands, where two aircraft were forced to aboard the mission. One B6N failed to take off as her undercarriage collapsed while a second got airborne but developed engine faults and had to return to Hachijo Jima. For the rest it was a long flight down to the target area but, as this was to be a one-way mission, that was not important. In the event all twenty-eight remaining aircraft reached the battle zone. They were first detected by the radar of the fleet carrier *Saratoga* while still about one hundred miles distant, but she mistook them for friendly aircraft and took no action. This was to cost the Americans dearly. Not until 1700 did F6Fs on the CAP identify the incoming group at Japanese. Six A6Ms attacked and while the ships guns shot down two of them the others hit, two more '… bouncing off the water into the starboard side, one hitting the flight deck forward, the fourth hitting a large crane …' Three of the bombs they carried detonated inside the *Saratoga*'s hull setting her ablaze. After a while the fires were brought under control but she was then struck by a third *Kamikaze*, which brushed her flight deck before crashing in the sea, but the bomb she carried penetrated the carrier's flight deck blowing a large hole in it. It took until 2000 before she was able to affect sufficient repairs to land back her airborne aircraft and she lost thirty-six of her aircraft, which were burnt out, while a further six had to ditch in the sea and were also lost. The carrier also suffered 123 of her crew killed and 192 wounded and she was forced to head back to Eniwetok and then all the way back to Bremerton to repair.

The *Kamikaze*s also hit the escort carrier, the *Bismarck Sea*, which was operating close-support air missions some twenty miles east of Iwo. Just before 1900, one of these smashed into her 'square abeam'. Fully fuelled up aircraft on her deck immediately started to burn, the blaze being fuelled by exploding ammunition. There was a twenty-two-knot wind over the fleet at the time, which rapidly spread the flames. Soon the whole ship was ablaze and the order to abandon ship was issued. While that was in progress the carrier detonated in a huge explosion and quickly sank. Many of her crew were picked out of the rough waters by her escorts but she lost 218 of her crew, 943 officers and men as well as most of her aircraft. The *Tenzans* went for another jeep carrier, the *Lunga Point*, but she avoided being hit. The naval auxiliary *Keokuk*, a net tender, was hit, set on fire and badly damaged with seventeen dead and forty-four injured. Two of the large Landing Ship Tanks (LCTs) *477* and *809* with 3 Marine Division artillery pieces embarked, were also hit and damaged.

The Americans later claimed that all of the about forty attackers had been destroyed, but this was not the case, in truth the *Mitate* group lost forty-three men killed in that attack, including five A6M pilots. After the battle, on their return, a group of F6Fs ambushed two of the fast D4Ys and damaged them, but both managed to land intact back safely at Hachijojima.

On 1 March 1945, one of these *Suisei* bombers sortied alone from Hachijojima toward Iwo Jima to make a lone suicide attack.

Okinawa

In April and May it was the turn of Okinawa as the Allies edged closer to Tokyo. The US Fleet had commenced heavy attacks on homeland airfields from 18 March onward and *Kamikaze* units struck back hard, badly damaging the fleet carriers *Intrepid*, *Wasp*, *Franklin*, *Enterprise* and *Essex*, battleships *New Mexico* and *West Virginia* and heavy cruiser *Indianapolis*, flagship of Admiral Spruance. The battleship *Yamato* was sacrificed on a one-way mission, with her fuel bunkers half-full and with no fighter protection. She was overwhelmed by almost eight hundred US carrier aircraft before she got anywhere close to the invasion beaches. The Americans had started landing on 1 April under Operation *Iceberg*. By now the American fleet had grown yet further to include fifteen fleet and light carriers, and it had the added assistance of the British Pacific Fleet with between four and six fleet carriers at various times during the battle with four light carriers *en route* to join them. The Japanese responded vigorously under the prepared Operation *Ten-Go*, which was put into effect on 25 March with 3 and 10 *Kōkū-kantai* working under Vice-Admiral Ugaki's 5 *Kōkū-kantai* based on southern Kyushu and 1 *Kōkū-kantai* from Formosa (now Taiwan). *Kamikaze* attacks began immediately, organized in *Kikusui* waves and during the course of the campaign reached a new intensity. Although they had lost the initial impact of surprise and found the Allies prepared, the scale of the attacks was large and the Japanese had also learnt a lot. The *Kamikaze* attacks were preceded by the dropping of foil strips to block Allied radars, by conventional diversionary attacks and by the ranks of suicide aircraft of all types. Losses of warships, but especially of the isolated picket duty destroyers out on the fringes of the fleet, were very heavy indeed. Fortunately for the Allies many of the fairly green young Japanese pilots simply attacked the first warships they came across, thus expending much of their fire-power on the destroyers, which saved the troopships, transports and landing craft untold casualties.

To undertake the defence of Okinawa 3 *Kōkū-kantai* began to concentrate all available units in the southern home island of Kyūshū within striking range. With the remaining carriers relegated to ferry duties or laid up, the A6Ms concentrated ashore and by 1 April 601 *Kōkūtai* at Kokubu air base had thirty-eight A6Ms on strength led by Lieutenant Hideo Katori. The 352 *Kōkūtai* (Kusanagi) previously engaged over northern Kyushu against B-29s from Chinese bases, also moved in with thirty-nine A6Ms commanded by Lieutenant Shinei Uematsu. The plan was to send wave after wave of *Kamikaze*s south to destroy the invasion fleet under Operation *Kikusui* (Floating Chrysanthemum). The principal role envisaged for the A6Ms was to conduct low-level strafing runs ahead of the main suicide units to clear the way for them to get through to the ships. On 3 April a force of thirty-two A6Ms and eight Kyushu J7W *Shidens* under Lieutenant Hideo Katori were dispatched on a sweep. These engaged American fighters over

Kikai naval airfield on Kikaiga Shima, off north-western Amani Island at the beginning of the island chain down to Okinawa on 3 April, claiming sixteen enemy destroyed for the loss of eight A6Ms. Another fierce air fight took place over Kikaiga Shima on 16 April with Lieutenant Kakichi Hirata leading twenty-six A6Ms and four J7Ws, which resulted in the loss of four fighters from each side. Four A6Mb aircraft led by Lieutenant (j.g.) Makio Aoki made an assault on the US Task Force off Okinawa the same day but all were lost. On 17 April after a fortnight's operations only nine A6Ms were left fit for duty and these were withdrawn to Hyakurigahara Air Base, at Higashiibaraki-gun, Ibaraki Prefecture, where its strength was built up to one hundred A6Ms, which were carefully husbanded ready for the final battle for the homeland but never actually employed again.

The principal -*tai* (units) in which the A6M were involved either as suicider or as escort, were the *Kamikaze Tokubetsu Kōgekitai Schichisei-, Shinken-, Shōwa-, Taigi-* and *Tsukuba-tai*. Estimated numbers of A6Ms were 208 despatched as suicide attackers with thirty acting as escorts. The biggest A6M fighter battles were fought on 3 April, when forty fighters were despatched on escort duties and claimed to have destroyed seventeen Allied aircraft for the loss of eight of their own; on 12 April, when seventy-five Japanese fighters were engaged, destroying an estimated twenty-five enemy for the loss of twelve; and on 16 April, when no fewer than ninety-three fighters went out and claimed to have destroyed a further twenty-three Allied machines for the loss of seventeen.

While the American carriers with their wooden decks were seriously damaged and had to retire to the West Coast to repair, the British carriers with their 3in (7.62cm) armoured steel decks, fared better and direct hits merely 'dished' the flight decks rather than penetrating into the aircraft hangars. The British carriers also had their aviation fuel ('Avgas' in American parlance) stored aboard in tanks contained within water-filled compartments under the armoured decks, which minimized the fireballs that had destroyed or crippled so many American and Japanese carriers. Where the British were second-best was in everything else; numbers of aircraft embarked were less than half those of American carriers; anti-aircraft weapons were fewer and less efficient; mobility was poorer due to the short-ranges of British warship design; the British fleet was slower, its refuelling techniques antiquated. The aircraft with which they fought were mainly Lend-Lease types, chiefly F4U Corsairs (which the Fleet Air Arm had pioneered as carrier-based fighters), F6F Hellcats, plus a few British Fairey Fireflies and the 'navalized' variant of the famous Supermarine Spitfire, known as the Seafire.

The twenty-four Seafire L.111/F.111s with which No. 894 Naval Air Squadron under Lieutenant-Commander (A) J. Crossman, DSO, RNVR, was equipped aboard the fleet carrier *Indefatigable*, had the powerful Merlin 55M in-line engine, with a single-speed, single-stage supercharger with a 'cropped' impeller for extra low-altitude boost, but had very short range and was principally used as a 'point defence' fighter over the fleet. It was also fragile and delicate and unable to withstand the rough-and-tumble of intensive carrier warfare, a fact known for at least two years. It suffered three times the number of losses from accidents than in combat.[16] Subsequently they were fitted with 45-gallon (170.34-litre) 'Slipper' tanks and later ex-RAAF 89-gallon (336.90-litre) P-40 tanks for longer-range missions. The Seafire's strength was the same as the A6M's, it was best at low altitudes and had a good rate of turn – a perfect duelling match had the quality of both pilots been similar at this stage of the war but such was rarely the case. The British Pacific Fleet was assigned the thankless and far from glamorous task of neutralizing the runways in the Sakishima Gunto off north-west Formosa, being used to ferry aircraft down from Kyushu to the Okinawa battlefield.

Nonetheless the Seafire, despite its faults, was credited with destroying eight A6Ms while serving with the British Pacific Fleet off Okinawa. The most prolific Zero killer was Sub-Lieutenant (A) Richard Henry Reynolds of No. 994 Naval Air Squadron. On 1 April he became embroiled with no fewer than three A6Ms. The first was a *Kamikaze* sighted at 0728, which penetrated the CAP and made a strafing run against both the carrier *Indomitable* killing one man and wounding five others, and then the battleship *King George V*. Unable to do any harm against this armoured monster the A6M continued on and Sub-Lieutenant Reynolds ignored standing orders and courageously entered the Gun Defence Zone in pursuit. The A6M had a good lead, however, but Reynolds managed to get in some long-range shooting using maximum deflection for his cannon and hit her in the wing root. Despite all the talk, the Zero did not explode, in fact seemed impervious and was able to gain a little altitude before flipping over and crash-diving hard into the base of the carrier *Indefatigable*'s bridge structure. The explosion killed four officers and ten men and wounded sixteen more and damaged three aircraft. The armoured deck was dented by 3 inches and was soon repaired.[17]

Reynolds resumed his patrol and at 0748 a second A6M, not a *Kamikaze* but a fighter-bomber, suddenly appearing out the overcast, penetrated through to the destroyer screen and dropped a 551lb (250kg) bomb close alongside the destroyer *Ulster*. The ship's midships side was opened up and she had to be towed back to Leyte for repairs. After the attack this aircraft was caught still at low level by Reynolds and, after two firing runs, she was shot into the sea. Within a few minutes yet a third A6M appeared and Reynolds once more engaged. This A6M was looking for a fight and attempted to trick Reynolds into a close-turning combat, which he wisely refused. Instead the Seafire maintained its high speed until within optimum firing range and using combat boost for the climbs thus dictated the action, with Reynolds finally managing to shoot her into the sea after five bursts, with almost his last remaining ammunition. This very able pilot was later to confirm his hat-trick against the A6M when he shared a kill with another Seafire on 4 May.[18]

It was estimated by the US Army survey, that some 1,900 *Kamikazes* sacrificed themselves off the Ryukyus. A total of twenty-six US vessels were destroyed off Okinawa, and a further ten had to be sunk after being badly damaged in *Kamikaze* attacks, a net loss of thirty-six ships. A massive further 368 ships were damaged, a large proportion of which were by *Kamikazes*. The Allies lost 763 aircraft, ninety-eight of them being British, while the US Army lost 4,907 men killed or missing and 4,824 wounded. The A6M was not only the first *Kamikaze*, it predominated in such actions and, of the 2,663 aircraft used by the IJNAF in this role, the A6M numbered 1,189 of them.

Preparation for the final battle

Once the Philippines had been cut off and Iwo and Okinawa taken the Japanese prepared themselves for the final defence of the home islands. Every attempt was made to assemble every possible aircraft and build up the air strength in readiness. The planes were secreted away as best they could be, to prevent them being destroyed piecemeal as at Guam and elsewhere, and in the main they were not committed, no matter what the provocation. Thus when the Allied fleets sent hundreds of aircraft to destroy what remained of the Japanese fleet at their anchorages, they met almost no aerial opposition as they methodically went about avenging Pearl Harbor. Even when Allied battleships closed the coast and shelled industrial targets close to Tokyo itself, nothing stirred. All was to be saved for the actual landing.

In the final analysis the *Kamikaze*s failed to save the Philippines, they failed to save Iwo Jima and they failed to save Okinawa. Whether they would have saved Japan itself had Operation *Olympic* ever been launched is harder to say. The policy to be adopted, that of attacking the troop transports rather than carriers or heavily armed warships as conducted in the earlier campaigns, would have most certainly led to very heavy Allied casualties. Already war-weary (the British had been fighting for six years, the Americans for four) such losses might have given pause, but it is doubtful whether the Allies would have been turned from their course, especially as their Soviet partner, who had ignored the Pacific totally during its colossal struggle with Germany, now sought to finalize things with Japan in Manchuria, China and Korea. It is as well that it never came to the test for tens of thousands of young men on both sides. When the Emperor ordered them to cease fighting, the greater majority did so, those who resisted being disarmed and the carefully stored aircraft made inoperational by the removal of their propellers etc. The war ended for most A6Ms not with a bang but a whimper.[19]

There were exceptions of course; some just could not accept they had been defeated. As related, the originators of the *Kamikaze* ideal, which had so involved many A6Ms and their pilots, took their own lives. Admiral Ōnishi composed a final poem, which can perhaps be taken as recognition of all the young Zero pilots who died that way.

I tell the spirits of the *tokkotai*
  I thank you from my heart for your brave fights.
  Even though you believe the final victory (of Japan) and Died gracefully like cherry blossoms, your faith has never been accomplished.
  I apologize to the spirits of my men and their bereaved families With my death.

Next, I bid obedience to all in Japan. It would be bliss if all of you realize that acting rashly, Throwing your life would only profit your enemy, and decide with Faith to follow the sacred order of the Emperor his majesty, and endure the pain.

While enduring your pain, do not forget the pride to be Japanese.

You all are the treasure of the country.

Yet in the time of the peace, adhere the spirit of *Kamikaze* and do your best for the welfare of the Japanese race and for the Peace of the people around the world.

Takijiro Onishi. Admiral Imperial Japanese Navy.[20]

Assessments

In the end 10,449 A6Ms were finally produced between March 1939 and August 1945, of the various models,[21] and, as the first Navy plane to out-perform land-based fighters by a wide margin, it was unique. This little aircraft formed 60 per cent of the IJN's fighter force when she went to war in 1941 and was still serving in the front line four years later. She had served aboard the aircraft carriers *Akagi, Hiryu, Hiyo, Hōshō, Junyō, Kaga, Ryūjō, Ryuho, Shōhō, Shōkaku, Sōryu, Zuihō* and *Zuikaku* and with the fighter component of every major land formation. Even a few JAAF units are rumoured to have used a few. With the massacre of the IJN carriers between 1942 and 1944, it became mainly a land-based aircraft itself at the end of the war, and, although its leading-edge had long since disappeared, it still commanded considerable respect in the hands of the dwindling band of expert and veteran flyers. The A6M illustrated perfectly the Japanese approach to war and typified the aggressive approach adopted up to and throughout World War II. The attack was the primary thought; the offensive was always to be maintained, even if it often resulted in heavy losses. A nation of one hundred million could, perhaps, afford a certain amount of sacrifice, and the modified and distorted version of the old Samurai code introduced into the military during the *Meiji-jidai* at the end of the nineteenth century, *bushido* ('way of the warrior'), imbued in generations a spirit of selfless self-sacrifice and unquestioning loyalty to the Emperor, and from 1882 onward was taken to extremes that western minds simply could not comprehend.[22]

However, in 1941 by simultaneously making war against the vast populations of China, the United States and the British Empire, and holding itself in readiness to embroil itself also with the Soviet Union as well, the rulers of Japan appeared set on a course of self-destruction.

Attack was the doctrine, and the A6M embodied that as no other aircraft of the period. With its clean and pure lines, its sensitivity to the pilot's touch, its superlative climb and its powerful armament, it fitted the Japanese Navy pilot like a glove and had the reach to project power to an undreamt of degree for a fighter aircraft. It could react in an instant – Allied pilots have related many times how they had an A6M in their sights and then, within seconds, it was on *their* tail. Its effect on the stunned Chinese, American and British Commonwealth pilots was as much psychological as anything. It became the great air benchmark of the Pacific War, and initial Allied tactics were to avoid it, or defend against it, to tackle it meant death. Joseph Jacob Foss, legendary US Marine Corps fighter pilot with VNF-121 of Guadalcanal's 'Cactus Air Force', recalled, 'I told my pilots that if you were alone and saw a Zero at the same altitude you were flying that you were outnumbered and should go for home. They were not a plane to tangle with unless you had an advantage.'[23] This mind block was even more remarkable in that it almost instantly displaced the distain that had hitherto dominated Allied thinking about Japanese military aircraft.

Excellent weapon though the A6M was, and timely as was its adoption on the eve of Japan's greatest challenge, it had many Achilles' heels and, once these had been fully evaluated and understood, its aura began slowly to fade, even in the minds of the Japanese airmen themselves.

The A6M remains a unique aircraft and will always have a special place in the aviation hall of fame as an aircraft that broke the mould and made history.

Museum A6Ms

These are of widely varying authenticity and more are being dug out of the Pacific jungles and atolls all the time. The most well-known examples reside at the Imperial War Museum, Duxford, Cambridge, UK; Auckland War Memorial Museum, Auckland, New Zealand; Australian War Memorial,

Canberra ACT, Australia; China People's Revolution Military Museum Beijing, China; Museum Dirgantara Mandala, Yogyakarta, Indonesia; Smithsonian National Air and Space Museum, Washington DC; Marine Corps Air Station Museum, Iwakuni, Japan; *Yamato* Museum, Kure, Japan; Yasukuni Shrine War Museum, Tokyo; Mitsubishi Heavy Industry Co., Nagoya Air and Space System Plant, in-house display; Fantasy of Flight, Polk City, Florida; Planes of Fame Museum, Chino Airport, California; Museum of Flying, Santa Monica, California; Naval Aviation Museum, Pensacola, Florida; National Museum of the United States Air Force, Wright-Patterson AFB, Dayton, Ohio; Pacific Aviation Museum, Pearl Harbor, Hawaii; San Diego Air and Space Museum, California, USA; Nagoya International Airport, Japan.

Appendix I

Basic Specification of the A6M2

Type: Single-seater carrier-born fighter aircraft.

Dimensions: Wingspan – 39 feet 5 inches × Overall length – 29 feet 9 inches × Height – 9 feet 7 inches (12m × 9.06m × 2.92m)

Wing area: 241.54 ft^2 (22.44m^2)

Weight: Empty – 4,235lb (1,912kg); Full – 5,423lb (2,460kg)

Maximum speed: 332mph (533km/h) at 14,930ft (4,550m); 282 mph (454 km/h) at sea level.

Cruising speed: 307 mph (333 km/h)

Climb rate: 53 ft/sec (16m/sec)

Service ceiling: 33,800 ft (10,000m)

Range: Internal wing-mounted tanks only – 183 gallons (693 litres) – 1,162 miles (1,870 km); with 73-gallon (330-litre) ventral drop tank – 1,930 miles (3,100km)

Armament: 2 × 0.303 (7.7mm) Type 97 machine-guns, cowling mounted, 500rpg. 2 × 20mm Type 99 wing cannon, 60 rpg.

Power plant: 1 × 959hp (708kW) Nakajima NK1C *Sakae-12*, 14-cylinder radial engine.

Propeller: *Sumitomo* three-bladed metal constant-speed.

Principal Variations of the A6M

A6M1 – Equipped with a 780hp (470kW) Mitsubishi Mk2 *Zuisei-13* radial engine.

A6M3 – Equipped with a 1,130hp (8,934kW) *Sakae-21* radial engine. Cannon upgraded to Type 99 Mk 2, increased muzzle velocity, 100 rpg. The wings were 'clipped' square (resulting in the temporary allocation of the separate Allied code-name of 'Hamp'.)

A6M5a – Cannon fitted were Type 99 Mk4, 85rpg. 2 × wing carried 132lb (60kg) bombs.

A6M5b – One 7.7mm machine-gun replaced by a 12. 7mm machine-gun.

A6M5c – Both 7.7mm machine-guns replaced by 13.2mm machine-guns – with option to fit an additional fuselage-mounted 13.2mm machine-gun. Armour protection for pilot introduced.

A6M7 – A Suicide (*Kamikaze*) variant designed for the job rather than the conversion, which substituted 1 × 551-lb (250kg) bomb for the drop tank.

A6M8c – Planned to be equipped with Mitsubishi *Kinsei-62* engine.

A6M2-N – Type 2 floatplane with centreline float and two outriggers. 327 built by Nakajima.

A6K – Two-seater Advance Trainer variant.

Appendix III

Production of the A6M

Date	Mitsubishi Jukogyo KK (Nagoya)	Nakajima Hikoki KK (Ota)	Sasebo Naval Arsenal	Hitachi	TOTAL
3/39–3/42	722	115	–	–	837
4/42–3/43	729	960	–	–	1689
4/43–3/44	1164	2268	–	–	3432
4/44–3/45	119	885	236	279	1519
TOTALS	3879	6570	236	279	10954

Notes

Introduction

1. Engel, Leonard, 'Japan is NOT an Air Power', article in *Flying and Popular Aviation*, January 1941 issue.
2. Zacharoff, Lucien, 'Japan's Bush-League Air Force', article in *Air News*, September 1941 issue.
3. See: Roskill, Stephen Wentworth, *Churchill and the Admirals*, London: 1977. William Collins.
4. Somerville to his wife, 1 March 1942. Somerville, Admiral Sir James, *The Somerville Papers*, edited by Michael Simpson, Aldershot: 1995. Navy Records Society/The Scholar Press.
5. Marder, Arthur J., *Old Friends, New Enemies: the Royal Navy and the Imperial Japanese Navy, 1936–45; Volume I. Strategic illusions, 1936–41*, Oxford: 1981. Oxford University Press.
6. Best, Antony, *British Intelligence and the Japanese Challenge in Asia, 1914–1941*, London: 2002. Palgrave Macmillan.
7. Aldrich, Richard J., *Intelligence and the War Against Japan*, Cambridge: 2000, Cambridge University Press.
8. Ford, Douglas, 'British Naval Policy and the War against Japan, 1937–1945: Distorted Doctrine, Insufficient Resources, or Inadequate Intelligence?' *International Journal of Naval History*, Volume 4 Number 1, April 2005.
9. 'In Search of a Suitable Japan: British Naval Intelligence in the Pacific Before the Second World War', article in *Intelligence and National Security 1*; No. 2, May 1986.
10. Dower, John W., *War Without Mercy: Race and Power in the Pacific War*, New York: 1986. Pantheon Books.
11. Sherrod, Robert, *History of Marine Corps Aviation in World War II*, Washington DC: 1952. Combat Forces Press.

Chapter 1

1. American sources continue to present the conference, which extended from 12 November 1921 to 6 February 1922, as a great achievement, and of course, to

them it was – see Goldstein, Erik, and Maurer, John, *The Washington Conference 1921–22: Naval Rivalry, East Asian Stability and the Road to Pearl Harbor.* London: 1994. Routledge. For Britain, it was a disaster that came home to roost eighteen years later, while for the Japanese to be frozen at 60 per cent of the western navies, was felt to be an humiliation.

2. So-termed because the programme would have seen the completion of eight battleships and eight battle-cruisers, all more powerful than contemporary western vessels.

3. Chalmers, Rear-Admiral W. S. *The Life and Letters of David, Earl Beatty.* London: 1951. Hodder and Stoughton.

4. This was paralleled by the conversion of the British battle-cruisers *Courageous* and *Glorious* and the American battle-cruisers *Saratoga* and *Lexington* in the same manner.

5. Genda Minoru, *Kaigun Kōkūtai shimatsuki (Record of Japanese Naval Air Service).* Tokyo: 1961–2. Bungei Shunjū.

6. Horikoshi, Jirō, *Eagles of Mitsubishi, The Story of the Zero Fighter*, Tokyo:1970. Kappa Books.

7. Compare this to the British Admiralty's request for 241 aircraft by 1941, to which the Air Ministry objected in the strongest possible terms! – Till, Geoffrey, *Air Power and the Royal Navy 1914–1945 – a historical survey.* London: 1979. Jane's Publishing Company.

8. Douhet, General Giulio, *The Command of the Air*, Tuscaloosa: 2009. University of Alabama Press.

9. Toshio Hijikata, *My Naval Aviation Experience*, Lecture dated 4 March 2005 at Kamakura. Transcribed by Naoaki Ooishi.

10. Hata, Ikuhiko and Izawa, *Yasuho, Nihon Kaigun Sentōki-tai* (later translated as *Japanese Naval Aces and Fighter Units in World War II* by Gorham Don Cyril), Tokyo: 1970. Kantōsha Publishers.

11. One such account was written post-war, claiming that the Japanese lost every one of its twenty-four fighters and twelve of its bombers for the loss of just eleven and two Russian fighters – see Caiden, Martin, *The Ragged, Rugged Warriors*, New York: 1966. E. P. Dutton. This would appear to be pure American hyperbole because the actual Japanese force appears to have been eighteen G3M bombers escorted by thirty A5M fighters, which were met by seventy to eighty Chinese and Soviet-manned fighters and even a Chinese source claims only a total of twenty-one Japanese machines for the loss of twelve of their own while the Japanese admit to only four losses, two fighters and two bombers.

12. Although not introduced until 1942, and then only gradually, a series of Allied code names were allocated to Japanese aircraft to enable easier identification by Allied military. Thus fighter aircraft were allocated boys' forenames, bombers were given girls' forenames, trainers were given the names of trees, while gliders had the names of birds. Under that system the G3M was dubbed the 'Nell', the G4M was called the 'Sally' and the A5M the 'Claude'.

13. The –12 designation reflecting the twelfth year of the reign of the *Shōwa* era, the reign of Emperor Hirohito – termed 'The Period of Japanese Glory'. See: Bix, Herbert P., *Hirohito and the Making of Modern Japan*, New York: 2000. Harper-Collins Publishing.

14. The carriers *Akagi* and *Kaga*, after their 1938 refits, came out at 36,500 tons and 38,200 tons standard displacement respectively and could each carry 91 aircraft. The recently completed *Sōryū* and *Hiryū*, built from scratch, displaced 15,900 tons and 17,300 tons respectively, and could only accommodate 63 aircraft; while the *Shōkakau* and *Zuikakū*, then under construction, had a designed stand tonnage of 25,675 tons and could carry 72 aircraft.

15. Contemporary Allied fighters were the American Curtiss P-36A Hawk with a top speed of 313mph (500km/h; and the British Hawker Hurricane with 340mph (547km/h).

16. Caiden, Martin, *Zero Fighter*, New York: 1969. Ballentine Books.

Chapter 2

1. This chapter relies heavily on Horikoshi's own account, Horikoshi, Jiro, *Eagles of Mitsubishi: The Story of the Zero Fighter*, Tokyo: 1970. Kappa Books (Kobunsha Co. Ltd), an updated, corrected English edition of which was translated by Shojiro Shindo and Harold N. Wantiez by University of Washington Press, 1992. Also reference has been made, but with great caution due to numerous factual errors, to Yoshimura, Akira, *Zero Fighter*, translated by Retsu Kaiho and Michael Gregson, Westport: 1996. Praeger.

2. Hisamitsu, Matsuoka and Masayoshi, Nakanishi, *The History of Mitsubishi Aero Engines 1915–1945*, Tokyo: 2005. Miki Press.

3. This landing gear was a development of that first fitted to the American Vought 143.

4. Japan, which had quit the League of Nations earlier over the Manchurian incident, had in 1936 renounced and then pulled out of all International Naval Limitation Treaties also and was re-arming as fast as she was able.

5. See: Somitomo Light Metal Technical Reports, *History of Extra Super Duralumin* – Part 1, Somitomo *Technical Review*, 51 No. 1, 2010.

6. Some people have tried to associate the magnesium content contained in ESD with the tendency for the A6M's wings to ignite easily under fire, the alleged 'flammable wing' problem, but even at the extreme range 2.8 per cent content (US modification 7075 being a modern equivalent), such solution heat treated aluminium alloys were never more vulnerable than any aluminium-clad aircraft, Japanese or Allied.

7. A = Carrier-based; 6 = sixth Navy fighter sequence; M = Mitsubishi; 1 = First version of the Prototype 12.

8. *Ki* – abbreviation of *Kitai* or airframe.

9. Horikoshi, Jiro, *A Research on the Improvement of Piloted Airplanes*, Report No. 396. Tokyo: 1965. Institute of Space & Aeronautical Science, University of Tokyo.
10. Yoshimura, Akira, *Zero Fighter*, Westport: 1996. Praeger.

Chapter 3

1. The unit was originally known as the Technical Intelligence Unit (TIU) and was based at McIntosh Building, Fortitude Valley, with the Enemy Equipment section headed by Lieutenant C. D. Gessel, but the name changed when an international team from the Royal Australian Air Force, Royal Navy, US Navy and US Army Air Corps combined in 1942. The actual code naming idea appears to have originated with a suggestion from Technical Sergeant Francis Williams. Like most other things in that area the idea became known as MacArthur Southwest Pacific Code Name System but soon became Pacific-wide once local variations had been ironed out.
2. 'Plane Facts: Zero-sen Ancestry', article in *Air Enthusiast*, Volume 3, No. 4. Stamford: 1976. Key Publishing.
3. The USAAS did not become the United States Army Air Force (USAAF) until summer 1941.
4. Boyd, Gary, 'Vought V-143, 1930 Technology Transfer', article in *Air Power History # 43* (Winter 1996). Clinton, Maryland: 1996. Air Force Historical Foundation.
5. *Air Classics*, April 2006.
6. Some comparison muzzle velocities included the Hispano–Suiza HS 404 at 880 m/s, the German MG 151/20 at 800 m/z, the British Hispano Mk. II at 880 m/s and the Soviet ShVak at 770 m/s.
7. Williams, Anthony G. and Gustin, Emmanuel, *Flying Guns of World War II*, Shrewsbury: 2003. Airlife Publishing.
8. All the inspection panels on the A6M were flush fitted and were manually opened by pressing a black dot with one finger, which opened the latch so the plate could be slid out.
9. Drake, Hal, 'Howard Hughes was a Liar!', article in *Air Classics*, Volume 12, No. 9, September 1976.
10. Matt, Paul R. and Rust, Kenn C., 'Howard Hughes and the Hughes Racer', article in *The Historical Aviation Album: All American Series*, Volume XVI. Temple City, Cal.: 1980. Historical Aviation Album.

Chapter 4

1. It should be remembered, however, that between January 1940 and March 1942 almost nine hundred A6Ms were produced.
2. Yoshimura, Akira, *Zero Fighter*, translated by Retsu Kaiho and Michael Gregson, Westport: 1996. Praeger.

3. Hata, Ikuhiko and Izawa, Yasuho, *Japanese Naval Aces and Fighter Units in World War II*, Annapolis: 1989. Naval Institute Press.

4. Burton, John, *Fortnight of Infamy*, Annapolis: 2006. United States Naval Institute Press.

5. Horikoshi described these as 'Army Type 96 bombers' but there were no such aircraft.

6. Okumiya, Masatake and Horikoshi, Jiro, with Caidin, Martin, *Zero! The Story of the Japanese Navy Air Force 1937–1945*, London: 1957. Cassell.

7. See Farrell, Brian and Hunter, Sandy, *The Great Betrayal! The Fall of Singapore Revisited*, London: 2020. Marshal Cavendish.

8. Nonetheless, Japan planned to produce a licence-built version of the He-100 and Hitachi was selected as the builder, but nothing ever materialized on this project, one of many mysteries surrounding this aircraft. See: Dabrowski, Hans-Peter, *Heinkel He 100, World Record and Propaganda Aircraft*. Atglen, Pen: 1991. Schiffer Publishing.

9. Pitot tube, named after Henri Pitot, is a pressure measurement device that measures fluid flow velocity. It was initially used to measure boat water speed and later modified to measure aircraft airspeed at a given moment.

10. Critical Altitude – the height at which an aircraft achieves her maximum speed with the engine work at full military power.

11. Gunston, Bill (ed.) *The Illustrated Book of Fighters*, New York: 1985. Exeter Books, and Jackson, Robert, *Mitsubishi Zero: Combat Legend*, Ramsbury: 2003. The Crowood Press.

12. Okumiya Masatake, and Horikoshi, Jiro, with Caidin, Martin, *Zero! The Story of the Japanese Navy Air Force 1937–1945*, London: 1957. Cassell & Company Ltd.

13. Board of Inspection and Survey Reports featuring Production Inspection Trials on both the F4F-3, Contact 68219, dated 23 January 1941, and the F4F-4, Contract 75736, dated 24 March 1942, reported that both failed to achieve their contractual requirement speeds of 350mph and 328mph respectively.

Chapter 5

1. Natingly, Major Robert E., USMC, *Herringbone Cloak – GI Dagger, Marines of the OSS*, Marine Corps Command & Staff College, 10 May 1979. Quantico: 1979. Marine Corps Command & Staff College.

2. Tuchman, Barbara, *Stilwell and the American Experience in China 1917–45*, New York: 1971. Macmillan.

3. Chennault, Claire Lee, *Claire Lee Chennault Papers 1941–1967*, Hoover Institution Archives, Stanford, Ca.

4. For other fighter tactics see Thompson, J. Steve, with Smith, Peter C., *Air Combat Manoeuvres: the Technique and History of Air Fighting for Flight Simulation*, Hersham: 2008. Ian Allan Classic.

5. Another example of the widespread ethnocentrism prevalent in the West at this time. See: Booth, Kenneth, *Strategy and Ethnocentrism*, London: 1979. Croom

Helm. The true story of the development of the Ki-46 can be found in: Ferkl, Martin, *Mitsubishi Ki-46 Dinah*, Cat.No. II-4002. Ostrava-Porkuba: 2005. Revi.

6. Prados, John, *Combined Fleet Decoded: The Secret History of American Intelligence and the Japanese Navy in World War II*, New York: 1995. Random House. See also: Stephen Jurika Papers 1926–1987. Collection Number 80035. Hoover Institution Archives, Stanford, Cal. 10 boxes and *Jurika, Captain Stephen, Jr, US Navy (Rtd) Volumes I and II*, US Naval Institute, Annapolis, MD. Volume 1 contains fourteen interviews conducted by Paul B. Ryan from October 1975 to April 1976.

7. Packard, Captain Wyman H., USN, *A Century of U S Naval Intelligence*, Washington DC: 1996. Office of Naval Intelligence and Naval Historical Center.

8. Presentation #433, see *The Japanese Army Wings of the Second World War*, Tokyo:1972. Koku Fan/Burin-do Publishers.

9. The AVG flew their first combat mission in China on 10 December 1941 and were principally engaged with the Japanese Army's 64 *Sentai*, flying the Nakajima Ki-43 *Hayabusa* (Peregrine Falcon), which the Allies were later to codename 'Oscar'. Also engaged were Nakajima Ki-27 (later allotted the Allied codename 'Nate'). These aircraft were invariably erroneously reported as the Zero, AVG pilots having dubbed it the 'Army Zero' due to its similarity in appearance to the Navy plane.

10. Note Chennault said 'leak-proof' and *not*, as some American historians have alleged, 'self-sealing'. See: Records of the War Department: General and Special Staffs – RG165. Records of the War Plans Division, WPD 4449-1, Archives and Records Administrations (NARA), College Park, MD.

11. Bland, Larry I. (ed.), *The Papers of George Catlett Marshall II*, Baltimore: 1986. Johns Hopkins University Press.

12. US Army FM-30-38, *Identification of Japanese Aircraft*, 10 March 1941. Washington DC: 1941.

13. Elphick, Peter and Smith, Michael, *Odd Man Out: The Story of the Singapore Traitor*, London: 1993. Hodder & Stoughton.

14. See JIC (41) 327, *Probable Scale of Japanese Air Attack on Malaya*, dated 13 August 1941. CAB 79/13, National Archives, Kew, London.

15. Aldrich, Richard J., *Intelligence and the War Against Japan: Britain, America and the Politics of Secret Service*, Cambridge: 2000. Cambridge University Press.

16. AIR40/1453, *ALO Weekly Intelligence Summary*, No. 30, dated 29 October 1940. National Archives, Kew, London.

17. AIR22/74, *AID Weekly Intelligence Summary*, No. 75, dated 6 February 1941, and AIR40/1448 Warburton (AA Chungking) to DAI (Director, Air Intelligence) No. 19, dated 22 April 1941. National Archives, Kew, London.

18. CAB101/160, National Archives, Kew, London.

19. Brooke-Popham, LHCMA 6/8/8, on Maltby (AM) report dated 18 November 1946.

20. Mollahan, Colonel David J., USMC; DeVine, Lieutenant-Colonel Thomas J., USA; Victor, Lieutenant-Colonel Ross A., USAF and Mayer, Commander

Edward, USN, *The Japanese Campaign in Malaya: December 1941 – February 1942: A Study in Joint Warfighting*, Joint Forces Staff College, Joint and Combined Staff Officer School, Class 02-3S, dated September 2002. Faculty Advisor: Captain Gary R. Chiaverotti, Seminar A.

21. It was not until late August 1943 that the A6M appeared in force in the area, when the 331 *Kōkūtai* arrived at Sabang, Weh Island, Sumatra, with thirty-two Zeros under Lieutenant-Commander Hideki Shingō. They had been transported from Saeki aboard the carrier *Junyō* and flown ashore despite the majority having had no previous carrier operating experience whatsoever! And it was not until December that twenty-seven of these A6Ms, moved into Magwe airfield, Burma, via Tavoy (now known as Dawei) on the south-west Burmese coast. They made their first sortie on 5 December, escorting bombers to attack Calcutta, and destroyed six Hawker Hurricanes IIC (AI) s without loss to themselves that day with Warrant Officers Sadaaki Akamatsu and Hirsohi Okano. Before they could add to that tally, pressure from the Americans in the central Pacific brought about their withdrawal almost before they had begun. They were re-designated as *Haikōti* 603 and moved to Mariaon, Woleai Atoll, in the Caroline Islands, on 24 March.

22. Sonokawa, Captain Kameo, IJN, Captain of *Genzan Kōkūtai*, *Operations of 22nd Air Flotilla in Malaya*, United States Strategic Bombing Survey (Pacific), Interrogations of Japanese Officials, OPNAN-P-03-100, Naval Analysis Division. Interrogation NAV NO.77, USSBS No.387, dated 14 November 1945.

23. Allied fighters comprised Brewster Buffalo 1, Curtiss Mohawk IV, Hawker Hurricane 1, 11a and 1b and Curtiss P40B/C Warhawk/Tomahawk and Curtiss P-40E Warhawk/Kittyhawk of the AVG. Despite some American internet historians' fevered imaginations, there were no Spitfires in the Far East at this time; the first arrived in September 1942 and flew her first mission on 10 October.

24. Now Yangon International Airport, Myanmar.

25. And not just at the beginning of the war. At the Battle of the Coral Sea in May 1942, American Navy pilots from both VF-2 and VF-42, like Lieutenant Noel Gayler, were reporting attacking, and being attacked, by German Messerschmitt Bf.109 fighters. One US pilot, Lieutenant-Commander Paul Ramsey, the commanding officer of VF-2, was even officially credited with shooting down a Bf.109! At the Battle of Midway a month later the same stories proliferated, with Ensign Albert K. Earnest of VT-8 claiming his aircraft was shot up by one. Even during the Battle of Eastern Solomons in August 1942, Bf.109s were being 'identified' by American pilots such as Ensign John Kleinman of VF-5 from *Saratoga*, while Ensign Francis Register of VF-6 aboard *Enterprise* claimed to have destroyed one in combat in that battle. Never mind that the Bf.109 was a land-based fighter not a carrier aircraft; nor that it had an in-line engine and not a radial engine; had a entirely different tail and empennage; different cockpit shape; that, in fact, it looked nothing at all like an

A6M. The US pilots 'saw' them, engaged them and claimed them! Nor were the Americans alone in this, as in April 1942 Admiral Somerville had reported Aichi D3A1 naval dive-bombers as German Junkers Ju.87 Stukas in a similar state of denial. During the fighting for Singapore Australian pilots of both No. 21 and No. 453 Squadrons recorded engaging both Bf.109s and even Junkers Ju.88 bombers, an incredible state of affairs.

26. See, for example, the many citations quoted in Shore, Christopher F., Cull, Brian and Izawa, Yasuho, *Bloody Shambles, Vol.1; The Drift to War to the Fall of Singapore*, London: 1992. Grub Street.

27. Willmott, H. P., *Empires in the Balance, Japanese and Allied Pacific Strategies to April 1942*, Annapolis: 1982. Naval Institute Press.

Chapter 6

1. Most of the Marshall, Caroline and Mariana Island Groups, other than the Gilbert Island (British) and Guam (American) in the western Pacific, had effectively been under Japanese control since 1917 and were officially League of Nations mandated from 1919 onward.

2. The CS40B propeller was almost 6in (15cm) smaller.

3. Unlike Hollywood's recent fantasies, taken as gospel by many, no American pilots had won the Battle of Britain single-handed and then gone on to destroy the IJN's attack force at Pearl Harbor immediately afterwards!

4. In mitigation, such was the case in the armed forces of all nations in the 1930s, an age when ruggedness of life was considered not just the norm, but essential if one was to perform well in battle and endure the toughness of combat. Also it was a starker and more basic age, and the accepted 'norms' of the twenty-first century military had not been softened by such things as 'human rights', counselling nor influenced by the inclusion of females in the front-line fighting forces, and so cannot be judged by modern standards. This was particularly so in the case in the Japanese armed services where the very concept of surrender was totally alien, hence the total lack of concern for the welfare of any defeated or captured enemy.

5. A note on the 'ace' system. Again, the Japanese differed from the Allies in how this status was recognized. Thus, no emphasis was ever given to totally establishing enemy losses to the nth degree, the mere hitting and consequent breaking off of an attack often being automatically credited. Similarly, the practice of attributing even absolutely absolute 'kills' was by no means universal in Japanese fighter groups, many of them crediting the unit itself rather than any individual, and this became more the norm as the war went on. Consequently the many tally totals assigned to certain pilots should always be taken with a grain of salt and a general rule of thumb of about 1-in-3 claims being accurate might be a more prudent and meaningful score line. Often promotion followed if a pilot proved outstandingly successful at his job. It should be also be stated, of course, that the Allied claims of Japanese losses were often more astronomically

misleading in the first year of the war and indeed were to remain so, especially under General Douglas McArthur's command – but no Air Force, Allied or Axis, had ever proved immune to this false accounting, just look at the absurd figures given during the Battle of Britain and a recent claim that during the last eight months of the war the US Navy suffered the loss of only two SB2Cs and five TBMs.

6. Hata, Ikuhiko, and Izawa, Yasuho, *Japanese Naval Aces and Fighter Units in World War II*, Tokyo: 1970. Kantōsha Publishers.

7. Neuman, Gerhard, *Herman the German: Just Lucky I Guess*, Bloomington, Ind: 2004. Authorhouse.

8. Both the Royal Navy and the United States Navy had operated two- and three-carrier formations pre-war, with the latter Navy even producing, in War Games, a remarkable foretaste of the actual Pearl Harbor attack. During the war the Royal Navy occasionally managed to scrape together sufficient aircraft carriers to mount three-carrier forces for specific events, for example the *Pedestal* convoy operation to Malta in August 1942 with three fleet carriers included in the escorting naval force, plus a fourth engaged in flying off fighter aircraft to the island. However, until 1944, such large assemblies of carriers in one fleet were rare achievements for the Allies, though they had been the norm for the Japanese between December 1941 and April 1942 when operating in both the Pacific and Indian Oceans. The Allied naval commanders became well aware of this fact from Intelligence and visual sightings during both operations, although some modern revisionists have sought to deny the fact that they knew.

Chapter 7

1. Nitaka (now re-named as Mount Chia-i) was the highest mountain in Japanese-owned Formosa, (now Taiwan) higher even than Mount Fuji.

2. Okumiya, and Horikoshi, Jiro, with Caidin, Martin, *Zero!: The Story of the Japanese Navy Air Force 1937–1945*, London: 1957. Cassell & Co. However, this version of events is disputed by Dan King who asserts '... there are no hangars, nor were there any hangars or buildings in the area in 1941.' See: King, Dan, *The Last Zero Fighter: Firsthand Accounts from WWII Japanese Naval Pilots*, Irvine, Ca: 2012. Pacific Press.

3. Smith, Carl, with Laurier, Jim, *Pearl Harbor 1941 – The Day of Infamy*, London: 1999. Osprey Publishing.

4. In addition the Navy lost a further five F4F Wildcats of VF-6 from the same carrier, which were subsequently were shot down by panicky 'friendly fire' while attempting to land at Ford later that day many hours after the last Japanese aircraft had departed.

5. Some doubts had already surfaced and it was planned to move some B-17s to Mindanao, but this was not done due to a party for top brass held on the eve of the Pearl Harbor attack.

6. Brereton, General Lewis Hyde, *The Brereton Diaries: The Air War in the Pacific, Middle East and Europe 30 October 1941 – 8 May 1945*, New York: 1946. William Morrow].

7. Sakai, Saburō, with Caidin, Martin and Saito, Fred, *Samurai!* London: 1957. William Kimber.

8. The Americans remained convinced that these *must* have been carrier-based and conducted fruitless searches accordingly.

9. Suburo Sakai, who chalked up his third kill that day by easily destroying a P-40 over Clark Field, claims only five A6Ms were lost, one to anti-aircraft fire and four others during the long flight home. 'But not a single plane was lost to an enemy aircraft.' Sakai, Saburo, *Samurai*, London: 1959. William Kimber & Co. Ltd.

10. Interestingly Lieutenant-General Walter Short, in command of the Army air units at Pearl found himself out of the service and working in a car factory within a few weeks of his errors of judgement, while MacArthur became a national hero despite, some would say, this far greater blunder.

11. Okumiya, and Horikoshi, Jiro, with Caidin, Martin, *Zero!: The Story of the Japanese Navy Air Force 1937–1945*, London: 1957. Cassell & Co.

12. Back in London, following the *Prince of Wales* and *Repulse* debacle, and the premature withdrawal of the RAF from northern Malayan airfields, the British Air Ministry's Air Intelligence Division (AID) was coming to the (rather belated) conclusion, that 'Events in the Far East suggest that Japanese naval aircraft may be worthy of closer study than has yet been undertaken' – Japan: Preliminary Report on T97/1. T97/2 Torpedo Bombers and T.99 Navy Dive Bomber, AI2c, 13 December 1941, AIR40/35, National Archives, Kew, London.

13. The twin-engined Martin 139 was the export version of the well-known B-10.

14. This pilot survived only to be killed with 230 fellow inmates during an attempted mass breakout at Cowra POW camp in 1944.

15. Lewis, Tom, *A War at Home. A Comprehensive Guide to the First Japanese Attacks on Darwin*, Darwin: 2003. Tall Stories.

16. Roskill, Captain S. W., DSC, RN, *The War at Sea 1939–1945, Volume II The Period of Balance*, London: 1957. Her Majesty's Stationery Office.

Chapter 8

1. The A5Ms were not replaced by A6Ms until 23 April, *after* the Bay of Bengal operation had been completed despite what some recent western sources state.

2. T/B = torpedo-bombers, she carried no fighters at all.

3. Somerville to Admiralty, 8 April 1942. Somerville, Admiral Sir James, *The Somerville Papers*, edited by Michael Simpson, Aldershot: 1995. Navy Records Society/The Scholar Press.

4. Both the Albacore and the Fulmar were considered among the poorest combat aircraft ever flown – see Winchester, Jim, *The World's Worst Aircraft; From*

Pioneering Failures to Multimillion Dollar Disasters, London: 2005. Amber Books.

5. Somerville, Admiral Sir James, *The Somerville Papers*, edited by Michael Simpson, Aldershot: 1995. Navy Records Society/The Scholar Press.

6. Officially Royal Naval Air Service, RNAS, but hardly anyone actually used that term, either then or since.

7. Popham, Hugh, *Sea Flight*, London: 1954. William Kimber.

8. Smith, Peter C., *Aichi D3A1/2 Val*, Ramsbury: 1999. Crowood Press.

9. See: *Senshi Sōsho* (War History) Volume 29. *Hōkutō Hōmen Kaigun Sakusen* (North-Eastern Area Naval Operations) Tokyo: 1969. Asagumo Shimbunsha.

10. Churchill, Winston S., *The Second World War: Volume IV. The Hinge of Fate*, London: 1949. Cassell.

11. Tomlinson, Michael, *The Most Dangerous Moment*, London: 1976. William Kimber. This author was actually consulted by the publisher at the time on the figures and I warned them that Japanese records showed only eighteen losses; they nonetheless went ahead and published the misleading figures without amendment.

12. Hata, Ikuhiko and Izawa, Yasuho, *Japanese Naval Aces and Fighter Units in World War II*, Annapolis: 1989. Naval Institute Press. Even an older British source, claims just eighteen Japanese losses; see Shores, Christopher and Cull, Brian, with Izawa, Yasuho, *Bloody Shambles: Volume Two – The Defence of Sumatra to the Fall of Burma*, London: 1993. Grub Street.

13. In 1948 an official British inquiry was undertaken in Tokyo with the sole purpose of establishing whether or not the Japanese had intended to invade at this time, and unanimously concluded it had not – the findings being reflected in Admiralty, Naval Staff History – *War with Japan, Volume II*. C.B.3303 (2). London: 1954. Admiralty Historical Section.

14. Somerville, Admiral Sir James, *The Somerville Papers*, edited by Michael Simpson, Aldershot: 1995. Navy Records Society/The Scholar Press.

15. SEEBEE from Naval Construction Battalion (CB) For a detailed account of their work see – Bureau of Yards and Docks, *Building the Navy's Bases in World War II*, Volume 1, Washington DC: 1947. United States Government Printing Office.

16. See Kahn, David, *The Code Breakers: The Story of Secret Writing*, London: 1966. Weidenfeld and Nicolson.

17. Wilmott, H. P., *The Barrier and the Javelin, Japanese and Allied Pacific Strategies – February to June 1942*, Annapolis: 1983. Naval Institute Press.

18. The *Shōhō* was the former submarine support ship *Tsurugizaki* and her sister, the *Zūiho*, was the former *Takasaki* whose conversion had been completed in December 1940.

19. Apparently she almost capsized on her return journey, which indicated heavier damage than generally admitted.

20. Speculation that, had she have been readied sooner it would have turned the tide at the Midway battle, are irrelevant, because Japanese signals indicated that,

even if her *Kōkūtai* had been ready to participate, which she was not, she had been allocated to join the Aleutians part of the force, and thus would never have had the opportunity to play any part in the main carrier-to-carrier battle itself.

21. Also known was the fact that the *Kidō Butai* operated its carriers as a single group, as the signals from the PBY Catalina and the eyewitness accounts from the debriefing of the surviving Blenheim pilots, both off Ceylon in April, were sent to the Americans under the COPEK mutual Intelligence exchange channel arrangement, which had been set up by OP-20-G (NEGAT) in January 1942 and extended to Melbourne at the end of March. Pearl Harbor and Melbourne shared the same Japanese Navy information. See: *A Priceless Advantage: U S Navy Communications Intelligence and the battles of Coral Sea, Midway, and the Aleutians.* (CH-E32-93-01) Washington DC. In addition, Premier Churchill had cabled President F. D. Roosevelt as early as 7 April that: 'According to our information, five, and possibly six, Japanese battleships, and certainly five aircraft-carriers, are operating in the Indian Ocean.'

22. Books, articles, discussions and embarrassingly bad motion pictures and TV documentaries pertaining to deal with the Battle of Midway are so numerous that it would be futile to try and list them all here in a book dedicated to the A6M Zero. More such books on this battle appear all the time; not all of them are very well researched, while a few appear to have agendas of their own and are very partisan. For a detailed, comprehensive and, more importantly, strictly neutral and objective account, researched from the viewpoint of *both* sides, see – Smith, Peter C., *Midway Dauntless Victory: Fresh Perspectives on America's Seminal Naval Victory of World War II*, Barnsley: 2007. Pen & Sword Maritime.

23. Actual Japanese bomber losses were nine with three damaged beyond repair.

24. Confidential – Action report - United States Marine Corps, Marine Fighting Squadron 221, Marine Aircraft Group 22, 2nd Marine Aircraft Wing, Fleet Marine Force, c/o Fleet P.O. San Francisco, Calif. A1-1/olg, dated 6 June 1942. *Enemy contact, report on.* Statements. Kirk Armistead, CO.

25. Japanese Self-Defence Agency, War History Office, *Senshi Sosho: Middowe Kaisen* (War History Series: Midway Naval Battle), No. 43. Tokyo: 1971. Asagumo Shimbun.

26. Admiralty, *Information on Midway Island Battle*, dated 11 August 1942. From DACD (Director, Airfields and Carrier Division) to various departments. A.C.D.1842. Contained in ADM 199/1302, National Archives, Kew, London. Main report contained in *Admiralty Weekly Intelligence Report*, No. 126, dated 7 August 1942. These records have been open to the public for many decades, despite claims to the contrary.

27. 'Sequence of Events', contained in ADM 199/1302, National Archives, Kew, London.

28. The B-17 crews became notorious for this throughout the Pacific theatre of war and it was a standing joke with US Navy pilots, who called it 'creative vision'.

29. Ringblom, Major Allan H., USMC, *Dive-Bomber Pilot's Narrative, Battle of Midway*, 1996: USMC Historical Section, Quantico, Va.

30. Modern-day armchair and internet theorists opine that the best move Yamaguchi could have made was to have put as much distance between himself and the American Task Forces as he could. This option does not take into account the mind-set of a leading exponent of Japanese Navy air power in 1942, even had it been practical. Nor were American naval officers throughout their history prone to cut-and-run, so why should the Japanese have acted differently? A modern example, maybe, of the same old dual-standard thinking?

31. King, Dan, *The Last Zero Fighter: Firsthand Accounts from WWII Japanese Naval Pilots*, Irvine, CA: 2012. Pacific Press.

Chapter 9

1. For example, Air Vice Marshal Paul Copeland Maltby was informed that the intelligence that had been gleaned about the A6M by the British in Malaya had not been passed down to individual units, '… due to a lack of junior intelligence staff'. Air Marshal Stanley Jackson Marchbank to Maltby, 21 September 1954, CAB101/156, National Archives, Kew, London. Even in Burma far later a Hurricane pilot was recording that they received very little useful information on the A6M. See: Hemingway, Kenneth, *Wings Over Burma*, London: 1944. Quality.

2. Kelly, Terence, *Hurricane Over the Jungle*, Leicester: 1993. Ulverscroft.

3. This occupation was never intended as a 'diversion' for the Midway operation, as is so often proclaimed – the whole purpose of the latter operation was to lure the American fleet to its destruction (with Midway's occupation merely as the bait), and *not* to divert parts of it away from Yamamoto's fleet.

4. By far the most detailed account of this incident and subsequent salvage and re-building work is contained in – Rearden, Jim, *Koga's Zero: The Fighter that Changed World War II*, Missoula, Montana: 1995. Pictorial Histories Publishing Company Inc., which despite the hyperbole of the sub-title, has been meticulously researched.

5. Willmott, Hedley Paul, *Zero: A6M*, London: 1980. Arms & Armour Press.

6. My italics. Considering the universal bad press the IJN's radio equipment has received this is a quite remarkable statement. Post-war it was found that although there were constant complaints about the falling standards of their radio equipment, little of this found its way back to the constructors and manufacturers.

7. Hammel, Eric, *Carrier Clash: The Invasion of Guadalcanal and the Battle of the Eastern Solomons August 1942*, St. Paul, Mn: 1999. Zenith Press.

8. Originally another carrier, the *Hiyō*, was part of this force but due to a fire in an engine generator room, which badly damaged the condenser, she had to be sent back to Truk with a two–destroyer escort on 22 October.

9. The remaining *Hiyō* aircraft, sixteen A3Ms and seventeen D3As, commanded by Takeshi Mieno, transferred from Truk to Rabaul and continued to pound Guadalcanal as a land-based unit and later moved to the forward airstrip at

Buin on 1 November and they did not rejoin their carrier at Saeki again until 18 December.

10. The relief felt ashore at Guadalcanal at Halsey's appointment was recalled by one who was present when the news broke: 'I'll never forget it. One minute we were too limp with malaria to crawl out of our foxholes, the next, we were running around whooping like kids.' – See: Potter, E. B., *Nimitz*, Annapolis, Md: 1976. Naval Institute Press.

11. The *Enterprise*, operating some distance away, being hidden by a rain squall, was not molested at this stage.

12. Fisher, Commander Clayton E., *Hooked: Tales and Adventures of a Tailhook Warrior*, Denver, Co: 2009. Outskirts Press.

13. The exaggerated Japanese claims continue to be presented as fact, for example Akira Yoshimura wrote in 1996 that the Japanese offensive had sunk one cruiser, one destroyer and thirty-five transports! The American publisher allowed this to stand without query. Yoshimura, Akira, *Zero Fighter*, Westport, Conn: 1996. Praeger.

14. It is asserted that '… command at Rabaul, believing that control of the air was completely on the Japanese side, had inadvertently reduced the number of escort aircraft. Also, the pilots of the six aircraft were not necessarily the best that might have been selected,' Hata, Ikuhiko and Izawa, Yasho, *Japanese Naval Aces and Fighter Units in World War II*, Annapolis: 1989. Naval Institute Press. However, the authors do not elaborate in any way as to who made these allegations.

Chapter 10

1. Shaw, Jr, Henry and Kane, Major Douglas T., *History of U.S. Marine Corps Operations in World War II: Volume II – Isolation of Rabaul*, 1963: Quantico, Va, Historical Branch, G-3 Division, Headquarters, US Marine Corps.

2. Letoumeau, Roger and Letoumeau, Dennis, *Operation KE: The Cactus Air Force and the Japanese Withdrawal from Guadalcanal*, Annapolis: 2012. Naval Institute Press.

3. Despite this brilliant piece of dive-bombing, an Americans Intelligence team later recovered five JN25D-13 to D-17 code-books and a complete Naval Call-Signs list from the wreckage, forcing the Japanese to immediately change all their codes.

4. The Japanese Navy had commenced the war with only 2,120 aircraft on strength and, by April 1943, still only had 2,980 machines of all types. Production increased considerably in the year that followed, and in April 1944 6,598 aircraft were available, but the casualty rate had equally soared and the standard of construction had fallen away severely.

5. Ugaki, Admiral Matome, *Fading Victory: The Diary of Admiral Matome Ugaki 1941–1945*, Pittsburg: 1991. University of Pittsburg Press.

6. (1) Interrogation No. 601 NAV No. 116. Naval Analysis Division, *Japanese Land Based Air Operations in Celebes and Rabaul Area*, Commander Nomura, Ryosuke, Imperial Japanese Navy (Ret.) Meiji Building, 28 Nov 1945.
7. See: Bergerud, Eric M., *Fire in the Sky: The Air War in the South Pacific*, Boulder, Colorado: 2000. Westview Press; and Saki, Saburo, *Samurai*, London: 1959. William Kimber.
8. Miyazaki, Commander Takashi Miyazaki, IJN, *Interrogation Nav.47*, Washington DC: 1946. United States Strategic Bombing Survey.
9. A good, if brief, account of Rabaul's final days can be found in – Sakaida, Henry, *The Siege of Rabaul*, Louisville: 1996. Phalanx Publishing.

Chapter 11

1. See: Paxton, John, 'Myth vs. Reality: The Question of Mass Production in WWII', article in *Economicst Business Journal*, Vol 1, No. 1, October 2008. Wayne State College.
2. These filters, the enormous Volkes model, which hung below the aircraft's nose, were responsible for a drag factor that reduced these Spitfires speed by at least 30mph. The RAAF pilots tried to replace them with an improvised version of more moderate dimensions, but failed.
3. The 'Killer' tag was applied by the Press after it became known that he had shot and killed several Luftwaffe pilots in the air after they had parachuted out of their aircraft. He was credited with over twenty-eight confirmed aircraft destroyed, including four A6Ms. See: Alexander, Kristen, *Clive Caldwell: Air Ace*, London: 2006 Allen & Unwin.
4. Morehead, James, *In My Sights: The Memoirs of a P-40 Ace*, Novato, Ca.: 1998. Presidio Press.
5. Hata, Ikuhiko, and Izawa, Yasuho, *Japanese Naval Aces and Fighter Units in World War II*, Tokyo: 1970. Kantōsha Publishers.
6. Chennault, Claire Lee, with Hotz, Robert, *Way of the Fighter*, New York: 1949. G P Putnam & Sons.
7. Baeza, Bernard, *Soleil Levant sur L'Australie (The Rising Sun over Australia)*, *Historie de L'Aviation No. 19*, Montreal: 2008 Editions Lela Presse.
8. See: Bergerud, Eric M., *Fire in the Sky: The Air War in the South Pacific*, Boulder, Colorado: 2000. Westview Press.
9. Under the 15 February 1944 re-organization the previous practice of aircraft-carriers being assigned their own *Kōkūtai* (Air Groups) had been abolished and autonomous independent *Kōkūtai* were formed, which were then allocated as required.
10. It was estimated that the US Pacific Fleet had more AA guns aboard its warships by this time than were available to defend the entire British Isles.
11. Dickson, W. D., *Sea Battles in Close Up: 11. The Battle of the Philippine Sea June 1944*, Shepperton: 1975. Ian Allan.

12. Tillman, Barrett and Coonts, Stephen, *Clash of the Carriers: The True Story of the Marianas Turkey Shoot of World War II*, New York: 2007. New American Library. Also Y'Blood, William T., *Red Sun Setting: The Battle of the Philippine Sea*, Annapolis, Md: 1981. Naval Institute Press.

13. Other surviving carriers were *Amagi*, *Junyō*, *Ryuho*, *Shinano* and *Unryū* but these were utilized as ferry carriers taking replacement aircraft south to the main battle area, in which capacity *Shinano* and *Unryū* were lost.

14. Originally the aircraft complement was to have been eleven Yokosuka D4Y *Suisei* dive-bombers (codename 'Judy') and eleven Aichi E16A *Zuiun* floatplanes (codename 'Paul'). Later this was changed with the establishment of 4 *Koko Sentai* with the two light carriers and this required the addition of 163 *Hikōtai* and 167 *Hikōtai*, both under Lieutenant Sumio Fukuda, each with an allocation of forty-eight A6M5s but an actual strength of about thirty fighters each, which began training at Tokushima airfield, Shikoku Island.

15. Willmott, H. P., *The Battle of Leyte Gulf: The Last Fleet Action*, Bloomington, Indiana: 2005. University of Indiana Press.

16. Okumiya, and Horikoshi, Jiro, with Caidin, Martin, *Zero!: The Story of the Japanese Navy Air Force 1937–1945*, London: 1957. Cassell & Co. Despite this one recent internet 'expert' has claimed that once the Zero's weaknesses were known and countered, even novice US pilots could easily shoot down superior Japanese pilots, adding that even in 1941 the Wildcat was superior!

17. 'Where is the rest of your crew!' a Royal Navy Pilot is said to have ribbed a US Navy Hellcat pilot on first seeing the F6F.

18. Some armchair internet jockeys in the USA claim that the A6M had a maximum speed of 309mph and that any higher speed would cause the skin to wrinkle.

19. See: *Japanese Radio Equipment* [E-08] – DS820.52U524 [E-08]; *Japanese Radio Apparatus Construction Methods* [E-18] DS20.S2 U524 [E-18] and *Japanese Insulation Materials* [E-23] DS20S2 U524-[E-23], Naval Historical Division, Operational Archives Branch, Washington DC, for further details. Of course Allied airborne radios were not much better and also the subject of constant complaint.

20. Tagaya, Osamu, Imperial Japanese Naval Aviator 1937–45, Wellingborough: 1988. Osprey.

21. Which used an almost equal combination of water and Methanol ($CH_3 OH$) – MW50.

22. *Combat Evaluation of Zeke 52 with F4U-1D, F6F-5, and FM-2*, TAIC Report No. 17 dated November 1944, Washington DC.

23. Minoru, Dr. Akimoto, *Oinaru Zereosen no eiko to kuto (Nihon gunyoki kokusen zenshi*, Tokyo: 1995. Gurin Aro Shuppansha.

24. Listed by some sources as the Model 55 – i.e. Okumiya, Masatake and Horikoshi, Jiro, with Caidin, Martin, *Zero! The Story of the Japanese Navy Air Force 1937–1945*, London: 1957. Cassel.

25. Navy Department, Bureau of Ordnance – *Japanese Explosive Ordnance*, OP 1667. 14 June 1946. Volume 1, Washington DC. Bennington, VT: 2011. Merriam Press.

Chapter 12

1. The two fleets essentially consisted of the same ships, only the title changing with the alternation of the C-in-C, with one controlling with his staff, while the other team prepared for the next offensive.
2. Ginjoro Fujiwara, a prominent industrialist, had been appointed in 1940 as Minister of Commerce and Industry, with a special brief to modernize Naval Procurement procedures. He determined upon tripling Japanese Navy aircraft production and soon introduced many practical steps to make improvements to the flow. A new airfield was constructed at Nagoya and river barges carrying five A6Ms at a time, replaced the primitive ox-cart method, still, incredibly, in use. With the completion of the Mizushima Aircraft plant at Okayama and the full operation of Kumamoto (Kengun) aircraft factory, A6Ms began coming off the line at one hundred a month at Nagoya and twice that number at Nakajima.
3. Hudson, J. ed., *The History of the USS Cabot (CVL-28): A Fast Carrier in World War II*, McAllen,Tx: 1986 Hudson.
4. Many years later, in June 2003 Iwashita met Nisi's family in Massachusetts. For the full story see – Taylan, Justin, *The Face of A Young Pilot Shot Down Over Iwo Jima*, pacificghosts.com.
5. Yasuho, Izawa and Shores, Christopher, 'Fighting Floatplanes of the Japanese Imperial Navy', article in *Air Enthusiast*, No. 31 (July–November 1986 edition).
6. The A6M-Ns were *never* embarked aboard the Japanese Armed Merchant Raiders *Aikoku Maru* and *Hokoku Maru* in the Indian Ocean as frequently claimed.
7. Smith, Peter C., *Kamikaze: To Die for the Emperor*, Barnsley: 2015. Pen & Sword Aviation.
8. She was to be claimed sunk yet again by the USAAF at Midway and several times more during the course of the war – but survived until July 1945.
9. Like Yamamoto, Ōnishi had served a stint in the USA and knew its awesome industrial potential. Also like Yamamoto, he had advised strongly against going to war with the USA, 'There is no nation this country should fight less.'
10. Ugaki, Admiral Matome, *Fading Victory: The Diary of Admiral Matome Ugaki 1941–1945*, Pittsburg: 1991. University of Pittsburg Press. Ugaki was roundly condemned later as one of the '… evil old men' who prolonged the war. In his own view, however, it was the ultimate sacrifice of pure patriotism and both he and Ōnishi were later to share the fate of those that went to their deaths, Ōnishi committing ritual disembowelment (*hara-kiri* or cutting the stomach), choosing the *seppuku* (ritual sacrifice) option and taking fifteen hours to die in slow agony in atonement, while Ugaki went to his death leading the very last *Kamikaze* mission of the war.

11. Hirikoshi, Jiro, *Eagles of Mitsubishi: The Story of the Zero Fighter*, Tokyo: 1970. Kappa Books (Kobunsha Co., Ltd).

12. The order failed to save Nishizawa, however, for he was killed *en route* to Tacloban as a passenger aboard a Shōwa LD2 transport plane intercepted by to VF-14 F6Fs from the carrier *Wasp* that same day. Ironically the LD2 was a licence-built version of the famous Douglas DC-3 Dakota.

13. The British AA cruiser *Euryalus* put two 5.25-inch shells into the carrier *Illustrious* in just one such incident on 29 January, killing eleven of her crew and wounding twenty-two more.

14. Iwantani, Lieutenant-Commander Taiyo (Ocean) magazine, March 1945, cited in Axell, Albert and Hideaki, Kase, *Kamikaze: Japan's Suicide Gods*, New York: 2002. Longmans.

15. Tadamichi Kuribayashi to Yoshii Kuribayashi, see Newcomb, Richard F., *Iwo Jima*, Austin, Tx: 1966. Holt, Rineheart and Winston.

16. Off Salerno, Italy, in 1943 106 Fleet Air Arm Seafires embarked in five carriers, destroyed just two German aircraft, frequently pursued USAAF A-36s by mistake for German machines (but could never catch them) and in return lost a grand total of forty-two Seafires destroyed or damaged beyond repair in deck landings!

17. Smith, Peter C., *Task Force 57: The British Pacific Fleet 1944–45*, London: 1959. William Kimber.

18. Nijboer, Donald, *Seafire FIII Vs A6M Zero: Pacific Theatre*, Wellingborough: 2009. Osprey Publishing.

19. A few A6Ms, scattered around the former Empire, saw limited post-war usage, for example by the French in Indo-China, the rebellious inhabitants of the Dutch East Indies, and in China itself, but these were few and their activities brief and poorly documented.

20. Report No. 46, *Tokko* translated by Mr Ishiguro.

21. The breakdown was: A6M1, A6M2, A6M3 – between March 1939 and March 1942 – Mitsubishi 722 – Nakajima 115 and between April 1942 to March 1943 – Mitsubishi 729 – Nakajima 960. A6M5, A6M6, A6M7, A6M8 – from April 1943 to March 1944 – Mitsubishi 1,164 – Nakajima 2,268; between April 1944 to March 1945 – Mitsubishi 1,145 – Nakajima 2,342; from April 1945 to Aug 1945 – Mitsubishi 119 – Nakajima 885.

22. Under this the taught mantra stressed *Chūsetsu* (Loyalty); *Reigi* (Politeness); *Buyū* (Bravery); *Shingi* (Trust) and *Shisso* (Thrift) – all admirable qualities for the military to uphold.

23. Foss, Joe, with Foss, Donna, *A Proud American: The Autobiography of Joe Foss*, New York: 1992. Pocket Books.

Index